Financing
the
Sport
ENTERPRISE

Thomas H. Sawyer
Michael G. Hypes
Julia Ann Hypes

Sagamore Publishing
Champaign, Illinois

Production Coordinator: Janet Wahlfeldt
Cover and Interior Design: Kenneth O'Brien
Interior Photos Courtesy of Michael Hypes
Cover Photos Courtesy of Photodisc

Library of Congress Cataloging-in-Publication Data
Sawyer, Thomas H.
    Financing the sport enterprise / by Thomas H. Sawyer, Michael Hypes, Julia Ann
Hypes.
        p. cm.
ISBN: 1-57167-520-5
    1. Sports--Finance. 2. Sports--Economic aspects. 3. Sports administration.
I. Hypes, Michael, 1960- II. Hypes, Julia Ann, 1961- III. Title.
GV716.S29 2004
796'.06'9--dc22   2004010752

Dedication

This book is dedicated to the memory of my mother–Mary Daughn Sawyer. Mom was an elementary school teacher for over 35 years and built for me the foundation to be a sound teacher and writer. Without her influence and patience I would not be what I am today.

CONTENTS

Acknowledgments

This book started out as a team project to develop a standard format for information to be covered in an undergraduate sport finance course that would meet all the standards established by the National Association for Sport and Physical Education (NASPE) and the North American Society for Sport Management (NASSM). After a number of years of developing the course materials it was obvious that the team should convert the basic work into a sport finance textbook.

At this time I would like to acknowledge the efforts of my co-authors, Dr. Michael Hypes (Morehead State University) and Julia Ann Hypes (Morehead State University). They were integral parts in the development and writing of this textbook. Without their efforts and expertise this book would have never seen the light of day. They have been members of the sport management professoriate for over twenty years.

With the aid of Joe Bannon, Sr. and his staff at Sagamore Publishing this book has entered the marketplace. The editorial assistance and support have been great. I greatly appreciate their patience and willingness to work with the authors. They are a great author-friendly publishing operation.

The quality of this book has been greatly enhanced by the assistance of Dr. Jerry Burnam. Dr. Burnam served as the developmental editor. He reviewed every chapter at least twice and made very useful and valuable suggestions as the book was being developed. He was very easy to work with and I greatly appreciated his insights.

All writers know how important it is to have a second set of critical eyes to read a manuscript and make sure it is reader-friendly. My second set of eyes is my wife and companion for life. Kathi is a former seventh grade English teacher and is a great copy editor. She makes sure the text is easy to read and comprehend. Without her expertise this book would not be as reader-friendly as it has become.

Foreword

Future sport managers must understand all aspects of financial management that will confront them once they become practitioners. It is our opinion that managers must assume proactive rather than reactive roles in confronting the fiscal challenges facing their organizations.

Further, it is evident that organizations that will be successful will have managers who adopt an entrepreneurial approach to financial management. The sport manager of the future will need to continuously seek new revenue resources and diversify those sources that already exist. Finally, the manager must ensure that their constituents, clients, and/or fans receive the most effective service or experience possible.

This book is intended to provide students in sport management curricula and professional practitioners with the first comprehensive survey coverage of the many traditional and innovative aspects of financial management. The focus of this text is on the basis of financial management including but not limited to diversification of revenue, acquisition of revenue resources, financial management, auditing, sponsorships, licensing, franchises, fundraising, and more. We believe the material in this text is different from what has appeared in other general finance texts.

The creation of this text has been a collaborative effort among the authors. Every aspect of the organization, research, and writing of the book has been a joint endeavor. Tom Sawyer, the lead author, was responsible for the chapters dealing with fundamentals of economics (1), organizing of the sport enterprise for financial management (2), accountability (5), revenue generation for facility development (8), concessions and merchandising (11), box office (10), fundamentals of fundraising (14), the booster or support organization (17), insurance (19), financial risk management (20), outsourcing services (13), and volunteers (18). Julia Ann Hypes prepared the chapters regarding financial analysis (3), the budget and financial planning (4). Mike Hypes developed the following chapters: purchasing (6), sponsorships (7), licensing (8), and the franchise game (9).

This text is aimed at upper division and graduate students in professional preparation curricula in sport management. Much of the information has been tested in our own classes. It has been revised in response to student feedback. Further, we believe this would be a useful book for practitioners in the field.

Foundations of Sport Finance

The ABC's of Economics: A Layman's Overview

Introduction

Once you have registered for this class, purchased this book, and begun leafing through its pages, you made a choice that cost you something—your time and money. There were other ways you could have spent your time and money, but the fact that you selected this class and the professor chose to require this book kept you from experiencing those other alternatives at this time in your life. Even now you must decide whether to continue reading this chapter or put the book aside and do something else. If you are still reading, it is natural to ask—why? Your answer might be that it is raining and there is nothing better to do. Hopefully, it is because you value your time reading this chapter more highly than you value alternatives such as watching TV, playing a computer game, going out on a date, sleeping, or studying for another subject. Otherwise, why would you continue reading as you are? And what about the cost (your time) that you are now incurring as a result of your decision to continue reading? It is a value you place on the most attractive of the many alternatives you now face. It is a cost because it is something that you must forego in order to do what you are doing.

The scenario above describes the process when one decides how to allocate resources. It is the underlying foundation of financial planning. It is simple economics at work.

Instructional Objective

After reading this chapter the student will be able to:
- understand the elements of a basic economic challenge,
- answer the question "What is economics?"
- explain key economic terms,
- discuss unionism in the United States, and
- describe the economic impact of venues and events on a city.

The Elements of a Basic Economic Challenge

The above example contains all of the essential elements of any economic challenge that will be faced by any sport manager. There are scarce resources—time and money—and many alternative uses of those resources. This creates a challenge of choice—an economic challenge. The decision must be made to utilize resources for a particular project and forego the opportunity of using them for another project. The project not chosen is the cost—the opportunity cost—of making the decision that was made.

If sport managers had open checkbooks, then financial management would be easy. However, the reality is that decisions need to be made and the sport manager needs to learn how to manage scarcity. Scarcity is a fact of life.

The challenge all financial managers face is how to allocate revenues among all possible competing uses. Choices must be made. This is a common economic problem worldwide. The common thread is scarcity of resources.

The ABCs of Economics

What is economics? Why do we have money? What determines the cost of the products we buy? Economics is the study of the market system. It is the study of how people make choices about what they buy, what they produce, and how our market system works. This chapter should clear up some of these mysteries with simple, common-sense answers. After reading it, you will have a better idea of what makes the economy tick.

The Science of Economics

Economics is the foundation for making sound financial decisions and developing solid financial plans and strategies. The sport manager needs to understand the science of economics in order to be successful. No sport enterprise can survive and grow without sound financial decision making in place.

Scarcity

People want many things in life; in fact, the more they have, the more they want. When a desire is fulfilled, another desire replaces it. Desires are infinite, but the resources to fulfill these desires are limited. There are not enough resources to give everyone what they want.

The concept of scarcity is one of the most important concepts in economics. If the resources existed to fulfill every desire, everybody would have everything they wanted; but life is not like that. There are limited resources, and decisions must be made about how to use those resources.

What are the Scarce Resources?

There are three common categories of resource—land, labor, and capital. The economist refers to them as factors of production. Land includes many forms: farmland, parkland, and open space. It also includes water, air, minerals, and fossil fuel resources. Finally, land is used as a receptacle for the deposit of waste materials.

Labor is a three-prong resource—time, muscle power, and brainpower. Peter Drucker indicates the most important worker group in society today and in the future is the "knowledge workers." Since the 1960s, Drucker has outlined three key themes relating to the labor force: (1) the primacy of knowledge and the knowledge worker, (2) the importance of hard to find information outside the organization, and (3) the need to fully use talents of older workers.

Capital is the produced resource. It refers to those produced factors of production (e.g., factory buildings, office buildings, machinery, equipment, roads, and bridges used in the production and/or distribution of goods and services). The capital stock consists of the sum total of those produced resources. Investment is the process of adding to the stock of capital.

If you apply the above definitions to a professional team, it would be as follows: the land is the land that the stadium, practice facilities, and offices and parking areas sit upon. The capital is the stadium, practice facilities, and offices and parking areas. The produced resources are the wins and losses of the team. The labor is considered the coaches, players, and management staff. The capital stock is the win/loss record of the team. The investment is the process of improving the win/loss record of the team.

Scarcity and the Decisions that are Made

Since resources are scarce (even for George Steinbrenner and the New York Yankees), it is critically important to use the resources strategically and wisely. In the American economy, resources are divided between the private sector and government (public sector). However, Drucker strongly suggests that managers need to keep a close view on global activities. Therefore, the sport manager needs to understand that in centrally controlled economic systems (e.g., European and Asian economies) government plays a major decision-making role.

There are four key components in economic decision making—what goods and services, how are they produced, for whom are they produced, and how extensively are resources used? What goods and services are to be produced by the organization that will blend into the economy is a very important decision to

be made by the organization. This is a fundamental decision and requires substantial knowledge of the economy past, present, and future.

Determining how to produce the goods and services is critical as well. A decision needs to be made for which resources are to be used in the production of the goods and services.

Prior to selecting the goods and services to be produced, the decision makers had already determined who the products and services were for. They also knew how to best engage these parties in the purchase of these products and services.

The final decision to be made focuses on how extensively the resources should be used. Whether some of the resources will remain idle or whether they will be fully employed for the production of the products and services must be considered.

Opportunity Costs

Since there are more desires than resources to fulfill them, we must choose one desire to fulfill over another. The opportunity cost of the decision is what you had to give up to have what you wanted. You may want a new stereo system and you may also want a television set but you do not have the money to buy both. If you choose to buy the stereo, the television set was the opportunity cost of that decision. You might decide to go out to dinner instead of going to movie. You might choose to stay up late studying for a final at the cost of some sleep. In each example, a choice was made; something was sacrificed; there was a cost, not necessarily a monetary cost.

Everything Has an Opportunity Cost

There are four basic questions that every economy must address. What should be produced? How many should be produced? What methods should be used?

How should the goods and services be distributed?

There are two kinds of economies: a command economy and a market economy. In a command economy, the government would answer all these questions. In a market economy, the marketplace decides how to answer the four basic questions. A market economy would answer these questions by saying that each producer can answer these questions themselves. A producer can make his own decisions, but these decisions would be determined by the marketplace. In other words, a producer makes decisions that will make his product sell and make him money. So the buying public really makes these decisions by choosing to buy, or not to buy, a product.

Here in the United States, we live in a market economy.

Characteristics of a Market Economy

There are five characteristics of a pure market economy: economic freedom, economic incentives, competition, private ownership, and limited government.

Economic Freedom

In a market economy, people have the freedom to make their own economic decisions. People have the right to decide what job they work at and their salary. A producer has the freedom to produce whatever product or products they want to and chooses what price to sell them. Everyone has the freedom to choose what is in their best interests as long as they don't interfere with the rights of others.

Economic incentives

While everyone has economic freedom, in practice it doesn't necessarily mean that people can simply do what they want. A producer has the freedom to charge an unreasonably high price for an item, but chances are people won't buy it. This is an example of an economic incentive. Economic incentives are the consequences, positive or negative, of making an economic decision. A positive incentive, such as making a profit on an item, encourages a producer to produce what the consumer wants. A negative incentive, such as a drop in profits or a boycott, would discourage producers from acting against the public interest.

Competition

There is competition in a pure market economy. This means that there isn't just one producer producing an item for the public. There are usually many producers of any given item. This gives consumers a choice in buying something. If they do not like the price or quality of a product made by one company, they can buy the product from another company. This encourages the producer to produce a quality product and charge a reasonable price for it. If they don't, they will lose business to "the other guy."

Private Ownership

In a market economy, the individual people or companies own the factors of production that they use to make their product as opposed to the factors of production being owned by the government.

Limited Government

A pure market economy requires a "limited" government; that is, a government that does not have absolute power over its people and plays no role in the economic decisions of the people. If the government was not limited, it would have control over the economy and there would be no economic freedom, and the economy would, by definition, be a command economy rather than a market economy.

The Factors of Production

To produce goods and services, resources must be used. These resources are the "factors of production:" These resources are Land, Labor, and Capital.

Land

The natural resources that people use: Forests, pasture land, minerals, water, etc.

Labor

The human ability to produce a good or service: Talents, skills, physical labor, etc.

Capital

Goods made by people to be used specifically to produce goods and services: Tools, office equipment, roads, factories, etc.

Another factor of production is Entrepreneurship. An entrepreneur is someone who puts all the factors of production together to make a good or service. Without any entrepreneurship, no good or service would be produced.

Circular Flow

In a market economy, there are two markets: The "factor market" and the "product market." In the factor market, the people who own the factors of production sell their services to the companies that produce products. In exchange, the companies give the workers wages, rent, and interest. In the factor market, the people are the sellers and the companies are the buyers. The people are selling their services to the production firms.

In the product market, companies sell the products they have produced to the people who pay money to the companies for them. The money is flowing in the opposite direction this time; people are buying products from the producing firms.

In this way, money flows through the economy in a circle. The money goes from the producers to the workers in the form of wages and the money then flows back to the producers in the form of payment for products.

The Invisible Hand

The Invisible Hand is the concept that producers will be guided as if by an "invisible hand" to produce what the public wants. The reason for this, ironically, is greed. A producer will produce what the public wants simply because that is what will create profit for him. Likewise, a producer also will not produce something harmful to the public since it would cause him to lose profits.

The Law of Demand

The Law of Demand states that when the price of an item goes down, the demand for it goes up. When the price drops, people who could not afford the item can now buy it, and people who were not willing to buy it before will now buy it at the lower price. Also, if the price of an item drops enough, people will buy more of the product and even find alternate uses for the product.

The benefits a person receives from a product depend on his/her goals. These goals are referred to as demand. The words "tastes," "wants," "needs," "preferences," and "usefulness" all refer to goals. When people's goals change, the amount of benefit they gain from the product changes and this will cause them to change the amount of the product they want to buy.

Goals, preferences or tastes, depend on many factors, including the age of people, the amount of education they have obtained, and the social customs. Social custom is an important determinant of preferences and can account for many differences in demand among groups.

The relationship between price and the amount of a product people want to buy is what economists call the demand curve. This relationship is inverse or indirect because as price gets higher, people want less of a particular product.

This inverse relationship is almost always found in studies of particular products.

There are various ways to express the relationship between price and the quantity that people will buy. Mathematically, economists say that quantity demanded is a function of price with other factors held constant, or:

$Qd = f(price, other factors held constant)$

Table 1.1 below captures this relationship. The numbers in Table 1.1 are what one expects in a demand curve: as price goes up, the amount people are willing to buy decreases. (Note: A widget is an imaginary product invented by an economist to use in illustrating an idea.)

Table 1.1

A Demand Curve	
Price of Widgets	Number of Widgets People Want to Buy
$1.00	100
$2.00	90
$3.00	70
$4.00	40

This same information can be plotted on a graph as a demand curve (see Graph 1.1).

Graph 1.1

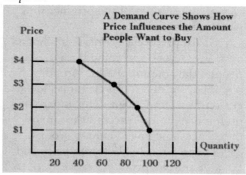

The Law of Supply

The relationship between the quantity sellers want to sell during some time period (quantity supplied) and price is what economists call the supply curve. Though usually the relationship is positive, so that when price increases so does quantity supplied, there are exceptions. Hence there is no law of supply that parallels the law of demand.

The supply curve can be expressed mathematically in functional form as:

$Qs = f(price, other factors held constant)$

It can also be illustrated in the form of a table (see Table 1.2) or a graph (see Graph 1.2).

Table 1.2

A Supply Curve	
Price of Widgets	Number of Widgets Sellers Want to Sell
$1.00	10
$2.00	40
$3.00	70
$4.00	140

Graph 1.2 shown below has a positive slope, which is the slope expected from a supply curve.

Graph 1.2

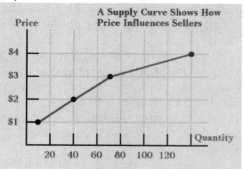

Supply curves as well as demand curves appear much more concrete on an economist's graph than they appear in real markets. A supply curve is mostly potential—what will happen if certain prices are charged, most of which will never be charged. From the buyer's perspective, the supply curve has more meaning as a boundary than as a relationship. The supply curve says that only certain price-quantity pairs will be available to buyers—those lying to the left of the supply curve.

Equilibrium Price

If a sample "demand graph" was drawn with price on the X-axis and quantity of a product demanded on the Y-axis, the graph would look like a downward sloping curve; as price increases, demand goes down. If a "supply graph" was drawn, it would be an upward sloping curve; as price increases, supply increases. If both curves are drawn on the same graph, the point at which they meet is the "Equilibrium Price" (see Graph 1.3). This is the price at which the amount of product demanded is equal to the amount of product supplied; in other words, if the price of a product is set at its equilibrium price, then for each individual product produced, there is a buyer for it. If the price of the product is set too high, then there will be more product produced than

bought; a surplus of goods would occur. If the price is set too low, there would be demand for a higher quantity of product than is being produced; a shortage would occur.

If a product turned out to suddenly become very popular and the total demand were to suddenly increase (that is, more people demand a product at any given price), the demand curve would shift up and right and the equilibrium price would increase. Likewise, if demand decreases, the demand curve would shift down and left and the equilibrium price would decrease.

If the total supply for a product were to increase, the curve would shift up and left and the equilibrium price would decrease. If the supply were to decrease, the curve would shift down and right and the equilibrium price would increase. This means the "demand goes up" (i.e., at a lower price more people are willing and able to buy it). Whereas when the "total demand goes up," the amount of demand at all prices goes up. If the price of an item drops and more people buy it, the demand for it goes up. If something has made the product more popular and more people are willing to buy it at any price, the total demand has gone up.

Graph 1.3 illustrates the concept with the estimated supply and demand for a snow cone in 2000 sold at the concession stand at the Indianapolis Indians, a triple A baseball club.

Graph 1.3

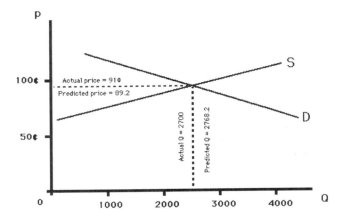

Third-party Costs and Benefits

When a business transaction takes place, there are two parties: (a) the seller who sells the product to the buyer, and (b) the buyer who buys the product from the seller. The transaction takes place between the two parties and no one else. Sometimes, however, a third party, someone who was not involved in the transaction, is either hurt or helped by the transaction. This is called a "third-party cost" or a "third-party benefit," respectively.

An example of a third-party cost would be a pack of cigarettes. There is the drug store owner as the seller, the smoker as the buyer, and the people who are offended by the smoker's smoking are the third party who are hurt by the transaction even though they had nothing to do with it.

A third-party benefit would be the nicotine patch. There's the seller of the patch, the smoker who buys the patch, and the third party who benefit are the people who no longer have to breathe the contaminated air from the smoker's cigarette.

Gross Domestic Product

The Gross Domestic Product is the total value of all goods and services produced in the country. In computing the GDP, only the value of the final goods and services are included. This means that only the value of the final product is included and not all the individual supplies that went into making that product. A house, for example, would only have its own value included in the GDP and not the lumber, brick, wire, glass, cement, and shingles that went into building it.

Business

In the American business environment ,,there are market structures that must be recognized and understood as well as different business types that are commonly employed. The sport manager needs to understand the various market structures and business types.

Market Structures

For any given product that is produced, its production market falls into one of four categories: pure competition, monopolistic competition, oligopoly, and monopoly (see Table 1.3 for a comparison of each). These categories are called the "market structures." The category that a product falls into depends on how many people are producing it.

In a purely competitive market, there are many buyers and sellers. It is easy for a new person to enter the market and the products are all pretty much identical. For example, an egg market that has 5,000 firms each make 10,000 eggs per year. 50 million eggs are being produced each year and each egg is the same as every other egg.

In a market with monopolistic competition, there is a large number of firms producing a product. Each firm has a small amount of control over the price and it is fairly easy for a new producer to enter the market. Each firm utilizes non-price competition; that is, they compete with the other firms, not by competing in price, but by trying to make their product unique, different from the products made by other companies in the market. This is called product differentiation. Examples of monopolistic competition are barbershops, restaurants, and bookstores. There are many firms in these markets. Each one is different and they compete with each other by emphasizing how their product or service is different from the others.

In an oligopoly, there are just a few large firms producing the product. There is limited entry into an oligopoly (in other words, it is difficult for a new firm to

Table 1.3

A Comparison of Four Types of Market Structures

Market	Number of firms	Control over price	Type of product	Entry	Competition
Pure competition	Very large	None	Standardized	Very easy	Price-based
Monopolistic competition	Large	Small	Differentiated	Fairly easy	Non-price
Oligopoly	Few dominant firms	Fair amount of control	Standardized or differentiated	Difficult	Non-price competition for differentiated products
Monopoly	One	Large	One	Blocked to other firms	Non-existent

enter into the market and be widely recognized and accepted), and oligopolies utilize non-price competition and product differentiation. An example of an oligopoly is the automobile industry where just a few large firms are producing the products.

In a pure monopoly, there is no competition at all, just one large firm making a given product. A monopoly can charge any price it wants for a product since there is no other producer with a lower price that consumers can go to. Since monopolies hurt consumers by not providing people with any choice of where to go, the government often breaks up monopolies.

Stocks and Bonds

When a corporation sells out a piece of itself, that piece is called a stock. Selling stocks is a way that corporations raise money to invest in their company. When a person buys a stock, he becomes part owner of the company. How big a part of that ownership is determined by how much stock he buys. Since a shareholder is part owner, he receives some of the profit of the company. Therefore, people invest in companies as a way to make money.

Another way that corporations raise money is to sell bonds. When a company sells a bond to a person, it is really borrowing money from that person with a promise to pay the money back, with interest, at a future date. A company that sells the bond must pay the value of the bond back when the payback date comes, even if they lose money. A bond, therefore, carries a lower risk which makes it more appealing to many investors.

There are two types of bonds: bearer bonds and registered bonds. When a person buys a bearer bond, he is given a coupon that he can turn in when it is time to collect on the bond. A person could buy a bond and give the coupon to someone else to turn in if he so desired. On the other hand, when a person buys a registered bond, the corporation keeps the bond on record so that only the person who bought the bond can collect on it. This adds a measure of safety against theft or loss.

The Stock Market

A number of teams in professional sports have gone public (i.e., Green Bay Packers) and have sold stock. There are interesting benefits (i.e., increased funding base) and challenges (i.e, stockholders to be accountable to for the bottom line) in becoming a public corporation. The sport manager must understand the impact of the stock market on financing the sport enterprise as a public and private entity.

Stock Exchange

A stock exchange is a place for businesses to sell stocks, pieces of owner-ship of the company, and for people to buy and sell stocks from each other. As more people buy a stock, the more valuable it becomes to shareholders and the price of the stock goes up. As people sell stock, the price of the stock goes down. The primary goal of a stock buyer is to buy the stock when the price is low and sell it later for a profit when the value of the stock rises. When a stock can be sold at a higher price than it was bought for, it is called a capital gain.

Common vs. Preferred Stock

There are two types of stock: com-mon and preferred. Owners of preferred stock are first in line for dividends and have a fixed dividend rate. Common stockholders are last in line for dividends and the dividend for a common stock-holder is variable. Common stockholders are allowed to vote for company directors so a common stockholder has a say in how the company is run. Preferred stockhold-ers, however, are usually not allowed to vote for the company directors. In short, common stockholders bear the greatest risk because they are last in line for dividends and their rate of dividend can drop.

Bull and Bear Markets

When people are optimistic and investment in the stock market is rising, it is called a "bull market." When people are pessimistic and investment is dropping, it is called a "bear market."

Buying on Margin

Buying on margin is when a person buys stock with borrowed money. A person buys stock on margin when he expects the price of the stock to go up. He can then pay back the loan out of the profit made on the stock.

Money and Inflation

Sport managers are always faced with making decisions regarding ticket prices and meeting payrolls. Understanding money and money flow is important when developing a solid financial plan for the sport entity. The sport manager must understand the impact of inflation on the overall financial picture for the sport entity.

What's So Wrong With Bartering?

The process of bartering is trading an item with a person for something in exchange. Before there was money, people simply traded some item to get what they wanted. There were many problems with bartering. One of the problems is that you cannot always find someone who has the item you want who wants something that you have. In fact, in many cases, both parties involved in a trade want the same thing and both have the same item to trade. Often the item you want is scarce and the items you have to trade are all abundant. If you have an abundant item, you cannot trade it for anything, since everyone has the item.

Another problem with bartering is that people might have to exchange a valuable item for an item of lesser value simply because they need the item and have nothing else to offer. For example, you may need a book for an economics class and the bookmaker wants a new car. The car is much more valuable than the book, but as you need the book to pass the class, you trade the car for the book because you have nothing else to trade.

However, if we have a system of money, you can simply put down money to buy the book. You do not have to trade something that is much more valuable than the item you want; you can just shell out the amount of money that represents the cost of what you want to buy.

Characteristics of Good Money

Money can come in different shapes, colors, and sizes. Money can be almost anything from salt to gold, but there are certain requirements for money to be a good medium of exchange. It needs to be easily recognized, easily divisible, portable, hard to duplicate, and it must be a good storer of value.

Money must be easily divisible. You need to be able to divide a large sum of money into smaller pieces in order to make a minor purchase. Gold is not easily divisible since a small amount is very valuable. You would have to shave off very small pieces with a knife to buy a soda at a convenience store and that small value would be hard to measure accurately.

Money also needs to be portable, meaning that it is easy to carry and transport. Salt would not make for very good money since you would have to carry a large and heavy amount around to make a small purchase. It would also be difficult to measure. You would need a measuring cup with you. Buying an item could turn into a major event.

Money must not be easily copied. If it were easy to reproduce, everyone would immediately make their own money and it would quickly lose value. Now we have special bars that go through bills so that they can be authenticated and special paper is used as well. Without all these precautions, money could be easily counterfeited and would be worthless.

Lastly, money must be a good storer of value. This means that you can put it away for a period of time and it will still be valuable when you need it. If you saved up a lot of money, but it had lost its value when you needed it the most, money would be useless.

Inflation

Inflation is when the cost of goods and services in the marketplace all go up at once. There are two main types of inflation: demand-pull inflation and cost-push inflation. Demand-pull inflation happens when people's incomes rise but the amount of goods and services in the marketplace remain the same. Since people have more money to spend, they

are willing to pay more for goods and services. In other words, the total demand will go up, which will cause prices to rise. Demand-pull inflation has been described as "more money chasing the same amount of goods." Cost-push inflation happens when the cost of producing the item goes up. This means that the total supply for an item goes down and again prices rise.

In general, inflation hurts people. When prices rise, people cannot buy as much with their money. People on a fixed income (i.e., an income that doesn't increase when the cost of living goes up) are especially hurt since the items they need to survive have increased in price but their incomes do not increase. Businesses are hurt since they cannot invest as much in the business and it is difficult to plan for the future if you do not know what the value of the dollar will be.

Some people are helped, however, and those people helped are people in debt (i.e., people who owe money). If someone borrows money and inflation causes the value of money to go down, then the money they pay back won't be worth as much as when they borrowed it. They essentially are paying less money back than they borrowed.

What is Economics Then?

Economics is the study of how scarce resources are allocated among alternative uses. It is the study of the choices people make with respect to the use of scarce resources and how they make their choices. It has, as its fundamental objective, the establishment of valid generalizations about the principles underlying the choices people make.

Macroeconomics (large) is concerned with the behavior of people in the aggregate, with the aggregate of consumers, the aggregate of business people, and with government overall.

Microeconomics (small) is the study of individual market participants (the individual consumer, the individual concern) and individual markets (the market for oil, the market for cars).

Economies of Scale

An important source of increased efficiency that often accompanies growth and greater mechanization is economies of scale. Economies of scale refers to the savings in resources made possible by increases in size—the scale—of the stadium or arena (i.e., increased seating, addition of luxury boxes, addition of club seating). When the scale of the stadium or arena is small, the addition of upscale restaurants and advanced technologies may not be profitable. When the stadium or arena is large, such luxury items are profitable and feasible.

Federal Reserve System

The Federal Reserve System (Fed) is the nation's central bank. It is structured like a pyramid. At the top sits the Board of Governors. Next is the Federal Open Market Committee, the monetary policy-making organ, followed by the 12 regional Federal Reserve Banks, and finally, the member and non-member depository institutions. The most important function of the Fed is to regulate the money supply and ensure an adequate supply of paper currency. Further, it performs check-clearing operations for depository institutions, supervises activities of financial institutions, and acts as a bank for the U.S. Treasury.

Law of Diminishing Marginal Utility

The law of diminishing marginal utility tells us that the extra utility diminishes with successive purchases. As more and more is purchased over a specific length of time, total utility will increase, but at a diminishing rate.

Law of Diminishing Returns (or the Law of Variable Proportions)

As equal amounts of one input are added to fixed amounts of the other inputs, total output will rise but at a diminishing rate. It is at a diminishing rate because one input will have less and less of the fixed inputs to work with. The amount of fixed inputs is reduced as other inputs are added, thus reducing the effect of the fixed inputs upon the overall return.

Law of Increasing (Opportunity) Costs

If resources are being used fully, the increased production of any one good will necessitate the reduced production of some other good(s). Therefore, with the production of any one good, resources must be withdrawn from employment elsewhere. There is a cost—an opportunity cost—to increasing the production of any one good.

Unionism in the United States

Unions are concerned with more than just the real wages of their members. They are concerned as well with how many of their members can obtain employment at the union wage scale; they are concerned with job security; they are concerned with job safety, job health, medical, insurance programs, and pension plans.

A Brief History

In the beginnings of the United States, most non-agricultural products were produced in small retail establishments called shops. Products were largely custom-made to meet the specifications of individual consumers. Apprentices (unskilled craftsmen) worked alongside journeymen (skilled craftsmen) and masters (journeymen owners). Most important was the fact that all apprentices, journeymen, and masters alike shared a common interest—maintaining the standards of the craft and product prices.

After the Revolutionary War, factories producing standardized products for the national market began to rapidly replace the craft shops. The shops could not produce a large quantity of products quickly enough for the consumer as could the factories; thus began the Industrial Revolution and the shift of apprentices and journeymen to the factories. As more and more factories were established, competition among producers became very intense. Accordingly, producers focused on holding down costs, which usually meant holding down wages, demanding longer hours for the same pay, and hiring cheaper labor. Many producers hired fewer journeymen and many more apprentices to be trained by the journeymen. As time went on, the producers tried to abolish the apprenticeship system replacing them with women and children who would work for less. This led the craftsmen to form unions to protect their rights.

Early Unions

The formation of the early unions began after the Revolutionary War and grew rapidly until the Great Depression. The earliest unions were formed (around the 1790s) as a consequence of specific disputes with employers over reduced wages and replacement of apprentices with women and children. Unions and labor societies were established early on for shoemakers (cordwainers), printers, carpenters, cabinetmakers, and masons. Later, unions for steamfitters and plumbers, miners, steelworkers, electricians, rail workers, and teamsters were formed.

Many unions tried to form closed shops (only union workers were employed). If the employers did not accede to the union's demands, the union would threaten to strike or to boycott the organization's products.

Employers strongly resisted union demands. Whenever unions would grow up, an employer's organization would spring up whose primary objective was to smash the unions. Employers sought assistance from the courts as well. The courts stripped the unions of their effective powers by declaring as illegal any of the actions unions might undertake in support of their cause—strikes, boycotts, and closed shops—on the grounds that those actions injured others—namely employers and nonunion members.

The employers continued to step up union-breaking efforts. They used many antiunion methods to discourage union development. The three most common methods used were the employment of strikebreakers (scabs), yellow-dog contract (workers agreed to not join or support a union), and the blacklist (a list circulated among employers with names of workers who should not be hired).

The union supporters continued their efforts to organize in spite of the antiunion methods. They formed the Knights of Labor (1869), which later became the American Federation of Labor [AFL] (1886). The purpose of the Knights of Labor was to make the labor force unified for social reform.

The AFL was concerned about only two areas—improving wages and working conditions for its members. It did not care about grand, utopian objectives or a program of social reform, which eventually caused the Knights of Labor to fold. The Achilles' heel of the AFL was that it only represented craft union workers and it could not capitalize on the growth opportunities that would have been possible had it appealed to the rapidly increasing numbers of unskilled industrial workers.

The heyday of unionism was between 1932 and 1947. During this period the union membership exploded, rising from three million to over 15 million.

Two factors were largely responsible for this dramatic change: the passage of new laws (e.g., Norris-LaGuardia Act which outlawed yellow-dog contracts, and the National Labor Relations Act which is referred to as the "Magna Carta of American unionism") passed by Congress that were decidedly prolabor, and the rise in industrial unions. Since the heyday, numerous pieces of legislation have been passed to pave the way for better labor relations such as the Taft-Hartley Act (known as the Labor Management Relations Act) and Landrum-Griffin Act (known as the Labor-Management Reporting and Disclosure Act).

The essence today of union-management relations is captured in the collective bargaining process. Professional baseball has seen more of its share of negative labor relations over the past two decades. Strikes by players and umpires have almost brought baseball to its knees. What factors influence the negotiators and therefore the ultimate contract? The factors are many and complex, including four considered to be central in every labor dispute: (a) financial status of employers and workers, (b) ease of passing on costs (to the consumer), (c) pattern of bargaining (other unions and other employers), and (d) government intervention.

The common contract issues that are central to the collective bargaining process include:
- Pay (e.g., piece work, profit sharing, wage differences, overtime compensation, bonuses, performance pay, and cost-of-living adjustments),
- Fringe benefits,
- Bonuses,
- Working conditions, and
- Job security (e.g., seniority, work rules, and grievance procedures).

Finally, the outcome of the collective bargaining process is a contract that spells out the wages and working conditions agreed to by employers and union members.

Economic Impact of Venues and Events

Unlike most studies commissioned by stadium advocates, the consensus in the academic literature has been that the overall sports environment has no measurable effect on the level of real income in metropolitan areas. Coates and Humphreys (2000) suggest that professional sports may be a drain on local economies rather than act as an engine of economic growth that advocates would have you believe. The evidence from numerous academic studies (Baade & Dye, 1990; Quirk & Fort, 1992; Rosentraub, Swindell, Przybylski, & Mullins, 1994; Crompton, 1995; Baade, 1996; Noll & Zimbalist, 1997; and Coates & Humphreys, 1999) suggests that attracting a professional sports franchise to a city and building that franchise a new stadium or arena will have no effect on the growth rate of real per capita income and may, in fact, reduce the level of real per capita income in that city.

The Coates and Humphreys (2000) study indicates that, "the presence of professional sports teams, on average, reduces the level of real per capita income in metropolitan areas." However, this result differs from much of the existing literature (Baade & Dye, 1990; Quirk & Fort, 1992; Rosentraub, Swindell, Przybylski, & Mullins, 1994; Crompton, 1995; Baade, 1996; Noll & Zimbalist, 1997) which generally has found no impact at all; but the Coates and Humphreys (1999, 2000) studies used a broader and longer panel of data and a richer set of variables reflecting the sports environment than the previous studies.

Coates and Humphreys (2000) used the following example to illustrate their findings:

"The arrival of a new basketball franchise in a metropolitan area increases real per capita income by about $67. However, building a new arena for that basketball team reduces real per capita income by almost $73 in each of the 10 years following the construction of the arena, leading to a net loss of about $6 per person. Similarly, in cities that have baseball franchises, the net effect of an existing baseball team playing in a 37,000-seat baseball-only stadium is a $10 reduction of real per capita income."

Finally, one thing is clear from the evidence on professional sport franchises: "owners are reaping substantial benefits in the value of their teams because they are skilled at the stadium gambit and cities are not gaining in the growth rate of the real per capita income and, in many cases, may see a reduction in the level of real per capita income" (Coates & Humphreys, 2000).

Summary

It is important for the sport manager to understand the fundamentals of economics and how economics relates to overall financial management. Good financial management requires the sport manager to make sound economic decisions in a world with scarce resources. The point sport managers need to understand is this: the sum of individual and collective wants far outstrips the resources that are available to satisfy those wants. No matter how well off an organization is, a long list can always be produced of unsatisfied wants and needs. These desires are unmet simply because the organization does not have the means to satisfy them. The American economic system is often described as affluent, but it is important to note that the quantities of goods and services produced and consumed would have to increase significantly if the average American were to be as well off as our nation's moderately wealthy people.

Finally, the economic impact of professional sports on the local economic development can be best explained by the following quote from Bill Veeck: "We play the Star-Spangled Banner before every game—you want us to pay taxes, too?"

References

Baade, R.A. (1996). Professional sports and catalysts for metropolitan economic development. *Journal of Urban Affairs*, *18*, 1.

Baade, R.A., & Dye, R.F. (1990). The impact of stadiums and professional sports on metropolitan area development. *Growth and Change, 12*, 1.

Coates, D., & Humphreys, B.R. (2000). The stadium gambit and local economic development. *Regulation, 23*(2), 15.

Coates, D., & Humphreys, B.R. (1999). The growth effects of sport franchises, stadia, and arenas. *Journal of Policy Analysis and Management, 18*, 601.

Crompton, J.L. (1995). Analysis of sports facilities and events: Eleven sources of misapplication. *Journal of Sports Management, 9*, 14.

Noll, R.G., & Zimbalist, A. (1997). *Sports, jobs, and taxes: The economic impact of professional sports teams and stadiums.* Washington, D.C., The Brookings Institution.

Quirk, J.P., & Fort, R.D. (1992). *Pay dirt: The business of professional team sports.* Princeton: Princeton University Press.

Rosentraub, M.S., Swindell, D., Przybylski, M., & Mullins, D. (1994). Sports and downtown development strategy: If you build it, will jobs come? *Journal of Urban Affairs, 16*, 221.

Organizing the Sport Enterprise

In small enterprises, organization may be informal and change from day to day. Boutiques, small family businesses, and other similar enterprises may not spend much time organizing at all. However, for large complex enterprises such as a professional sport franchise, athletic shoe and apparel company, or sporting goods manufacturer with larger and more complex objectives, sound organization is a prerequisite for operational effectiveness.

Organizing is the process by which employees and their jobs are related to each other for accomplishing enterprise objectives. It consists of dividing work between groups and individuals and coordinating group and individual activities. Further, organizing involves establishing appropriate managerial authority. Keeping this description in mind, note the following points since each is a crucial aspect of organizing:

Goals

Setting goals creates order out of chaos. Since all enterprises are composed of individuals, they are subject to chaos. Organization is important because it helps clarify enterprise goals as they relate to individual employees and work units.

Formal Relationships

A second aspect of organizing is informing employees of what must be done and how individual jobs relate to each other. Without formal relationships, no one would know who was supposed to do what and how jobs were to be coordinated to achieve an enterprise's objectives.

Stable Relationships

Effective organization has solid stable relationships. An enterprise cannot claim to be organized if each time an expense voucher is submitted it is routed to a different person in a different department. The result would be chaos. Effective organization requires reasonably long-lasting relationships among jobs even if employees change.

Authority

A final aspect of organizing is establishing appropriate managerial authority over various work units. In the absence of authority, organized action would be impossible. Managers need authority not only to perform their managerial roles but also to direct and coordinate subordinates. In this regard, the formal relationship between a superior and subordinate is solely based on managerial authority.

Before considering three introductory questions, let us first consider how enterprises formalize their structure. If you were to ask the manager of a self-service gas station and convenience store how it is organized, chances are the manager's response would be phrased in general terms. "The attendants stock the shelves, rotate the dairy products in the freezer, prepare deli sandwiches, ring-up the sales, and keep the store area clean," the manager might say. As long as the enterprise's organization is well conceived and clearly communicated to all employees, this may be quite adequate. What is most vital for effective organizing is a thorough understanding by all employees of the formal relationships involved.

Most large and many medium-size sporting enterprises formalize their structure through the use of organization charts and organization manuals to achieve this understanding among their employees. The chart portrays an enterprise's structure graphically, while the manual describes it in writing. Organizational charts and manuals are used because it is often difficult to communicate verbally the structural relationships that comprise an enterprise.

Learning Objectives

After reading this chapter the student will be able to:
- Identify a formalized form of departmentalization,
- Recount the advantages and disadvantages of a formalized, product, territorial, and customer departmentalization,
- Clarify what is meant by "chain of command",
- Distinguish between "delegation" and "decentralization/centralization" as they relate to authority,
- Differentiate line units from staff units,
- Define the term "unity of command",
- Organize a sport enterprise for financial management, and
- Design a small business.

Organizational Chart or Blueprint

Organizational charts are the most common method of formalizing the sport enterprise management structure. Occasionally referred to as a table of organization, an organizational chart is a graphic representation or blueprint of all the work units and jobs in a sport enterprise and how they are structurally related. No organizational chart can ever totally reflect the enterprise it is meant to depict. Generally omitted are the informal relationships between employees who have no reporting responsibility to one another but must nevertheless coordinate their activities.

Also omitted are the informal group and individual coalitions that come and go in any well-established enterprise.

In this regard, it often has been noted that organizational charts are, at best, windows into the dynamic process of enterprise life. The information they convey is an important means for formalizing an enterprise's structure.

The Organization Manual or Handbook

Some enterprises further formalize their structure by preparing an organization manual or handbook, which usually contains:
- A statement of objectives,
- Enterprise history,
- An organization chart,
- Job descriptions for top managers,
- Personnel policies and procedures,
- Terms and conditions of employment (e.g., pay, hours, transfers, and promotions),
- Holidays and vacations, and
- Employee benefits and services (e.g., health insurance, life insurance, disability insurance, and retirement).

If prepared in a professional manner, manuals or handbooks can be expensive and difficult to maintain. Charts and manuals do provide a beginning point for formalizing an enterprise's structure. Thus, if properly prepared, they help define structural relationships between jobs and people.

Organizing into Structures or Work Units

After designing jobs, the first question a manager must answer is, "How can jobs be effectively organized into work units?" To understand how this is accomplished, we will consider how jobs are grouped into work units as an enterprise grows. There are six common structures found in corporate America: primitive structure or agency form, functional, product, territorial, customer, and mixed or hybrid structures.

Primitive Structure or Agency Form

As an illustration, imagine a family owned and operated Triple "A" baseball franchise in a mid-sized metropolitan area. Initially, its founder and owner sold the tickets, advertising, sponsorships, hot dogs, popcorn, and beer, maintained the field and facility, handed out programs, coached and managed the team, provided sport injury care, and drove the bus with the help of his wife and children. As the franchise grew, he hired high school students to work part-time each afternoon and on Saturdays and Sundays. Soon he had five full-time employees, then 10, then 15. At this point, the firm could be depicted as a boss and several employees (a primitive structure). All employees report directly to the boss and s/he provides the necessary coordination through personal supervision. Thus, each acts as an agent or extension of the boss who coordinates all the company's activities and performs all managerial tasks. Employee authority derives directly from the boss. It is as his agents that employees perform their duties. They can be asked to do whatever is required. Such a structure is quite flexible. At the same time, it is notably constrained in its ability to cope with complexity since all coordination depends on the boss whose capacity is necessarily limited (see Figure 2.1).

Figure 2.1

Primitive Structure
Small Town USA

"A" Baseball Franchise
Organizational Chart

Founder

Employees

Functional Structure

As the franchise grew and increased in complexity, the boss could no longer coordinate all the activities and also effectively perform other necessary managerial tasks. So, informally, he asked one employee to help with sales (probably calling on minor accounts), another to help schedule work hours, and another to order supplies. They became his assistants. Eventually this structure became formalized; that is, the assistants became full-time specialists and the company developed functional departments similar to that shown in Figure 2.2.

The functional structure was developed at the turn of this century in response to the increasing size and complexity of business undertakings. A functionally structured enterprise groups its activities into separate units or departments of which each undertakes a distinctive function such as business manager, marketing/sales manager, player development coordinator, field and facility superintendent, sport medicine director, field manager, coaches, transportation manager, and more. A deeper specialization and focused concentration on functional activities is even more apparent. As might be expected, the principal strength of functional structure is its emphasis on functional interests within specialized departments. With enterprise growth, there is a multiplication of employees performing the same function and an ever-increasing refinement of specialized skills. The result is a gain in economics of scale and overhead. For instance, once all sales and marketing people are grouped into a central marketing department, it is possible to distinguish between marketing, advertising, promotion, and sales specialties.

Among other advantages of functional structure are:
- Provides a simple communication and decision network,
- Facilitates measurement of functional output and results,
- Simplifies training of functional specialists,
- Gives status to major functional areas,
- Preserves strategic control at the top management level,
- Maximizes functional interests within departmental units, and
- Results in efficient use of resources.

Figure 2.2

Functional Structure

"AAA" Baseball Franchise
Organizational Chart

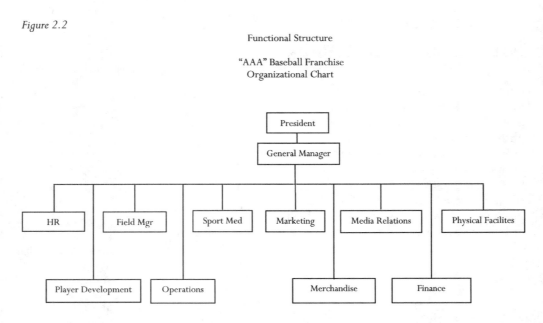

The major shortcoming of functional structure is that the larger the number of departments, the more difficult it becomes to achieve coordination between specialties. Under such circumstances, interdepartmental cooperation can emerge as a problem. This, in turn, fosters a parochial emphasis on departmental objectives with a minimal appreciation of broader enterprise goals.

Other disadvantages of functional departmentalization include:
- Cost of coordination between departments can be high,
- Employee identification with specialist groups makes change difficult,
- Preparation of broadly trained managers is limited,
- Coordination between functional areas is difficult,
- Limited preparation of broadly trained managers,
- Encourages interdepartmental rivalry and conflict, and
- Client satisfaction can be low.

Product Structure

Grouping activities on the basis of product lines began in early 1920s. This was brought about as a solution to two major structural problems faced by many corporations: (1) inadequate strategic responsiveness to the demands of the market and (2) lack of a broad perspective necessary to efficiently coordinate an ever-increasing number of specialized inputs. The common response to these problems was a structure whose primary basis for grouping was by product rather than function. With product structure, each major product line is administered through a separate and semi-autonomous division. The result is a structure that provides both strategic responsiveness and efficient coordination of a larger number of specialized inputs. To this end, specialists of different types are grouped together to perform all the duties necessary to produce an individual good or service. For example, Nike, Reebok, Fila, Converse, Polo Ralph Lauren, Tommy Hilfiger, Rockport, and Greg Norman Collection have athletic footwear and attire divisions and Adidas-Salomon has athletic footwear, attire, and hardware sport products which are structured along product lines. A majority of the world's largest corporations (i.e., General

Figure 2.3

Product Structure

XYZ Sporting Goods Company

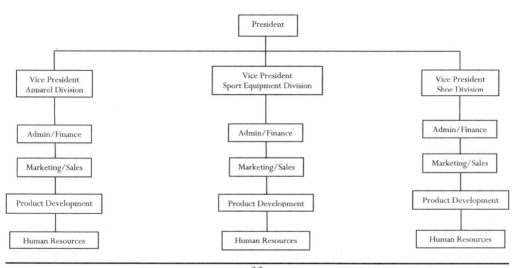

Motors, Ford, General Mills, Proctor and Gamble, Hewlett-Packard, Sears, Du Pont, Westinghouse Electric, General Electric, etc.) are structured according to product structure (see Figure 2.3).

Each separate unit (for example, Nike Corporation – apparel, equipment, and shoes) in a firm that is structured by product is a replica of an individual, functionally organized enterprise. A major difference, however, is that although each department in a functional structure can only be assessed as an expense (i.e., expenditures or costs) center or revenue (i.e., income) center, in a product firm, departments can be evaluated as profit (i.e., the amount of money that exceeds total expenditures) centers since they have identifiable cash flows comprised of revenues and expenses. Moreover, product departmentalization is better able to accommodate growth than its functional counterpart. The addition of new product departments (whether acquired from outside or generated within) is relatively straightforward. New departments can be added on a self-contained basis having a similar relationship to headquarters as do existing departments.

Additional benefits of product structure include:
- Facilitates coordination between functions for rapid response,
- Focuses on client needs and thus leads to greater customer service and satisfaction,
- Develops broadly trained managers,
- Evaluates departments as autonomous profit centers, and
- Adds flexibility to an enterprise's structure.

The major disadvantage associated with product structure is the dilemma of coordination between product areas. A lack of clarity in responsibilities and a decrease in professional contacts between product specialists are likely to develop as structural complexity increases. As a result, coordination problems typically occur as a result of communication difficulties arising between units separated into product departments.

Other disadvantages of product structure are:
- Leads to a decrease in professional communication between functional specialists,
- Contributes to a duplication of services in functional areas such as marketing research and financial analysis, and
- Increases coordination problems between specialized product areas.

Territorial Structure

Territorial structure is appropriate for large enterprises whose activities are physically dispersed. Territorial structure groups activities based on geographic location. Boundaries are determined by distance, natural, legal, political, and cultural considerations. Its principal advantage is that it allows units operating in different environments to adapt to local circumstances. For this reason, territorial structure is popular not only among enterprises that are geographically dispersed, but also among those that operate in several regions with different legal, political, or cultural environments. A classic illustration would be Nike and other sporting goods companies, which operate in many international locations. Adapting to national differences is of extremely critical importance. This advantage, however, is not without cost. Since territorial structure requires a large number of general managers, it can lead to duplication of services (i.e., finance, human resource, marketing, and distribution activities) and often presents increased problems for top management control over local operations.

Territorial structure is particularly suited for multinational business corporations such as Nike, Spalding Sporting Goods, Wilson Sporting Goods, Adidas-Salomon, Fila, Reebok, Rockport, Russell-Southern, and Riddell. In this structure, each division manager is responsible for various units, which might

Figure 2.4

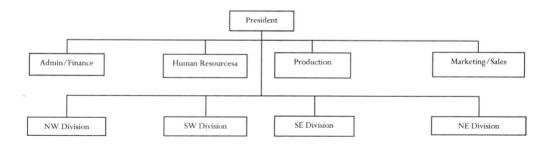

Territorial Structure

XYZ Sporting Goods Company

include accounting, human resource management, marketing, and so on (see Figure 2.4).

Customer Structure

This form is often selected when an enterprise's clients have very different needs and the enterprise seeks to cater to the specific requirements of different buyers.

A university may offer on-campus, off-campus, or extension courses, day and night classes, undergraduate and graduate classes, which are all designed to meet the specific needs of the various customers it hopes to serve. A marketing department within a sport franchise may very well be divided into groups (i.e., group sales, luxury box sales, club seating sales, sponsorships, and advertising). (See Figure 2.5.)

While customer structure has the advantage of tying performance to requirements of key market segments, it is not without disadvantages. Given the diverse nature of the client groups served, establishment of consistent and uniform company-wide practices is quite difficult. As a consequence, pressure often develops for special treatment of various buyers. Such preferential consideration may or may not be merited. An additional drawback emerges when customer groups develop at an unequal pace. During periods of recession, for example, banks may find the number of new construction loans to be processed is so low as to make it uneconomical to staff a separate department to serve that segment. However, during expansion, that same segment may grow at such a rapid pace that managing staffing and arranging facilities to meet the demand becomes a problem. Either

Figure 2.5

Customer Structure

XYZ Sporting Goods Company

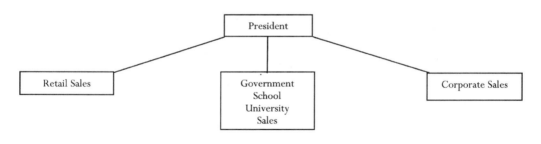

instance will likely result in the underutilization of facilities and personnel.

Mixed Structure

It is common to mix the various types of structures into hybrid forms. For example, Nike, a sporting goods company, has three major product groups (apparel, equipment, and shoes), which are organized into three product divisions (product structure). Each division is organized into three departments: production, distribution, and finance (functional structure). Finally, each division has broken the world into regions including the United States, Canada, Europe, Far East, Asia, and so on (territorial structure). In the XYZ corporation case there are three common structures combined to form the corporation's organizational structure. This type of blending is found in most major corporations (see Figure 2.6).

Internal Factors Influencing Structure

There are three common internal factors that can influence structure: (1) size, (2) product diversity, and (3) employee characteristics.

Size

Size, as determined by the number of employees, is an influence on structure. Research on the relationship between size and structure underscores three major findings. First, as size increases, structure becomes more standardized and formalized. That is, there is greater use of rules and procedures (standardization) and an increased reliance on paperwork (formalization) to coordinate activities. Both standardization and formalization become necessary when an enterprise grows too complex to control by informal means.

Figure 2.6

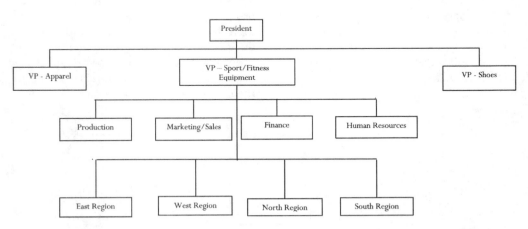

Mixed Structure

XYZ Sporting Goods Company

Note: The structure under the VP for Apparel and VP for Shoes would be the same as the VP for Sport/Fitness Equipment in a mixed structure.

Second, as size increases, the number of managerial levels typically increases. As this occurs, relationships among managers at different levels are likely to become increasingly abstract and impersonal. Managers occupying similar positions at the same level may interact to an increasing extent according to simplified job definitions associated with their titles. Federal employees, for example, often refer to one another and interact according to their GS level.

Third, as size increases, the proportion of employees engaged in administrative activities decreases. The relationship between size and the proportion of employees in administrative positions is known as administrative intensity. As an enterprise increases in size, economies of scale in administration are typically achieved. Economies of scale occur for several reasons:

- Larger enterprises generally can use labor saving machines and methods more efficiently (i.e., computers and standard record keeping) to handle routine administrative matters. The cost of such technology may not be justifiable in smaller enterprises.
- Despite an enterprise's size, different types of people must usually be hired to perform different administrative tasks. Except in the very smallest enterprises, a marketing manager, for example, would not be expected also to handle financial concerns. Consequently, smaller enterprises often find themselves underutilizing the administrative services of their employees. This idle capacity can only be fully utilized with increases in size. Therefore, an increase in output may require additional operative employees but not necessarily more administrative personnel. As size increases, spans of control can often be increased, thus making more complete use of existing administrative services.

- The benefits of division of labor (occupational specialties), standardization, formalization and departmentalization tend to increase with size. The advantages of a well-designed structure are usually more fully realized in larger enterprises.

Product Diversity

An enterprise is said to have a diverse product line if it produces a large number of goods and services. An increase in product diversity is typically accompanied by an increase in structural complexity. Compare, for example, the structure and product diversity of Nike with that of any Fortune 500 corporation or imagine how the structure of Nike has changed from the time it was a small manufacturer of one product—athletic footwear—to its current status as a multimillion dollar manufacturer of many more products.

Employee Characteristics

The characteristics of an enterprise's employees are the third internal factor that influences structure. In assessing the appropriateness of a structure, potential employee reactions must be considered. Employees typically have expectations of how an enterprise should operate. The more accurately managers understand these expectations, the more likely it is they will design a structure that will foster effective performance.

The New York Yankees need a pitcher, Nike needs designers, the University of North Carolina needs a head athletic trainer, and the NFL needs a lawyer. The type of structure appropriate for each must not only match its specific strategy but also reflect the expectations of its employees. For instance, employees who are highly creative, achievement-oriented, accept responsibility, and understand and identify with an enterprise's objectives will probably respond most favorably to a loose structure. A rigid structure built on excessive rules and procedures is likely to stifle their effectiveness.

Chain of Command

There are generally three levels of management: (1) first-line, (2) middle, and (3) top. As noted, the degree of managerial authority varies as one moves between levels. The higher the management level, the greater the authority. The line of vertical authority that starts at top management with a president and progresses down to first-line management is known as an enterprise's chain of command. A chain of command exists whenever one individual is made a subordinate of another. In addition to defining different levels of authority, a chain of command routes directives and other information up and down an enterprise. Figure 2.7 depicts the chain of command of a typical university athletic organization. Actual chains of command vary widely.

Delegation of Authority

The process by which authority passes from one managerial level to another is known as delegation. It is especially important to realize that by delegating authority, managers do not reduce their own accountability. They remain responsible for their own actions and those of their subordinates. Delegation of authority, however, does extend a manager's reach. The captain of a baseball team may be an excellent pitcher, but he can't play all nine positions. In the same sense, no manager has time to personally perform all the work in his or her department. Delegating authority enables a manager to identify and utilize employee talents.

Experience suggests that, despite the necessity to do so, managers are often reluctant to delegate authority. They commonly lack trained subordinates to whom they can delegate authority, or they believe that only they themselves are capable of doing a task. Managers also fear

Figure 2.7

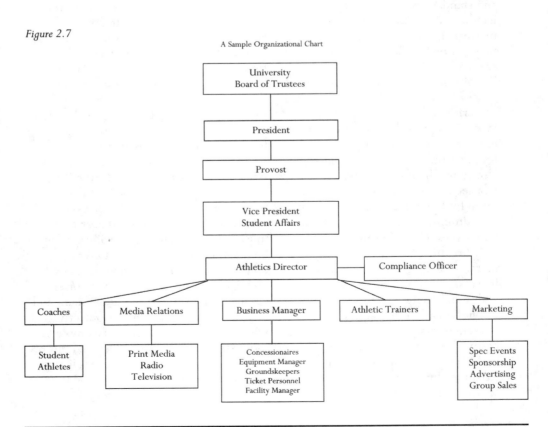

A Sample Organizational Chart

that subordinates will make mistakes; although, if someone handles a task well, a manager may fear the person as a competitor. Some managers fear that delegation of authority makes them look lazy. Others find it so difficult to communicate directions clearly that they take what seems the easier approach and do everything themselves.

Of course, if subordinates are unwilling to accept delegated authority, managers may have no choice but to take on the work themselves. Managers most commonly encounter resistance of this kind because their employees:

- Have not received proper job information,
- Have not been properly trained to perform a task as required,
- Lack self-confidence and fear personal failure,
- Have not been provided the proper equipment or tools to carry out a task.
- Are not certain of the extent of authority they have been given,
- Are not convinced there is anything to gain by accepting authority, and
- Find it easier to let the manager make all decisions.

Given these hurdles, here are several pointers to assure effective delegation:

- Be sure that delegates are willing to accept authority,
- Be sure they understand what you expect them to do,
- Be sure they possess the knowledge, skills, and abilities required to perform a task as required,
- Establish policies delegates can use to guide their decisions,
- Specify deadlines; avoid generalities,
- Establish controls to evaluate delegate performance,
- Reward delegates who get things done, and
- Admit that others can do a task as well as you can.

An enterprise is considered centralized to the degree that authority is not delegated but is concentrated at higher levels of management. In contrast, to the degree that authority is delegated, an enterprise is considered decentralized. The terms centralization and decentralization are only meaningful in a relative sense. An enterprise could not operate on a completely decentralized basis since all authority to make decisions would rest at the lowest managerial level, and it would lack the coordination essential to operating efficiency. Nor could an enterprise, other than perhaps a very small and simple firm, be completely centralized since all authority would be reserved for top management, and it would lack the needed flexibility to ensure that a variety of work is accomplished.

Line Units and Staff Units

Delegation of authority has direct implications for the activities of different enterprise members. In this regard, it is important to distinguish between line and staff managers. In any enterprise, the degree of a manager's authority is affected by many factors. One of the most important of these is the nature of the position the manager holds. In most large enterprises, a distinction is made between line units and staff units. Line units are those that contribute directly to accomplishing an enterprise's objectives. Thus, production, marketing, and finance are considered the major line units in a manufacturing firm because they contribute directly to achieving the objectives of producing and selling goods at a profit. Similarly, infantry, artillery, and armor are line units in an army because they contribute directly to achieving the objectives of meeting and defeating an enemy.

Staff units are those that contribute indirectly to accomplishing an enterprise's objectives. That is, they provide advice and expertise to assist line units in achieving their objectives. Any number of staff units can exist. For example, in the previously mentioned manufacturing firm, labor relations, accounting, logistics, administrative services, management information systems, research and development, public relations, and legal affairs would be considered staff units because they provide advice and expertise to assist line units. One way of determining whether a unit is line or staff is to ask, "Does this unit contribute directly to achieving an enterprise's objectives?" If the answer is yes, it is line. If the answer is no, it is staff.

In preparing organization charts, staff units are traditionally positioned to the right of line units. Since staff units provide advice and expertise, but have no authority over line units, they are customarily indicated with a dotted hash mark. This is to show that they fall outside an enterprise's direct chain of command. Line units are so-called because they are on "the line of authority" from an enterprise's president. Staff units are so called because they provide support, much like a shepherd's staff.

Centralization

Centralization has the following advantages to be considered:
- A greater uniformity in decisions is possible,
- Top-level managers are more aware of future enterprise plans and thus more likely to make decisions in an enterprise's best interests,
- It requires fewer skilled (and higher paid) managers, and
- It requires less extensive planning and reporting procedures.

Decentralization

Decentralization has the following advantages to be considered:
- Lower-level managerial problems can be dealt with on the spot,
- It provides lower-level managers with an opportunity to develop their decision-making skills,
- The motivation of lower-level managers is greater when they are entrusted to make decisions rather than always following orders issued at a higher level, and

- It spreads an enterprise's work load and allows top-level managers more time for strategic planning.

Organizing a Sport Enterprise for Financial Management

As enterprises grow in scope and complexity, a point is generally reached when it becomes necessary to seek the assistance of a specialized support staff. Emergence of staff units represents another aspect of a seemingly irresistible trend toward a greater and greater division of labor in a society becoming ever more complex.

A sport enterprise's ability to secure funds for a particular sport business depends on how the sport enterprise is structured for financial management. Funding alternatives differ depending on the sport business industry segment. Sources of funding differ for not-for-profit sport enterprises, for profit sport businesses, sport stadia and arenas, and park and recreation operations.

Sport managers interested in opening sport enterprises (i.e., bowling alleys, ice or roller skating rinks, miniature golf courses, par three golf courses, skateboard parks, aquatic facilities, health and fitness clubs, etc.) must decide early on the business structure providing the optimal benefits. The type of business structure selected for the sport entity will influence short-and long- term operations. The traditional business formations include not for-profit, for profit, sole proprietorship, general partnership, limited partnership, limited liability partnership, limited liability corporation, the S corporation, and the C corporation. This chapter will examine the various businesses structure mentioned above. However, the sport enterprise developers should consult an attorney before proceeding too far down the road.

For-Profit Business

There are endless for-profit sport-related business ventures, including but not limited to, the retail or wholesale of recreation and sporting goods, health/fitness clubs, recreation and sport manufacturers, bowling facilities, golf courses, aquatic facilities, ice or roller skating rinks, tennis complexes, skateboard parks, and more. A for-profit business is one that is generally incorporated. Its main function is to make a profit by selling products, producing products, providing entertainment, or providing needed services.

Not-for-Profit Business

Not unlike the for-profit sport enterprises, there are scores of not-for-profit sport-related business ventures including, but not limited to, youth sport leagues (e.g., Pop Warner Football, Little League Baseball, American Legion Baseball, Youth Soccer, Miss USA Softball, AAU basketball, and more), YMCA instructional sport leagues, YWCA sport programs, city or county park and recreation programs, and Boys and Girls Club sport leagues. A not-for-profit sport-related business is generally incorporated and tax-exempted [501 (c)(3)] or is a governmental agency. Its main function is to provide programming and break-even or to show a small profit.

What Is a Sole Proprietorship?

A form of business organization in which an individual is fully and personally liable for all the obligations (including debts) of the business is entitled to all of its profits and exercises complete managerial control.

What Is a General Partnership?

One of two kinds of partnership is a limited partnership. A general partnership has the right to participate in the management of the partnership and has unlimited personal liability for its debts.

What Is a Limited Partnership?

A partnership that has two kinds of partners: limited partners who provide financial backing and have little role in management and no personal liability, and general partners who are responsible for managing the entity and have unlimited personal liability for its debts.

What Is a Limited Liability Company?

A limited liability company, like a corporation, is a legal entity existing separately from its owners. A limited liability company is created when proper articles of organization (or the equivalent, under the laws of a particular state) are filed with the proper state authority and all fees are paid. State laws typically impose additional pre or post-creation requirements as well.

A limited liability company is not a partnership or a corporation, but it combines the corporate advantages of limited liability with (normally) the partnership advantage of pass-through taxation.

What Is a Limited Liability Partnership?

The Limited Liability Partnership (LLP) is essentially a general partnership in form with one important difference. Unlike a general partnership in which individual partners are liable for the partnership's debts and obligations, an LLP provides each of its individual partners protection against personal liability for certain partnership liabilities.

The limit of an individual partner's liability depends on the scope of the state's LLP legislation. Many states provide protection only against tort claims and do not extend protection to a partner's own negligence or incompetence or to the partner's involvement in supervising wrongful conduct. Other states provide broad protection, including protection against contractual claims brought by the partnership's creditors.

What Is a Professional Limited Liability Partnership?

A partnership that renders specific professional services may form an LLP and register as a professional limited liability partnership (PLLP). A PLLP is generally the same as an LLP except that it is an association solely of professionals. Each state specifies the qualifying professions for a PLLP. This business form is typically available to attorneys, physicians, architects, dentists, engineers, and accountants.

What Is an S Corporation?

Unlike C corporations, an S corporation is a corporation that elects to be treated as a partnership for tax purposes and is, therefore, not subject to double taxation. There are, however, certain restrictions:

- The corporation must not have more than 75 stockholders. (Husband and wives are treated as one stockholder.)
- Each stockholder must be a citizen or resident of the United States.
- The corporation must have only one class of stock (however, voting differences within a class of stock is permissible).
- The corporation must use the calendar year as its fiscal year unless it can demonstrate to the IRS that another fiscal year satisfies a business purpose.
- Not more than 25 percent of the corporation's income can be from passive activities, such as annuities, dividends, rents, royalties, etc.

What Is a C Corporation?

A C corporation is an organization formed under state or federal law. It is an artificial entity legally separate from its owners.

- Shareholders own the corporation.
- The percentage of stock owned by a shareholder determines how much control that shareholder has in the corporation.
- If a shareholder owns 51 percent of the voting stock, that shareholder holds controlling interest.
- To form a corporation, only one shareholder is required.
- Shareholders elect the Board of Directors.
- The Board of Directors control overall corporate policies and procedures.
- The Board of Directors elect corporate officers: President, Vice-President, Secretary, and Treasurer.
- The corporate officers run the day-to-day business affairs of the corporation.
- In small corporations, it is not unusual for the shareholders, Board of Directors, and corporate officers to be the same people.

Comparison of Advantages and Disadvantages of Business Structure Formations

Table 2.1 outlines the common advantages and disadvantages of each business structure formation. According to Miller (1997), the sole proprietorship remains a popular business structure for many sport business owners as evidenced by the fact that sole proprietorships accounted for 19 percent of all public golf courses, 14 percent of all membership sports and recreation clubs, 32 percent of all sporting goods and bicycle shops, and 20 percent of all physical fitness facilities in 1992. Ten years later, this picture has changed very little. However, the trend is an increased number of LLC's and LLP's which provide greater flexibility and less liability.

How to Start a Small Sport Business

Starting and managing a business requires motivation, desire and talent. It also takes research and planning. Like a chess game, success in small business starts with decisive and correct opening moves and although initial mistakes are not fatal, it takes skill, discipline, and hard work to regain the advantage.

To increase your chance for success, take the time up front to explore and evaluate your business and personal goals, then use this information to build a comprehensive and well-thought-out business plan that will help you reach these goals. The process of developing a business plan will help you think through some important issues that you may not have considered yet. Your plan will become a valuable tool as you set out to raise money for your business. It should also provide milestones to gauge your success.

Getting Started

Before starting out, list your reasons for wanting to go into business. Some of the most common reasons for starting a business are:

- You want to be your own boss,
- You want financial independence,
- You want creative freedom, and
- You want to fully use your skills and knowledge.

Next you need to determine what business is "right for you." Ask yourself these questions:

- What do I like to do with my time?
- What technical skills have I learned or developed?
- What do others say I am good at?
- Will I have the support of my family?
- How much time do I have to run a successful business?
- Do I have any hobbies or interests that are marketable?

Then you should identify the niche your business will fill. Conduct the

Table 2.1

Advantages	Sole Proprietor	Gen Partner	Ltd Partner	S corp	C corp	LLC	LLP	PLLP
Total control over decision making	x							
Single taxation of revenues	x			x				
Ease of formation	x					x	x	x
Great flexibility	x							
Reduced legislative restrictions	x							
Individual retention of profits	x							
Limited liability			x	x	x	x	x	x
Greater access to capital		x			x			
Pass-through taxation		x	x			x	x	x
Ease of raising capital			x	x				
Avoidance of the alternative minimum tax					x			
Lower tax liabilities					x			
Access to capital								
70% tax-free dividends paid to a corporation					x			
Unlimited number of members						x		
Members can include corporations and partnerships						x		
Ease of parent-subsidiary structures						x		
Disadvantages								
Limited access to capital	x							
Unlimited liability	x							
Limited longevity	x	x						
Joint and several liability		x						
Limited capital		x						
Inability of the limited partner to participate in management			x					
Size limited to 75				x				
Only one type of stock issues				x				
Prohibition of employee-shareholders borrowing from pension				x				
Limited employee benefit deductions				x				
Double taxation					x			
Extnsive corporate formalities and government review					x			
Conversion expense						x	x	x

necessary research to answer these questions:

- What business am I interested in starting?
- What services or products will I sell?
- Is my idea practical, and will it fill a need?
- What is my competition?
- What is my business's advantage over existing firms?
- Can I deliver a better quality service?
- Can I create a demand for my business?

The final step before developing your plan is the pre-business checklist. You should answer these questions:

- What skills and experience do I bring to the business?
- What will be my legal structure?
- How will my company's business records be maintained?
- What insurance coverage will be needed?
- What equipment or supplies will I need?
- How will I compensate myself?
- What are my resources?
- What financing will I need?
- Where will my business be located?
- What will I name my business?

Your answers will help you create a focused, well-researched business plan that should serve as a blueprint. It should detail how the business will be operated, managed, and capitalized. One of the most important cornerstones of starting a business is the business plan. SBA offers a tutorial on preparing a solid plan with all its essential ingredients. Be sure to review and peruse this section.

Once you have completed your business plan, review it with a friend or business associate. When you feel comfortable with the content and structure, make an appointment to review and discuss it with your banker. The business plan is a flexible document that should change as your business grows.

The Role of Politics in Financial Management

Howard and Crompton (1995) indicate that most public sector investment into the sport industry comes through subsidization and construction of facilities in which the sports teams play. The money for many of these facilities comes through issuing bonds and establishing higher or new taxes. Chapter 14 describes the financing of sport facility development through the use of public funds as well as private sector partnerships.

It is imperative that sport enterprise managers work with their counterparts in the public sector to gain public support for funding of the sport enterprise. Many state and local governments across the United States are not in strong financial positions; therefore, they are not willing to support the sport enterprise. This requires the sport enterprise to be creative in its public relations programs and the strategies used to convince legislators of the importance of sport within the community at large.

Finally, most recent stadium and arena projects have involved joint participation by the public and private sectors. Team owners are now sharing in varying degrees the cost of development. Yet, typically, the public sector's contribution is much greater than the amount contributed by a professional franchise. Critical to understanding the potential of joint ventures is a recognition that each sector has resources not possessed by the other. A joint venture is a collaborative agreement fusing the complementary benefits of each sector to the mutual advantage of all parties involved. The complementary assets of public-private sector joint-venture agreements include on the public side, substantial land bank, low-cost capital, tax savings, and control over zoning and permit process, and on the private side, access to capital, specialized management expertise, reduced liability risks, and reduced labor costs.

Summary

Organizing the sport enterprise for financial management is critical to a successful operation. Presently sport at every level appears to be financially healthy. Indications of fiscal viability are evident in the escalation of broadcast rights fees for sport properties, professional player contract increases, and reports that more young people are participating in youth and interscholastic sports than ever before. However, as each of these indicators increase, the need for an understanding and skillful approach to organizing the sport enterprise for financial management in order to produce a quality sport offering also increases.

Sport managers interested in opening sport enterprises must decide early on the business structure providing the optimal benefits. The type of business structure selected for the sport entity will influence short- and long-term operations. The traditional business formations include not-for-profit, for-profit, sole proprietorship, general partnership, limited partnership, limited liability partnership, limited liability corporation, the S corporation, and the C corporation.

There are numerous ways of funding the sport enterprise, including personal savings or equity capital, family, friends, bank loans, government loans and programs, venture capital, issuing private stock, public offerings, trade credit, factoring companies, and franchising and licensing options. The funding alternatives differ depending on the sport enterprise project.

It is imperative that sport enterprise managers work with their counterparts in the public sector to gain public support for funding of the sport enterprise. Many state and local governments across the United States are not in a strong financial position. Therefore, they are not willing to support the sport enterprise. This requires the sport enterprise to be creative in its public relations programs and the strategies used to convince legislators of the importance of sport within the community at large.

References

Bedeian, A.G. (1984). *Management.* New York: Dryden Press.

Downward, P., & Dawson, Alistar (2000). *The economics of professional team sports.* New York: Routledge.

Florida, R., & Kenney, M. (1990). *The breakthrough illusion.* New York: Basic Books.

Gorman, J., & Calhoun, K. (1994). *The name of the game: The business of sports.* New York: John Wiley & Sons, Inc.

Miller, L.K. (1997). *Sport business management.* Gaithersburg, MD: Aspen Publication.

Organization in the United States. Ph.D. Dissertation, University of California, Berkeley.

U.S. Small Business Administration [on-line] http://www.sba.gov

Financial Accountability and Planning

Financial Accountability and Analysis

Introduction

Employees are responsible for safeguarding and using those organization resources entrusted to them to carry out their assigned duties in accordance with the organization's goals and objectives as expressed in polices, establishing what should be accomplished, and procedures to effect the policies. Goals and objectives can be thought of as being separated into three distinct categories: effectiveness and efficiency of operations, reliability of financial reporting, and compliance with applicable laws and regulations.

Accountability is the culmination of the organized summarization of transactions representing economic events taking place within various business operating cycles throughout the organization. Employees working in financial areas are therefore responsible for appropriately managing and safeguarding the organization's assets that contribute to the preparation of reliable financial information.

In addition to a specific organization's policies, certain assertions are generally recognized as being embodied in all summarized financial data up to and including financial statements. Employees contributing to financial reports at any level are therefore making implied representations to all users or potential users of the data concerning the financial information they worked with. Users throughout the organization and outside the organization have a reasonable expectation to rely on the representations made. These representations then become the minimum goals and objectives of the organization regarding financial reports. This chapter will assist the future sport manager in understanding the importance of accountability and how to guarantee financial accountability.

Financial analysis is designed to aid sport managers through the process of evaluating past and current financial data. This analysis is necessary to evaluate performance and estimate future risks as well as financial potential. By reviewing balance sheets, income statements, and cash flow statements, a manager can obtain an overview of the financial solvency of the organization and its ability to withstand economic hardship. By properly analyzing revenue and investment potential, along with costs, the manager can better utilize the financial resources of the organization.

This chapter will review accountability issues, basic financial statements, cash flow, and the financial analysis process.

Instructional Objectives

After reading this chapter the student should be able to:
- Describe what accountability is in general,
- Understand the concept of financial responsibility,
- Describe the difference between a financial statement and financial reporting,
- Design an internal audit process,
- Develop a strategy for an external audit,
- Understand the role of financial analysis within an organization,
- Identify a basic financial statement, and
- Explain cash flow and its importance to an organization.

Accountability

Accountability is defined as the state of being accountable, subject to the obligation to report, explain, or justify something; responsible, answerable. Most academicians use a narrow definition that involves the not-for-profit answering to a higher authority in the bureaucratic or inter-organizational chain of command.

The public and the media tend to use a broader definition of accountability. Generally, this definition holds the organization accountable to the public, media, donors, clients/customers, stockholders, and others. The public and media have a greater expectation that the

organization will have a certain level of performance, responsiveness, ethics, and morality.

The organization's views on accountability will play a key role in developing an organization's standards of accountability. The sport manager should answer two questions when defining accountability for the organization: to whom is the organization accountable and for what activities and levels of performance is the organization held responsible.

Financial Accountability

The financial manager makes the following assertions regarding the execution and summarization of financial transactions that are found in various financial reports:

Existence and occurrence

The assets and liabilities actually exist at the report date and transactions reported actually occurred during the reporting period covered. There is physical security over assets and transactions are valid.

Completeness

All transactions and accounts that should be included in the reports are included and there are no undisclosed assets, liabilities, or transactions.

Rights and obligations

The organization owns and has clear title to assets and liabilities, which are the obligation of the organization. Transactions are valid.

Valuation and allocation

The assets and liabilities are valued properly and the revenues and expenses are measured properly. Transactions are accurate.

Presentation and disclosure

The assets, liabilities, revenues, and expenses are properly classified, described, and disclosed in financial reports.

Since employees and management involved with financial processes are making (implying) the above representations (assertions), management, at various levels, needs internal controls to ensure that financial data compiled is not false, misleading, incomplete, or inaccurate.

Users have every reason to believe the data and reports you give them are accurate and reliable. These minimum financial reporting objectives therefore become the internal control objectives used in designing an effective system of internal control that ensures reliable financial reporting. The uniquely designed internal control procedures within the organization are there to achieve these objectives.

Everyone in the organization has some responsibility for internal control even though it is often supervisors and/or managers who design the internal control procedures within their area of influence. This is true from two perspectives. First, almost all employees play some part in effecting control. They may produce information used in the control system or take other actions needed to effect control. Any weak link in the organization's structure can create a weakness in the control system. Second, all employees are responsible to communicate problems in operations, deviations from established standards, and violations of the organization's financial policy.

By definition, internal control is a process designed to provide reasonable assurance regarding the achievement of the organization's financial reporting objectives. Within this definition there are fundamental concepts relating to internal control including: (a) it is a process, not one event, but a series of actions that permeate the organization's activities and are inherent in the way business is transacted; (b) it is affected by the people of the organization in what they do and say and they must therefore know their responsibility and the limits of their authority; (c) it provides reasonable, not absolute, assurance regarding the achieve-

ment of objectives and should be cost effective; and (d) it is geared to the achievement of the organization's objectives.

In determining the control procedures to achieve the objectives, the process usually starts with a management-directed self-evaluation at the business operation cycle level and applies the "objectives" to groups of similarly processed transactions (types of transactions). The objectives for each group are achieved by a judgmentally determined mix of procedures from the following components of internal control. The mix may be different for each type of transaction within a financial area based on the relative risk and significance of the amounts involved. Also, some components cover a number of transaction types. The overriding purpose is that there is not a high risk of significant errors getting through the accounting process that would not be caught by a control procedure performed by an employee performing his/her regular duties.

Components

There are five major components of a control procedure including:

Control Environment

It is the responsibility of the sport financial manager to establish an environment that encourages integrity and ethical values. The financial manager's leadership philosophy, competence, and management and operating style communicate to the employees a sense of control consciousness in the sport organization.

Risk Assessment

The process of identifying financial risks and the consequences of such risks as related to control activities.

Control Activities

Those procedures designed to see that objectives are met and the risks identified in step two are reduced to a reasonable level. Control techniques include procedures to ensure that:

- Transactions are executed in accordance with management's general or specific authorization;
- Transactions are properly recorded to permit the preparation of financial reports in conformance with generally accepted accounting principles and to maintain accountability for assets.

Information and communication

Surrounding the control activities are information and communication systems. These enable the organization's employees to capture and exchange the information needed to conduct, manage, and control operations. A large part of the communication system is the accounting system, which consists of methods and records established to identify, assemble, analyze, classify, record, and report the organization's transactions in accordance with generally accepted accounting principles and maintain accountability for recorded assets and liabilities. At a minimum, the system must meet the following requirements:

- Be able to identify types of transactions executed (revenues, expenses, assets, and liabilities),
- Accumulate (record) economic events in the appropriate accounts at the correct amounts, and
- Record the economic events in the correct accounting period.

Monitoring

The entire process must be monitored and modified as necessary to react to changing conditions. The monitoring process should be performed at several levels. A supervisory review of activities should be on a regular basis as part of the normal management function. Periodic special reviews should be by management, internal auditors, and external auditors.

The process used to fulfill responsibilities and determine the level of internal control necessary should follow the above outline and be documented.

Not-for-profit Organizations' Accountability

Not-for-profit organizations are defined as private, self-governing organizations that exist to provide a particular service to the community (i.e., American Legion Baseball, AAU Basketball, Boys Clubs, Community soccer leagues, Girls Club, Little League Baseball, YMCA, YWCA, and many more). The term not-for-profit refers to a type of organization that operates without the purpose of generating a profit for owners.

As government continues to decline in providing services due to legal and budget constraints, not-for-profits have been filling the void by providing these needed services, but unlike government agencies, not-for-profits have not always been held to the same public scrutiny.

As scandals over not-for-profit accountability (i.e., American National Red Cross, United Way) make their way to the headlines of widely read newspapers, not-for-profit credibility wanes. As a result, not-for-profit organizations' images suffer, causing much of the public to decrease donations to all not-for-profit organizations, although many of the accusations against not-for-profits are spurious. Today, not-for-profits face powerful accountability pressures and are asked by donors and the public to justify their delivered services and operations.

The Financial Manager

A common feature among all large sport entities is that the owners (the stockholders) are usually not directly involved in making decisions, particularly on a day-to-day basis. Instead, the corporation employs managers to represent the owners' interests and make decisions on their behalf. Those managers would include, but not be limited to: general manager, facility and grounds manager, concessions manager, human resource manager, risk manager, and financial manager.

The financial manager has the responsibility to answer key questions including:

- What long-term investments should the organization consider?
- What lines of business will the organization be in?
- What sorts of facilities, machinery, and equipment will the organization need?
- Where will the organization secure the long-term financing to pay for investment?
- Will the organization bring in additional investors?
- Will the organization borrow the funds needed?
- How will the organization manage everyday financial activities such as collecting from customers, paying suppliers, and meeting payroll?

The financial management function is usually associated with a top officer of the firm, such as the chief financial officer (CFO) or the vice president of finance. The top financial officer may have two key subordinates called controller and treasurer. The controller's office handles cost and financial accounting, tax payments, and management information systems. The treasurer's office is responsible for managing the firm's cash flow and credit, its financial planning, and its capital expenditures.

> In small organizations the responsibility for financial accountability, budgeting, and planning becomes the duty of the executive director or general manager.

The Role of Financial Analysis

An organization must review and revise its financial status just as it reviews its programs and facilities. Through financial analysis, managers can review financial statements, assess cash flow, and determine if the organization is financially sound. There is no real difference in reviewing your personal finances and the finances of an organization. An organization will have more and different categories to review, but the purpose of the analysis is the same.

Financial analysis allows an organization to determine when, and if, capital projects may be undertaken as well as take advantage of investment opportunities. Missed opportunities or great financial risk can result from poor financial analysis. Budget reductions often occur during economic downturns, and knowing and understanding your financial status is essential in maintaining organizational solvency.

> Capital projects are often defined as major building projects, building acquisitions, or major equipment purchases.

When analyzing financial statements, it is essential that good judgment prevails. It is more appropriate for you to compare the financial statements of similar organizations so you can obtain realistic information for present and future financial growth. The current performance of an organization should be compared with its performance in previous years. This will aid the manager in setting realistic goals and objectives for future growth.

Financial Reporting

Financial reporting can be seen as a summary of the organization's performance, or capacity, in raising, handling, and using public money. Another way of expressing the role of financial reporting is to say it goes hand in hand with accountability. Accountability is often considered one of the cornerstones of good democratic governments. Officials are given authority and responsibility, and it is the task of the officials to clearly convey actions taken and whether these actions fall within the prescriptions of the law and community wishes.

Assessing performance or accounting with respect to raising, handling, and using public or private money is a complex issue. The criteria are many, diverse, and sometimes conflicting. In some cases, there is a recognized rule or standards-making body that can cover selected aspects of financial accountability. In general, however, there may be more than one rule-making body.

Conceptual Framework for Financial Reporting

Historically, rules for accounting and financial reporting were developed as new pressures arose. An alternative to reacting to pressures as they arise is to produce a conceptual framework and to derive the accounting rules or standards from this framework so that standards have one common reference point. With a common reference point, one standard should not conflict with another. Such a goal is attractive in theory, but often falls short in practice.

The Balance Sheet

The balance sheet, income statement, and cash flow statement all summarize some aspect of an organization's finances at a given point in time. The balance sheet summarizes the financial position of an organization at a particular point in time and is considered one of the most important financial statements. According to Parkhouse (2001), the four main uses of the balance sheet are that it shows (1) changes in the business over a period of time, (2) growth or decline in various phases of the business, (3) the business's ability to pay debts, and (4) through ratios the financial position.

The balance sheet is a snapshot of the firm. It is a convenient means of organizing and summarizing what an organization owns (its assets), what an organization owes (its liabilities), and the difference

between the two (the organization's equity) at a given point in time. Figure 3.1 illustrates how the balance sheet is constructed. As shown, the left-hand side lists the assets of the organization, and the right-hand side lists the liabilities and equity.

Assets: The Left-Hand Side

Assets are classified as either current or fixed. A fixed asset is one that has a relatively long life. Fixed assets can either be tangible such as a lawn mower, computer, or weight equipment, or intangible such as a trademark or patent. A current asset has a life of less than one year. This means that the asset will convert to cash within 12 months. For example, inventory of licensed team products would normally be purchased and sold within one year and is thus classified as a current asset. Cash itself is a current asset. Accounts receivable (money owed to the organization by its customers) is also a current asset.

Liabilities and Owner's Equity: The Right-Hand Side

The organization's liabilities are the first items listed on the right-hand side of the balance sheet. There are classified as either current or long-term. Current liabilities, like current assets, have a life of less than one year (meaning they must be paid within one year) and are listed before long-term liabilities. Accounts payable (money the firm owes to its suppliers) is one example of a current liability.

A debt that is not due in the coming year is classified as a long-term liability. A loan that the organization will pay off in five years is one such long-term debt. Organizations borrow long-term money from a variety of sources (see Chapter 4).

Finally, by definition, the difference between total value of the assets (current and fixed) and the total value of the liabilities (current and long term) is the shareholders' equity, also called common equity or owners' equity. This feature of

Figure 3.1

A Balance Sheet

Hannibal River Rats

Balance Sheet as of December 31, 2002 and 2004

($ in thousands)

	2003	2004		2003	2004
Assets			Liabilities and Owner's Equity		
Current Assets			Current Liabilities		
Cash	104	160	Accounts payable	232	266
Accounts receivable	455	688	Notes payable	196	123
Inventory	553	555	Total	428	389
Total	1,112	1,403			
Fixed Assets					
Net Plant and					
Equipment	1,644	1,403	Long-Term Debt	408	454
			Owner's Equity		
			Common Stock and		
			Paid-in Surplus	600	640
			Retained earnings	1,320	1,629
			Total	1,920	2,269
Total Assets	2,756	3,112	Total Liabilities & Owner's Equity	2,756	3,112

the balance sheet is intended to reflect the fact that, if the organization were to sell all of its assets and use the money to pay off its debts, then whatever residual value remains belongs to the shareholders. So, the balance sheet "balances" because the value of the left-hand side always equals the value of the right-hand side. That is, the value of the organization's assets is equal to the sum of its liabilities and shareholders' equity:

Assets = liabilities + shareholders' equity

This is the balance sheet identity or equation, and it always holds, because shareholders' equity is defined as the difference between assets and liabilities.

Liquidity

Liquidity refers to the speed and ease with which an asset can be converted to cash. Gold is a relatively liquid asset; however, a sport facility is not. Liquidity really has two dimensions: ease of conversion versus loss of value. Any asset can be converted to cash quickly if we cut the price enough. A highly liquid asset is therefore one that can be quickly sold without significant loss of value. A non-liquid asset is one that cannot be quickly converted to cash without substantial price reduction.

Liquidity is valuable. The more liquid an organization is, the less likely it is to experience financial distress (difficulty in paying debts or buying needed assets). Unfortunately, liquid assets are generally less profitable to hold.

For example, cash holdings are the most liquid of all investments, but they sometimes earn no return at all. Therefore, there is a trade-off between the advantages of liquidity and forgone potential profits.

Debt versus Equity

The first claim to the organization's cash flow generally goes to creditors. Equity holders are only entitled to the residual value, the portion left after creditors are paid. The value of this residual portion is the shareholders' equity in the firm, which is just the value of the organization's assets less the value of the organization's liabilities:

Shareholders' equity = Assets – Liabilities

This is true in an accounting sense because shareholders' equity is defined as this residual portion. It is also true in an economic sense. If the organization sells its assets and pays its debts, whatever cash is left belongs to the shareholders.

The use of debt in an organization's capital structure is called financial leverage. The more debt an organization has (as a percentage of assets), the greater is its degree of financial leverage. Debt acts like a lever in the sense that using it can greatly magnify both gains and losses. So financial leverage increases the potential reward to shareholders, but it also increases the potential for financial distress and an organization's ultimate failure.

Cash Flow

Cash flow refers to the flow of cash into and out of an organization over a given period of time. Outflow of cash is measured by the payments that will be made for expenses such as salaries, suppliers, and creditors. The inflows are the revenues brought in from customers, lenders, investors, and sponsors.

It is important to understand that it is possible to show a profit on an organization's income statement but have no money to pay the bills. This is why cash flow is one of the most important financial issues within an organization. A successful organization will always have sufficient cash available to cover operating expenses and labor costs.

In sport, cash flow is of particular importance because of each sport's unique revenue status at the collegiate level. Some sports can be quite profitable (such as football and basketball) and assist in funding other sports (cross country, wrestling, or intramurals) within the organization. A sport manager must always prepare for weak revenues from those peak-generating sports due to external factors beyond their control such as weather or poor win-loss records. These factors, and others, could have devastating effects on cash flow (Sawyer & Smith, 1999).

The sport manager must be certain that the available funds are being used in the most efficient manner for both short- and long-term financial planning. The organization does not just want to have money sitting in the bank when that money could be used in a more profitable manner. It is the sport manager's responsibility to maintain an adequate cash-flow balance.

It is important to note that cash flow does not tell the manager the financial condition of the organization, nor does it show profits or losses of the organization. It merely shows how much cash has come into the organization and how much is going out (Parkhouse, 2001).

Organizations commonly generate cash and spend it. Cash is generated by selling: (a) a product (i.e., the game or entertainment, licensed products, sports equipment and clothing, etc.), (b) an asset (i.e., a ball player), or (c) a security (i.e., selling a security involves either borrowing or selling an equity interest in the organization). Cash is spent by paying for: (a) materials and labor to produce products (i.e., Nike purchasing materials to produce the products to be sold), (b) assets such as professional players (i.e., baseball, basketball, football, ice hockey, or soccer players), and collegiate players (i.e., scholarships), (c) operational expenditures (i.e. other personnel, telephones, printing, advertisement, supplies, rentals, insurance, etc.), (d) payments to creditors, and (e) spending cash.

Generally, the cash activities of an organization can be summarized by a simple formula:

Cash Flow from Assets = Cash Flow to Creditors + Cash Flow to Owners

The formula above summarizes the total cash result of all transactions the organization engaged in during the year.

Statement of Cash Flows

The statement of cash flows is historically called the statement of changes in financial position. It is presented in terms of the changes in net working capital rather than cash flows. Figure 3.2 is a sample format for a statement of cash flow.

The basic idea is to group all the changes into one of three categories: operating activities, financing activities, and investment activities. The exact form differs in the detail from one preparer to the next. The key point to remember in the case in Figure 3.2 is that the organization started the year out with $84,000 in cash and completed the year with $98,000 for a net increase of $14,000. The statement outlines what events led to the change.

Standardized Financial Statements

It is important to be able to compare one organization to another. In order to accomplish this task, financial statements must be standardized. Generally, this is accomplished by using percentages rather than total dollars. This standardization is commonly noted in common-size statements.

Common-Size Statements

One useful way of standardizing financial statements is to express each item on the balance sheet as a percentage of assets and to express each item on the income statement as a percentage of sales. This type of financial statement is called common-sized statements.

Figure 3.2

Hannibal River Rats

2002 Statement of Cash Flows

($ in thousands)

Cash, beginning of year	$ 84
Operating activity	
Net Income	363
Plus:	
Depreciation	276
Increase in accounts payable	32
Less:	
Increase in accounts receivable	- 23
Increase in inventory	- 29
Net cash from operating activity	$619
Investment activity	
Fixed asset acquisitions	-$425
Net cash from investment activity	-$425
Financing Activity	
Decrease in notes payable	- 35
Decrease in long-term debt	- 74
Dividends paid	- 121
Increase in common stock	50
Net cash from financing activity	- 180
Net increase in cash	14
Cash, end of year	$ 98

Common-size Balance Sheets

A common-size balance sheet can be expressed as a percentage of the total assets. The Hannibal River Rats common-size balance sheets are shown in Figure 3.3

This type of financial statement is relatively easy to read and compare. In reviewing Figure 3.3 of the two balance sheets for the Hannibal River Rats, current assets were 19.7 percent of current assets in 2003, up from 19.1 percent in 2002. Current liabilities declined from 16.2 percent to 15.1 percent of the total liabilities and equity over the same time period. Similarly, total equity rose from 68.1 percent of total liabilities and equity to 72.2 percent. Overall, the Hannibal River Rats' liquidity, as measured by current assets compared to current liabilities, increased over the year. At the same time, indebtedness diminished as a percentage of total assets.

Common-sized Income Statements

A common-sized income statement can be expressed as a percentage of the total sales. The Hannibal River Rats' common-size income statement is shown in Figure 3.4.

This income statement outlines what happens to each dollar in sales. For the Hannibal River Rats, interest expense accounts for $.061 out of every sales dollar and taxes take another $.081. It appears that $.157 of each dollar is net income and that amount is split into $.105 retained in the business and $.052 paid out in dividends.

These percentages are very useful in comparisons. For example, a very relevant figure is the cost percentage. For the Hannibal River Rats, $.582 of each dollar in sales goes to operations costs. It would be interesting to compute the same percentage for the Hannibal River Rats' main competition to see how they compare in terms of cost control.

Future Financial Status

Sport managers need to be able to project the future financial status of the organization. These same financial statements are developed on a pro forma or projection basis. This involves expected profits or losses on a proposal for future operation, a new venture, or some type of organizational enterprise. The manager is able to gain better control and make wiser decisions for the future of the organization. Data from past operations is projected into the future. Caution must be used and the assumptions upon which the prediction is made should be clear. The prediction, or pro forma, statement requires objective reasoning and analysis of a proposal. The manager must be fully prepared to defend any and all of their projections. This process, however, can lead to better control and decision making within the organization (Bridges & Roquemore, 1996).

Financial Ratio Analysis

Financial ratios are used in comparing organizations of different sizes. Using ratios eliminates the size problem since the size effectively divides out. However, the sport manager needs to be cautious when using financial ratios since different people and different sources frequently do not compute the ratios in exactly the same way, and this can lead to some confusion.

There are five common types of financial ratios including: (a) short-term solvency or liquidity ratios, (b) long-term solvency or financial leverage ratio, (c) asset management or turnover ratios, (d) profitability ratios, and (e) market value ratios. The definitions that follow may or may not be the same ones as the reader has seen before or will see elsewhere. Therefore, if the sport manager uses ratios as a tool for analysis, he/she should be careful to document how each one is calculated and if comparing numbers to another source, be sure to understand how the other source computed the numbers.

Figure 3.3

Hannibal River Rats

Common-Sized Balance Sheets

December 31, 2002 and 2003

	2002	2003	Change
Assets			
Current Assets			
Cash	2.5%	2.7%	+ .2%
Accounts receivable	4.9	5.2	+ .3
Inventory	11.7	11.8	+ .1
Total	19.1	19.7	+ .6
Fixed Assets			
Net plant and equipment	80.9	80.3	- .6
Total Assets	100.0	100.0	0
Liabilities and Owners' Equity			
Current Liabilities			
Accounts payable	9.4	9.6	+ .2
Notes payable	6.8	5.5	- 1.3
Total	16.2	15.1	- 1.1
Long-term debt	15.7	12.7	- 3.0
Owners' Equity			
Common stock and paid-in surplus	14.8	15.3	+ .5
Retained earnings	53.3	56.9	+ 3.6
Total	68.1	72.2	+ 4.1
Total liabilities and owners' equity	100.0	100.0	0

Figure 3.4

Hannibal River Rats

Common-Sized Income Statement

2003

Sales	100.0%
Cost of operations	58.2
Depreciation (i.e., plant and equipment)	11.9
Earnings before interest and taxes	29.9
Interest paid	6.1
Taxable income	23.8
Taxes (34%)	8.1
Net Income	15.7

Addition to retained earnings	10.5%
Dividends	5.2

Short-Term Solvency or Liquidity Measures

Short-term solvency ratios as a group are intended to provide information about the organization's liquidity, and these ratios are sometimes called liquidity measures. The primary concern is the organization's ability to pay its bills over the short haul without undue stress. Consequently, these ratios focus on current assets and current liabilities.

Liquidity ratios are particularly interesting to short-term creditors. Since the sport organization's financial managers are constantly working with banks and other short-term lenders, understanding of these ratios is essential.

One of the best-known and most widely used ratios in this category is the current ratio. The current ratio is defined as follows:

$$\text{Current ratio} = \frac{\text{Current Assets}}{\text{Current Liabilities}}$$

For the Hannibal River Rats, the 2003 current ratio is:

$$\text{Current Ratio} = \frac{\$708}{\$540} = 1.31 \text{ times}$$

Since current assets and liabilities are, in principle, converted to cash over the following 12 months, the current ratio is a measure of short-term liquidity. The unit of measurement is either dollars or times. It could be said the Hannibal River Rats has $1.31 in current assets for every dollar in current liabilities or has its current liabilities covered 1.31 times over.

Long-Term Solvency Measures

This group of ratios is intended to address the firm's long-run ability to meet its obligations or, more generally, its financial leverage. The two most common ratios in this group are total debt ratio and total capitalization versus total assets.

The total debt ratio considers all debts of all maturities to all creditors. The most common definition for this ratio is as follows:

$$\text{Total debt ratio} = \frac{\text{Total assets} - \text{Total equity}}{\text{Total assets}}$$

$$= \frac{\$3,588 - 2,591}{\$3,588} = .28 \text{ times}$$

The financial manager for the Hannibal River Rats can say the organization uses 28 percent debt. This means that the organization has $.28 in debt for every dollar in assets. Therefore, there is $.72 in equity ($1.00-.28) for every $.28 in debt.

Frequently, the financial manager is more concerned about the organization's long-term debt than its short-term debt since the short-term debt will constantly be changing. The long-term debt ratio is calculated as follows:

$$\text{Long-term debt ratio} = \frac{\text{Long-term debt}}{\text{Long-term debt} + \text{Total equity}}$$

$$= \frac{\$457}{\$457 + 2,951} = \frac{\$457}{\$3,048} = .15 \text{ times}$$

The lower the ratio, the stronger the financial position of the organization. The $3,048 in total long-term debt and equity is sometimes called the organization's total capitalization.

Asset Management or Turnover Measures

The measures that follow are often called asset utilization ratios. There are two important current assets that should be reviewed, namely inventory and receivables. The first ratio is called inventory turnover and days' sales in inventory. For this ratio and the one to follow, we will use Nike as an example. During the year, Nike has a cost of goods sold of ($ in millions) $1,344. Inventory at the end of the year was $422. With these numbers, inventory turnover can be calculated as:

$$\text{Inventory turnover} = \frac{\text{Cost of goods sold}}{\text{Inventory}}$$

$$= \frac{\$1,344}{\$422} = 3.2 \text{ times}$$

In a sense, Nike sold off or turned over the entire inventory 3.2 times. As long as Nike is not running out of stock and thereby foregoing sales, the higher this ratio is, the more efficiently Nike is managing inventory.

If Nike turned over inventory 3.2 times during the year, then Nike can immediately figure out how long it takes to turn the inventory over on average. The result is the average days' sales in inventory:

$$\text{Days' sales in inventory} = \frac{365 \text{ days}}{\text{Inventory Turnover}}$$

$$= \frac{365}{3.2} = 114 \text{ days}$$

This calculation informs Nike that inventory sits 114 days on average before it is sold. Further, assuming current values were used in the calculation, it will take about 114 days to sell off current inventory.

Receivables Turnover and Days' Sales in Receivables

Receivables turnover is defined in the same way as inventory turnover:

$$\text{Receivable turnover} = \frac{\text{Sales}}{\text{Accounts Receivable}}$$

$$= \frac{\$2,311}{\$188} = 12.3 \text{ times}$$

In this example, Nike collected outstanding credit accounts and re-loaned the money 12.3 times during the year. This ratio is more useful if it is converted into days, so the days' sales in receivables is:

$$\text{Days' sales}_{\text{in receivables}} = \frac{365 \text{ days}}{\text{Receivables Turnover}}$$

$$= \frac{365}{12.3} = 30 \text{ days}$$

This ratio informs Nike that, on average, it collects credit sales in 30 days or Nike has 30 days' worth of sales currently uncollected. This ratio is frequently called the average collection period.

Profitability Measures

There are three common measures of profitability, including profit margin, return on assets, and return on equity. The focus of these measures of profitability is on the bottom line, net income.

Profit Margin

The Hannibal River Rats generates less than 16 cents in profit for every dollar in sales. The profit margin is calculated as follows:

$$\text{Profit margins} = \frac{\text{Net income}}{\text{Sales}}$$

$$= \frac{\$363}{\$2,311} = 15.7\%$$

All things being equal, the Hannibal River Rats would like to generate a high profit margin. In order for this to happen the organization must lower expense ratios relative to sales.

Return on Assets

Return on assets (ROA) is a measure of profit per dollar of assets. It is generally defined as follows:

$$\text{Return on assets} = \frac{\text{Net income}}{\text{Total assets}}$$

$$= \frac{\$363}{\$3,588} = 10.12\%$$

Return on Equity

Return on equity (ROE) is a measure of how the stockholders fared during the year. This is the true bottom line measure of performance for the stockholders. It is measured as:

$$\text{Return on equity} = \frac{\text{Net income}}{\text{Total equity}}$$

$$= \frac{\$363}{\$2,591} = 14\%$$

For every dollar in equity, the Hannibal River Rats generated 14 cents in profit.

Since return on assets and return on equity are commonly cited numbers, it is important to remember they are accounting rates of return. Therefore, they should be called return on book assets and return on book equity. Sometimes ROE is called return on net worth.

Market Value Measures

There are two market value measures commonly used: price/earnings ratio and market-to-book ratio. These measures are based on the market price per share of the stock. This information is not necessarily contained in financial statements and these measures can only be calculated directly for publicly traded companies. For these examples, it will be assumed that the Hannibal River Rats have stock that is publicly traded.

It will be assumed that the Hannibal River Rats have 33,000 shares outstanding and the stock sold for $8.80 per share at the end of the year. The net income for the Hannibal River Rats was $363,000, then its earnings per share (EPS) were:

$$\text{EPS} = \frac{\text{Net income}}{\text{Shares outstanding}} = \frac{\$363,000}{33,000} = \$11$$

Price/Earnings Ratio

The price/earnings (P/E) ratio is defined as:

$$P/E\ Ratio = \frac{Price\ per\ share}{Earnings\ per\ share}$$

$$= \frac{\$88}{\$11} = 8\ times$$

It could be said that the Hannibal River Rats shares sell for eight times earnings, or the shares have a P/E multiple of eight. In general, the P/E ratio measures how much the average investor is willing to pay per dollar of current earnings. The higher the P/Es are often taken to mean the firm has significant prospects for future growth.

> However, if a firm had no or almost no earnings, its P/E would probably be quite large. Therefore, care should be taken in interpreting this ratio.

Market-to-Book Ratio

The market-to-book ratio is expressed as:

$$Market\text{-}to\text{-}book\ ratio = \frac{Market\ value\ per\ share}{Book\ value\ per\ share}$$

$$= \frac{\$88}{(\$2,591/33)} = \frac{\$88}{\$78.5} = 1.12\ times$$

It is important to remember the book value per share is an accounting number. It reflects a historical cost for the organization. The market-to-book ratio compares the market value of the organization's investments to their cost. Generally a value less than 1 could mean the organization has not been successful overall in creating value for its stockholders.

Auditing

Auditing is a field of accounting activity that involves an independent review of general accounting practices. Most large organizations employ their own staffs of internal auditors.

Definition of Internal Auditing

Internal auditing is an independent, objective assurance and consulting activity designed to add value and improve an organization's operations. It helps an organization accomplish its objectives by bringing a systematic, disciplined approach to evaluate and improve the effectiveness of risk management, control, and governance processes.

Internal control is a process affected by the board of directors, senior management, and all levels of personnel. It is not solely a procedure or policy that is performed at a certain point in time; rather, it is continually operating at all levels within the organization. The board of directors and senior management are responsible for establishing the appropriate culture to facilitate an effective internal control process and for continuously monitoring its effectiveness; however, each individual within an organization must participate in the process. The main objectives of the internal control process can be categorized as follows:

- Efficiency and effectiveness of operations (operational objectives),
- Reliability and completeness of financial and management information (information objectives), and
- Compliance with applicable laws and regulations (compliance objectives).

Operational objectives for internal control pertain to the effectiveness and efficiency of the bank in using its assets and other resources and protecting the organization from loss. The internal control process seeks to ensure that personnel throughout the organization are working to achieve its objectives in a straightforward manner without unintended or excessive cost or placing other interests (such as an employee's, vendor's or customer's interest) before those of the organization.

Information objectives address the preparation of timely, reliable reports needed for decision making within the organization. They also address the need for reliable annual accounts, other financial statements, and other financial-related disclosures, including those for regulatory reporting and other external uses. The information received by management, the board of directors, shareholders, and supervisors should be of sufficient quality and integrity that recipients can rely on the information in making decisions. The term reliable, as it relates to financial statements, refers to the preparation of statements that are presented fairly and based on comprehensive and well-defined accounting principles and rules.

Compliance objectives ensure that all business of the organization is conducted in compliance with applicable laws and regulations, supervisory requirements, and internal policies and procedures. This objective must be met in order to protect the organization's reputation.

Internal control consists of five interrelated elements:
- Management oversight and the control culture,
- Risk assessment,
- Control activities,
- Information and communication, and
- Monitoring activities.

The problems observed in recent large losses at organizations can be aligned with these five elements. The effective functioning of these elements is essential to achieving an organization's operational, information, and compliance objectives.

Although the board of directors and senior management bear the ultimate responsibility for an effective system of internal controls, supervisors should assess the internal control system in place at individual organizations as part of their ongoing supervisory activities. The supervisors should also determine whether individual organization management gives prompt attention to any problems that are detected through the internal control process.

Roles and Responsibilities of External Auditors

Although external auditors are not, by definition, part of an organization and therefore are not part of its internal control system, they have an important impact on the quality of internal controls through their audit activities, including discussions with management and recommendations for improvement to internal controls. The external auditors provide important feedback on the effectiveness of the internal control system.

While the primary purpose of the external audit function is to give an opinion on, or to certify, the annual accounts of an organization, the external auditor must decide whether or not to rely on the effectiveness of the organization's internal control system. For this reason, the external auditors have to conduct an evaluation of the internal control system in order to assess the extent to which they can rely on the system in determining the nature, timing, and scope of their own audit procedures.

The exact role of external auditors and the processes they use vary from country to country. Professional auditing standards in many countries require that audits be planned and performed to obtain reasonable assurance that financial statements are free of material misstatement. Auditors also examine, on a test basis, underlying transactions and records supporting financial statement balances and disclosures. An auditor assesses the accounting principles used and significant estimates made by management, and evaluates the overall financial statement presentation. In some countries, external auditors are required by the supervisory authorities to provide a specific assessment of the scope, adequacy, and effectiveness of an organization's internal control system, including the internal audit system.

One consistency among countries, however, is the expectation that external auditors will gain an understanding of an organization's internal control process. The extent of attention given to the internal control system varies by auditor and by bank; however, it is generally expected that the auditor would identify significant weaknesses that exist at an organization and report material weaknesses to management orally or in confidential management letters and, in many countries, to the supervisory authority. Furthermore, external auditors may be subject to special supervisory requirements that specify the way that they evaluate and report on internal controls.

Accountability (accountable) is similar to responsibility (i.e., a position of power due to recognizing one's causative activity). Accountability implies the willingness to acknowledge responsibility to others and the willingness to fully accept responsibility for one's actions and their implications.

Information included in accountability reports is used to make decisions. These decisions may affect a large number of people and involve millions of dollars. It is important that this information meets certain standards.

Performance information in traditional financial statements must conform to Generally Accepted Accounting Principles (GAAP). GAAP are the standards for determining profit, which is the key measure of performance in the private sector. Equivalent standards of performance do not yet exist in government and the not-for-profit sector. Experience is required before appropriate standards can be established. Nevertheless, we can draw on standards set for financial information to help us determine the basic characteristics for performance information standards in government. These basic characteristics are as follows:

Understandability

The information is presented in a way that can be understood by users and is sufficient to provide an appropriate understanding of an organization's performance. Explaining the appropriate use of the information, how it was compiled, uncontrollable influences, and other factors may assist in understanding the information.

Relevance

The information presented is significant to the assessments and decisions to be made. Relevance includes the assertion that the information is timely.

Reliability

The information is free of material error, is unbiased, and is verifiable. The information can be relied upon by the user to represent that which (a) it purports to be or (b) it can reasonably be expected to represent.

Comparability

Users are able to compare information from year to year and among similar organizations.

Cost Beneficial

Providing accountability information has a cost. The cost of obtaining the information should not exceed the benefits. Analysis of benefits should not be limited to benefits within an organization, but should also include those benefits realized by key users of the information.

Summary

Sport managers or their financial managers play a critical role in the management of revenue and expenses within an organization. Through proper analysis of financial records, a manager can determine cash flow, sales revenue, and project future earnings. These reports and statements can help the organization realize capital budget projects and plan for the future.

Every organization must be concerned with sound business practices and financial responsibility. The need to develop and follow such practices is essential to the current and future financial stability of the organization.

References

Bridges, F.J., & Roquemore, L.L. (1996). *Management for athletic/sport administration.* Decatur, GA: ESM Books.

Horine, L., & Stotlar, D. (2003). *Administration of physical education and sport.* (5th ed.) Dubuque, IA: Wm. C. Brown Company.

Parkhouse, B.L. (2001). *The management of sport: Its foundation and application.* (3rd ed.) Dubuque, IA: McGraw-Hill.

Sawyer, T.H., & Smith, O. (1999). *The management of clubs, recreation and sport: Concepts and applications.* Champaign, IL: Sagamore Publishing.

Suggested Readings

Brigham, E.F., Gapenski, L.C., & Ehrhardt, M.C. (1999). *Financial management: Theory and practice* (9th ed.). Philadelphia: The Dryden Press.

Helfert, E.A. (2003). *Techniques of financial analysis: A guide to value creation.* Dubuque, IA: McGraw-Hill.

Lumby, S. (1995). *Investment appraisal and financial decisions.* New York, NY: Chapman and Hall Publishing.

Ross, S.A., Westerfield, R.W., & Jordan, B.D. (2001). *Fundamentals of corporate finance* (5th ed.). Chicago: Irwin.

Financial Planning

Introduction

The goal of financial planning or management is to maximize the current value of the organization. This often is represented as maximizing the current value per share of the existing stock. The financial planner for a sport organization needs to link together the organization's goals and objectives and the short- and long-term financial plan.

Budgets, an integral part of financial planning, are designed to help guide an organization through a financial calendar year, budget cycle, or a fiscal year. Budgets aid an organization in determining what funds are available after fixed costs, routine or annual expenses, and how much money may be available for special projects.

A fund is a sum of money set aside for some particular purpose.

When used as a guide, budgets can aid an organization in utilizing its available funds in the most effective and efficient manner possible. They also help eliminate waste and unnecessary spending practices.

This chapter will review the traditional budgeting process, preparation of budgets, revenues, and expenditures, and the components necessary for sound financial planning and provide the sport manager with the necessary tools for a successful contribution to the financial future of an organization.

Instructional Objectives

After reading this chapter the student will be able to:
- Understand the role of financial planning within an organization,
- Identify environmental factors that affect financial planning,
- Explain short- and long-term financial needs of an organization,
- Discuss the impact of financial planning on an organization,

•Understand the role of the budget within an organization,
•Identify different budget types,
•Discuss the budgeting process,
•Identify revenue sources, and
•Explain expenditures.

What is Financial Planning?

Effective financial planning is the foundation upon which an organization can build a successful future. It is much easier for decisions to be made in a proactive manner rather than as a reaction to unplanned situations. Risks are reduced and the organization's competitiveness is increased (Horine & Stotlar, 2003).

A sport organization must develop a sound strategic plan that includes establishment of the organization's objectives, design of the organization's structure, recruitment and selection of qualified employees, inducing individuals and groups to cooperate, and determining whether or not the organization's objectives have been obtained. Financial planning is an integral part of any strategic plan. A strategic plan specifically for financial planning should be developed to integrate into the overall organizational strategic plan. All revenue and expenditures need to be planned for well in advance in order to ensure success of the organization.

When planning for financial success, the sport manager must consider many facets of finance including cash planning, profit planning, capital budgeting, long-term planning, short-term financing, asset management ratios, forecasting, evaluating the environment, and risk management. The sport manager must be able to determine revenue streams and flow in order to cover expenditures in a timely fashion.

Financial planning can also help provide appropriate solutions for many of the problems that a sport business may face every day such as:

•Funding of capital projects,
•Developing new products and services,
•Retiring products and services,
•Selling assets,
•Purchasing assets,
•Protecting assets,
•Moving an organization to a new location, and
•Tax liabilities.

The financial staff's task is to acquire, and then help employ resources so as to maximize the value of the organization. Here are some specific activities:

•Forecasting and planning,
•Major investment and financial decisions,
•Coordination and control,
•Dealing with the financial markets, and
•Risk management.

Cash Planning

Determining the amount of cash needed at a particular point in the budget year can be accomplished by gathering data from both internal and external sources. Internal data are data generated by the organization itself and may include areas such as past budgets, sales records, and human resources reports. This type of data is primary data. The organization generates the data, analyzes it, and compiles reports from the data gathered within the organization. Internal data can also be gathered from personal observation or conversations as well as customer and employee surveys.

External data may be gathered from resources outside of the organization to help determine the impact of factors such as the local, state, national, and world economy, and demographic and geographic information. These external factors may impact sales and trends within the industry and the organization must be able to respond to the changing consumer needs. External data are often referred to as secondary data because it is compiled and published by another organization.

Because the nature of sport is seasonal, the manager should utilize previous budget records to determine how much cash will need to be on hand during particular points in the budget year. During times of revenue prosperity, cash should be held back to pay for expenditures during the "off-season" or other low revenue points. Cash planning should also include capital projects, those projects that require large sums of money to complete, as well as daily operation expenses.

> Cash is any medium of exchange that a bank will accept at face value, including bank deposits, currency, checks, bank drafts, and money orders.

Cash Flow

Cash flow is the difference between the number of dollars that came in and the number that went out. For example, a sport manager would be very interested in how much cash that was actually taken out of the organization in a given year.

Operating Cash Flow

Operating cash flow is an important number because it tells the sport manager whether or not an organization's cash inflows from its business operations are sufficient to cover its everyday cash outflows. For this reason, a negative operating cash flow is often a sign of trouble.

> Cash flow budget is a forecast of cash receipts and disbursements for the next planning period.

Cash Flow Budget

The cash flow budget is a primary tool in the short-run financial planning. It allows the sport financial manager to identify short-term financial needs and opportunities. Importantly, the cash flow budget will help the manager explore the need for short-term borrowing. The concept behind a cash flow budget is simple: it records estimates of cash receipts (cash in) and disbursements (cash out). The result is an estimate of the cash surplus or deficit.

> Profit is the sum remaining after all costs, direct and indirect, are deducted from the revenue of an organization.
>
> In general, revenue is the amount charged to customers for goods or services sold to them. There are alternative terms used to identify revenue including sales, fees earned, rent earned, or fares earned.

Profit Planning

The bottom line for an organization is the ability to generate revenue at such a pace that continued growth could be both sustained and achieved. If an organization has shareholders, this growth should include rewards, or dividends, for those shareholders.

While making a profit is the ultimate goal of any business, the mission, goals, and objectives of the organization should not be forsaken in order to obtain profit. By determining the short- and long-term goals of an organization and keeping them in mind during all phases of financial planning, resources can be better allocated to achieve these goals. Short-term goals are those goals that you want to achieve in the near future. The time frame for short term is no more than one to two years. Long-term goals are priorities that are set for a three to five year period in the future and they often require more time and resources to bring to reality. These goals should move to the short-term goal list as their deadline approaches and resources become available. By properly planning where your profits will be allocated, the manager can allocate funds for these various short- and long-term projects.

To properly plan for where and when our profits will be spent, we must first know where they are obtained and how stable that revenue generation will be over a longer period of time so the manager can better determine the profit margin. Revenue generation (see Chapter 6) is not the only area of concern when determining profits. The manager must also forecast costs and plan for unforeseen emergencies in order to determine profit margin.

There are several commonly used measures of profitability. These include profit margin on sales, return on total assets, return on common equity, and return on investment. Profit margins, gross and net, are determined by dividing profits by revenue. Net profit margins use net income or income after taxes and interest and gross profit margin uses earnings before taxes and interest have been paid.

Margin is the difference between the cost and the selling price of goods produced and services rendered. This is sometimes called a margin on sales or sales margin.

Profit margin is a profitability measure that defines the relationship between sales and net income. The result is a percentage of profit. Some items have a high percentage of profit margin and others have a lower percentage. The sport manager uses the profit margin measure to determine what the price of the service or product should be to be competitive and allow the organization to make a profit.

Common equity is the sum of the par value (i.e., the principal amount of a bond that is repaid at the end of the term), capital in excess of par, and accumulated retained earnings. Community equity is usually referred to as an organization's book value or net worth.

Return on assets (ROA) is another profitability measure of profit per dollar of asset.

The return on total assets (ROA) is determined by dividing profits by average assets for a given reporting period. The average assets (i.e., an average of an organization's assets over a prior period of time) can be located on the balance sheet. The return on investment (ROI) is often referred to as the ROA because it reflects the amount of profits earned on the investment in all assets of the firm. These terms are interchangeable.

The balance sheet is a snapshot of the organization. It is a convenient means of organizing and summarizing what an organization owns (i.e., assets), what is owed (i.e., liabilities), and the difference between the two (i.e., equity) at a given point in time. If the difference between assets and liabilities is positive, then the organization is profitable.

The return on common equity (ROE) is similar to the ROA; however, it is concerned with stockholder equity. The ROE is determined by dividing the net income by the average stockholders' equity in the organization. The ROA and the ROE can be effective in comparing the financial status of businesses of similar size and interest.

Return on equity is yet another profitability measure of how the stockholders did during the year. It is the true bottom-line measure of performance.

Capital Budgeting

Capital budgeting deals with investment decisions involving fixed assets (i.e., equipment, buildings, accumulated depreciation for equipment and buildings). The term "capital" is defined as long-term assets used in production, and "budget" means a plan that details projected inflows (amount of dollars coming into the organization) and outflows (amount of dollars leaving the organization to cover expenses) during some future period. Thus, the capital budget is an outline of planned investments in fixed assets and capital budgeting is the process of analyzing projects and deciding which ones to include in the capital budget.

> A fixed or permanent asset is one that is long-lived. These assets are tangible in nature, used in the operations of the business, and not held for sale in the ordinary course of the business but are classified on the balance sheet as fixed assets.

Long-Term Planning

Long-term planning is considered any type of planning that is at least five years into the future. All sport managers need to establish a long-term plan for the organization. This plan can be five to 15 years in length. The plans need to be revised annually, extending the plan for one additional year into the future. Each department within the organization needs to be involved in the long-term plan and each department's plan needs to be an integral part of the overall organization's long-term plan. Those organizations who do not plan well into the future generally are not around for the long haul. An organization cannot plan too much. Planning must be an integral part of the organization's culture.

Short-Term Financing

Most sport organizations in the private sector use several types of short-term debt to finance their working capital requirements including bank loans (e.g., line of credit, revolving credit agreement,

promissory note), trade credit (i.e., accounts payable), commercial paper (i.e., unsecured promissory note issued by the organization and sold to another organization, insurance company, pension fund, or bank), and accruals (i.e., accrued assets). Short-term credit is generally cheaper, quicker, and more flexible than long-term capital, but it is a riskier, less dependable source of financing. For example, interest rates can increase dramatically, and changes in an organization's financial position can affect both the cost and availability of short-term credit.

Asset Management Ratios

The asset management ratios measure how effectively the organization is managing its assets. These ratios are designed to answer this question: does the total amount of each type of asset as reported on the balance sheet seem reasonable or too high or too low in view of current and projected sales levels? If a sport organization has excessive investments in assets, then its capital costs will be unduly high and its stock price will suffer. However, if a sport organization does not have enough assets, it will lose sales, which will hurt free cash flow and the stock price. Therefore, it is important to have the right amount invested in assets. The sport manager needs to continually evaluate the organization's assets, including fixed assets, total assets, free cash flow, debt ratios, profitability ratios, and market value ratios. Finally, the sport manager needs to analyze trends in ratios and compare the results to other like organizations. The latter is known as benchmarking.

Evaluating the Environment

Evaluating the environment in which your organization competes is vital to its long-term financial stability. From terrorist activities that may affect event planning to advances in food preparation for concession sales, the competitive environment in which an organization operates must be monitored to avoid missed opportunities as well as financial disaster.

There are numerous ways to evaluate the environment of an organization. The manager must first look internally for components that may be easily altered to bring about a more profitable future. Internal aspects may include employee benefits, workloads, staffing, and policies. All of these areas work together to provide a pleasant work environment, which in turn increases productivity. By reviewing benefit expenses, it can be determined, for example, if less expensive health coverage could be provided to save both the organization and the employee money without reducing services. Workloads may be reassigned or new staff hired to reduce overtime and tension of overworked employees. Policies may need to be altered as an organization grows both in size and as its financial status changes. All of these components are controlled within the organization and take little effort to monitor, evaluate, and change.

The external environment in which an organization operates is not as easy to monitor, and therefore necessary change may be slow; however, its importance is vital to the future financial success of an organization. The international political environment, such as terrorism, war, and government stability, must be monitored to determine if events must be moved or cancelled. The marketing environment for sport products and services must be analyzed so opportunities in the marketplace will not be lost. Demographics and geography should be reviewed to determine new market potential and current market change. Such information can be found in census reports conducted by the government. Market research is the foundation for reviewing the environment in which an organization operates.

Forecasting Sales

Financial planning is often based on the successes and failures of previous years' sales. Along with the present market analysis, managers can use previous sales to forecast future sales. A market analysis will include a SWOT analysis of the organization and its competition. SWOT is the acronym for strengths, weaknesses, opportunities, and threats. When properly conducted, a SWOT analysis can show the position of a product within the market and can help the manager realize future market potential and opportunities within the market place. Strengths and weaknesses are internal components that can be controlled and corrected within the organization, whereas opportunities and threats are external factors that are influenced by areas such as the economy, trends, fads, culture, and the environment.

By realistically forecasting sales, an organization can better plan for cash flow and conduct both long- and short-term planning.

Financial Risk Management (See Chapter 20)

As sport enterprises become increasingly complex, it is becoming more and more difficult for the sport manager to know what problems might lie in wait. The sport manager needs to systematically look for potential problems and design safeguards to minimize potential damage. There are 12 major sources of risk common to sport organizations including business partners (i.e., contractual risks), competition (i.e., market share, price wars, antitrust), customers (i.e., product liability, credit risk, poor market timing), distribution systems (i.e., transportation, service availability, cost), financial (i.e., cash, interest rate), operations (i.e., facilities, natural hazards, internal controls), people (i.e., employees, independent contractors, training, staffing inadequacy), political (i.e., change in leadership, enforcement of intellectual property rights, revised economic policies), regulatory and legislative (i.e., antitrust, licensing, taxation, reporting and compliance), reputations (i.e., corporate image, brand), strategic (i.e., mergers and acquisitions, joint ventures and alliances, resource allocation, planning), and technological (i.e., obsolescence, workforce skill-sets) (Teach, E. 1997. "Microsoft's Universe of Risk," *CFO*, 69-72).

Preparing a Financial Plan—Building the Case

When preparing a financial plan, the manager must review all aspects of the organization and make decisions for its future stability and profitability. Financial planning will allow an organization to sustain itself through inflation, recession, cash flow shortages, and other economic situations that can be devastating to any business.

Without a sound financial plan, investors and lenders will not place their trust and resources into an organization. Research should be conducted looking at both past and present budgets, revenue generation resources, and capital outlay projects. This research of both internal and external factors will provide the manager with an overview of the past and current financial condition and help to make future decisions for improved financial stability.

The Role of the Budget

The budget is a part of the foundation upon which an organization justifies its mission. It establishes financial parameters through which the organization can determine its objectives and attain its goals. The mission statement for the organization establishes guidelines that help construct the budget. The mission statement is the statement of purpose for the organization that establishes goals that the organization wants to achieve. Without a mission statement, an organization would not function in an effective and efficient manner. There would be no direction, goals, or means of obtaining those goals. An organization without a budget could be likened to someone setting out on a cross-country road trip to visit relatives without a map or plan for which direction to drive first. A budget is an estimate of revenue and expenses for a given period of time, usually one to two years. Budgets anticipate or predict cash flow as well as control cash flow. Effective cash flow budgeting involves estimating when income and expenses occur to ensure that no times arise when a shortage of income means that an agency is unable to pay its expenses (Crompton, 1999). In sport, there are many periods when an organization may not be generating income sufficient to cover expenses. Monthly bills continue to become due and renovation projects are often undertaken during this "off season" period. When cash flow problems are anticipated and planned for within the budget, the organizations can easily attend to routine monthly bills as well as continue with maintenance schedules and renovation projects.

> The budget of the organization is determined by the organization's goals and objectives. Essentially, the budget is a restatement of the organization's objectives in financial terms.

Budget Types

There are numerous approaches to budgeting. The organization's board of directors, accountants, and managers can only determine the approach that is right for your organization. The five most frequently used budget types that will be discussed here are line item, program, performance, zero-based, and entrepreneurial budgeting systems (Crompton,

1999). While each approach has strengths, they also contain constraints that may not prove efficient for your organization. A combination of two or more of these budget approaches may be necessary for your organization to maintain an efficient and effective use of resources.

Line-item budgeting is the oldest and most common form of budgeting, which has its roots firmly planted in government. One reason behind its extensive government use is that it allows for financial control and accountability. In the line-item budget, a specific dollar amount is appropriated for each expenditure listed in the budget. The organization is limited to spending that pre-set amount of money for each expenditure area. For example, a line-item budget for an athletic team would contain expenditures for salaries, equipment, telephone, office supplies, and travel. Each of these areas for that team would be allotted a certain amount of money at the beginning of the fiscal year. When the team had spent all of its funds for equipment, there would be no more money for equipment.

This budget type offers an easy way to review expenditures and determine where budgets can be cut and where they may need to be expanded. A drawback to this type of budgeting is that it does not allow the administrator to account for direct relationships between expenses and benefits from dollars spent. Using the example above, we would know only of the amount of money spent on total telephone use and would not have a breakdown of how much of that telephone usage went to the recruitment of potential student-athletes, setting up travel, or scheduling. Another type of phone log would be necessary if the administrator wished to understand the break down and relationship.

Line-item budgets have three basic weaknesses. First, they offer little information when budgeting for services. The nature and level of services and the resources needed to provide a level of service are not apparent when using a line-item budget. Second, no formal process exists when being forced to make choices between services and programs. Third, there is no way to predict what impact changes in funding will have on performance or service level (Compton, 1999).

Program budgeting presents expenditures in the form of department functions or activity areas. It emphasizes outcomes rather than cost inputs. When utilizing this type of format, the organization must first identify all of the programs offered. The next step is to determine all costs associated with each program. The line-item budget is often incorporated under each program area. Although it provides more information than a line-item budget, a program budget still does not provide the administrator answers to key questions regarding the impact of their programming in relation to the amount of money spent on each program.

A performance budget will help the administrator answer the questions regarding the relationship between dollars spent and program impact. The emphasis with this type of budget is on what is achieved with the dollars spent. With a performance budget you hope to get more "bang for your buck" when allocating funds. By measuring each program outcome, the administrator can see how much is being accomplished with each dollar spent. The program outcomes must be stated in a measurable way using mission statements, objectives, and performance indicators. Types of performance indicators may include program size or volume, how efficiently funds are being spent (output per dollar spent) and how well a program meets an objective.

The emphasis on performance budgeting is on the programs, services and benefits rather than on the amount of money spent. With the line-item budget, we are concerned with control of funds in a performance-based budget. The central focus is the management of funds. The performance budget is particularly useful when presenting information to a board of directors, stockholder, or committee that is not directly associated with the daily operation of an organization. This type of budget clearly indicates where dollars have been spent and the relationship between those funds, and the performance of the programs.

With line-item and performance-based budgets, funds left over from one year are often allowed to be carried over to the next annual budget.

Zero-based budgets are a variation of the performance budget. Instead of using the traditional appropriations, organizations will start from zero each year. This could mean that an item that was funded in the current budget may not be funded in the upcoming budget year. Each year the programs, both existing and proposed, are reviewed, and it is determined how funds will be best allocated and which programs will be funded.

With zero-based budgeting, it is essential that an organization prioritize decisions and programs through evaluation and ranking. Since each program and decision is competing for the same funding, it is necessary to determine where funds will be most effectively allocated. This process is time consuming and can contribute to low staff morale. The ranking of projects may contribute to a feeling by staff that their programs are not as important to the organization and therefore cause uncertainty and discourse. The zero-based budget does, however, provide greater insight for staff on the usefulness of programs. Many organizations have developed modified versions of the zero-based budget and often use it to review and revise programs on an occasional basis. Zero-based budgets are especially effective in determining between the funding of marginal programs and new opportunities.

Entrepreneurial budgeting systems (EBS) are often called expenditure-controlled, target-based, or envelope budgeting. Their appeal is based partially on the ability of elected officials to maintain control over the bottom line.

Along with staff, the director of an agency is given authority to develop and implement programs and services within the budget limits. Elected officials are likely to require strong evidence that an agency is achieving its goals and objectives efficiently and effectively.

There is strong performance accountability with the entrepreneurial budgeting system. It ensures that elected officials maintain control over what goals to pursue while the administration decides how to pursue the goal. In contrast to a zero-based budget, the entrepreneurial budget is a top-down process. The top establishes priorities and forces those priorities onto those at the bottom of the organization.

The EBS is likely to have accounts for the major program areas of the organization. If an opportunity arises or an emergency occurs, money can be shifted from one account to another. Instead of focusing on how to spend a particular line-item amount, managers review where the funds are needed and if money could be saved and used elsewhere. This empowers managers and agencies to pursue missions and goals without worrying about previous budget priorities and frees managers to move revenue as needs change. These freedoms often stimulate motivation and allow managers to combine resources while, at the same time, holding them accountable for program results.

Budgeting Process

There are five steps that are commonly used in the budget process: (a) collecting data relative to the needs, strengths, and resources of the organization then applied to the mission of the organization, and goals of the previous year, (b) analyzing the data collected, comparing it to past experiences and present requirements, (c) identifying other factors that may impact operations, (d) preparing the document according to stipulations and requirements of the

Table 4.1

A Comparison of the Advantages and Disadvantages of Various Budget Types

Budget Type	Advantages	Disadvantages
Line Item	Financial control and accountability	Little information when budgeting for services
	Expenditures can be easily reviewed	Cannot identify direct relationships between expenses and benefits
		No formal decision making process
Program	Expenditures based on departmental functions	Does not provide information regarding the impact of the programming
	Emphasizes outcomes rather	

Continued

Table 4.1 Continued

	cost inputs	
	Separates costs (expenses) by	
	each program	
Performance	Measures program outcomes	Does not emphasize control regarding amount of money spent overall
	Central focus management of program funds	
	Clearly indicates the relationship between funds spent and program performance	
Zero Based	Prioritizes funds	Process time consuming
	Provides greater insight for decision making	Contributes to low staff morale

Continued

Table 4.1 Continued

Entrepreneurial	Controls expenditure by linking goals and objectives to expenditures	Reduces emphasis on previous budget priorities
	Increases accountability	
	Empowers managers to pursue mission and goals	
	Frees managers to move and combine revenues	

organization's governing budget including reviewing the document for accuracy and feasibility, soliciting a third party to review the draft document, and preparing for anticipated questions during the formal budget review, and (e) implementing the approved budget and auditing the budget at the conclusion of the fiscal year (Horine & Stotlar, 2003).

When collecting data for budget preparation, sport managers should use a variety of resources. Statistical information should be considered when preparing a budget. Statistics that a manager needs are: how income and expenses compare for a given period of time (variance analysis), usage and participation data, program evaluation reports, inventory levels, and other sources as appropriate (Sawyer & Smith, 1999).

Management must also look to employees for input on budgetary needs. Since employees are the users of equipment and supplies, they have first-hand knowledge regarding what is most effective and efficient in the production of goods and services. Management should provide all workers with the opportunity to share their knowledge and experience and contribute to budgeting decisions.

To build a budget, management must be able to forecast or predict, with some degree of confidence, what expected revenues and expenses will be for the next fiscal period. Forecasting must be made for both existing programs as well as anticipated new programs (Sawyer & Smith, 1999).

When looking at other factors that may or have impacted the budget, we can explore trend analysis. Past budgets should be examined to attempt to identify financial trends that have developed. This can be accomplished by examining the financial statement for the current month and comparing with past months of the fiscal year, comparing the current month with the same month last year, comparing year-to-date with the same information of the previous year, and actual performance year-to-date with budget year-to-date (Horine & Stotlar, 2003).

There are internal and external factors that can also impact budget preparation. Internal factors come from within the organization such as policy changes, personnel changes, and cost-of-living salary increases. These internal factors are within the organization's control. Those elements over which the organization has little or no control are termed external factors. These factors occur outside the organization and can include the economy, tax structures, trends, and changes in the law.

After all data have been collected and analyzed, dollar amounts should be calculated and applied to various ac-counts. Expenses should be based on input from the three methods of forecasting (i.e., employee, statistical, and managerial input). Revenue can be forecast using those methods as well. Most managers estimate expenses based on anticipated increases in the cost of living and/or suppliers forecasts for price increases. Income, on the other hand, is usually projected to be somewhat less than actually hoped for (Sawyer & Smith, 1999).

After the budget has been completed, it should be reviewed with as much staff involvement as is possible and practical. The staff should be aware of the financial status of the organization for the upcom-ing budget year and management should feel confident that the budget appears reasonable and that justifications for expenditures are clearly stated. It is essential that questions and concerns be addressed at this level before the budget is sent forward to the governing board for approval. The budget should be sent forward for presentation and all staff should believe that the budget has been developed with the best available data, experience, and forecasting possible.

Budget Preparation

Effective budget management is the result of continuous long-range planning, review, evaluation, and preparation. Before one can begin to plan for the future of an organization, a budget must be prepared. A typical budget begins with the establishment of a budget calendar and manual. The calendar denotes the beginning and the end of the budget cycle and establishes a time schedule for completing each phase in the budget. Organizations operate on different fiscal calendars such as July 1-June 30, October 1 – September 30, and January 1-December 31. The approval process for the budget takes approximately two months, thus the process needs to begin at least six months prior to the operational date of July 1, October 1, or January 1.

Sample Budget Cycle

July 1 – June 30 Fiscal Year Cycle

Implementation Phase	Monitoring Phase	Data Gathering Phase	Preparation Phase	Approval Phase
July 1- June 30	July 1- June 30	January 1 - February 28	March 1 - April 30	May 1 - June 30

The organization's chief financial officer prepares the manual and its main purpose is to facilitate a consistent understanding of what is expected from all involved in the budget planning process. The manual is distributed to all department heads so that there is a clear understanding of deadlines and expectations. Depending on the magnitude and scope of the organization, the process for developing a budget will be different and the number of staff involved will vary. The budget must still be established by the appropriate staff, approved by administration, and followed by all members of the organization.

For example, a collegiate athletic budget would be prepared by the athletic director with input from all the head coaches, head athletic trainer, equipment manager, assistant athletic directors responsible for compliance, scheduling and travel, facility and game management, and marketing and promotion. Once all data have been gathered and included in the overall budget and the athletic director reviews and makes adjustments, the budget is forwarded to the next level of administration for review, modification, and approval, then forwarded to the Board of Trustees for final approval. After the budget has been approved, it is implemented and monitored by the athletic director and the departmental staff.

The first step in preparation of a budget is the establishment of fiscal, operational, and policy guidelines that will affect the preparation of the budget. These include items such as salary increases, establishment of program priorities, personnel increases or decreases, and facility maintenance. These guidelines will be submitted to department heads. The department head, with consultation from the employees, will develop the details for the next budget year as well as priority programs.

After the guidelines are received, the divisions (i.e., in a collegiate athletic program divisions might include each sport offered, sports medicine, facilities and equipment, game management, scheduling and travel, marketing and promotion, compliance) are asked to submit budget requests to department heads. These requests should include a rationale for the requested funding and be in a priority order. Funding for special programs and services should also identify sources for additional revenue and potential new markets for the program or service. Each department head is responsible for reviewing program requests and "pulling together" the priorities for funding to most efficiently and effectively utilize available resources. The department head is charged with submitting a comprehensive department budget that will encompass routine operating expenses as well as allow for growth and development of the department and the organization. The budget document should include a justification for expenditures so when presented to the governing body all questions and concerns regarding the budget can be effectively answered.

Sample Explanation for an Expense

Printing	$45,000	25,000 football programs — 5,000/game/5 games
		84,000 basketball programs — 7,000/game/12 games
		10,000 baseball programs — 500/game/20 games
		5,000 softball programs — 250/game/20 games
		10,000 department brochures
		10,000 business cards

Preparation of the budget is a year-round process. While the director and agency staff may be involved formally in the mechanics of preparing and presenting the budget for only a six-month period each year, effective budget development is the result of continuous long-range planning, review, and evaluation (Crompton, 1999).

Revenue Sources

The types of revenue sources available will depend upon the type of organization and program involved. The primary sources of revenue generation are: (1) membership fees, (2) ticket sales, (3) admissions fees, (4) food concessions, (5) sponsorship agreements, (6) licensing agreements, (7) leases/rentals, (8) parking, and (9) merchandise sales (Sawyer & Smith, 1999).

A club or agency, to control access to facilities, programs, etc., collects membership fees. Those who have paid the membership dues are allowed entry. Membership fees may be collected on an annual, semi-annual, monthly, weekly, or per-program basis.

Ticket sales can be applied to any single event or a series of events (season tickets) and can usually be purchased in advance of the event. Ticket events differ from events charging an admission fee in that ticketed events are most often associated with spectator events, whereas events with admission fees are usually those where the customer is a participant or user of a facility such as a swimming pool, theme park, campground, etc. Admission fees, therefore, are those fees charged at the time a person enters a facility and includes authorization to use most, if not all, services within the facility (Sawyer & Smith, 1999).

The terms "concessions" and "food service" are used interchangeably. A well-operated concession plays a vital role in the revenue generation of an organization. Management must be concerned with serving good food at a reasonable price

and creating a pleasant atmosphere. Menu boards should be well organized with prices, brands, and pictures of items being served. Concessions should be well organized to eliminate customer confusion regarding where to order, pay, and pick up food. It is important that employees be well trained to handle crowds and keep lines moving. Disposable packaging, containers, and utensils have aided the concessions industry in delivering safe, convenient, high-quality foods. In most facilities, there should be sufficient numbers of concession stands to serve the total number of seats with each patron being able to reach the nearest stand within 40 to 60 seconds of leaving his or her seat (Farmer, 1996).

There are two types of concessions, in-house and contracted. (See Chapter 13 Outsourcing for detailed information.) The advantage of managing in-house concessions is that it provides total control. The facility manager can decide what prices to charge, the quality of the goods/products sold, and whether or not to open an area without having every decision become a negotiating session with the concessionaire. Many managers feel they are maximizing their revenues by cutting out the middleman, the concessionaire (Sawyer & Smith, 1999). Managers who do not want the headaches associated with organizing, planning and scheduling concessions often opt for contracting with outside organizations that specialize in concession management. A facility manager may not have the resources to efficiently and effectively operate concessions, so contracting out is a convenient and viable option.

Corporate sponsorship (see Chapter 7 for greater detail) is the purchase of rights from an organization either in cash, products, or services to pursue corporate communication or targeting objectives through predetermined activities and through the use of any images and symbols associated with the organization's activities to the benefit of the corporation (Sawyer & Smith, 1999). Sponsors agree to become involved for various reasons. These reasons include positive public relations for their organizations, increased sales, the generation of favorable media for their organization, competition, and good citizenship. The reason for involvement may also dictate their level of involvement. There are four common levels of involvement for sponsors: exclusive, primary, subsidiary, and official supplier. An exclusive sponsor has the sole financial commitment for the event. They may even own an event and, if not, they still have a major say in its organization. A primary sponsor shares the financial commitment to the event with one or more companies. Each company has a smaller financial commitment; therefore, they are better able to maximize exposure with minimal financial risk. These sponsors still have major input in how the event is organized and managed. A subsidiary sponsor is a company that has exclusive rights in a product category. Their financial commitment is smaller than the primary sponsor and their sponsored service is frequently essential to the event. An official supplier is on the same level as the subsidiary sponsor; however, their products are not crucial to the competition. Like the subsidiary sponsor, the official supplier generally has exclusive rights within a product category.

Colleges and universities and a number of large high schools have established licensing programs (see Chapter 8 for greater detail) as a means of generating revenue. The growth in consumer demand for licensed apparel has generated $4 billion in annual retail sales and has provided an opportunity for professional and amateur sport programs to benefit through licensing agreements. Several institutions, such as Notre Dame, Michigan, and Penn State, are generating nearly $1 million annually from licensing (Sawyer & Smith, 1999). A second party is granted the right to produce merchandise with an organization's logo for a royalty fee, usually 10 percent of the manufacturers wholesale price. Licensing

agreements can be complex and should be administered by a qualified, full-time licensing director. If your organization does not have the resources or does not wish to hire the necessary staff to administer a licensing program, a professional licensing agency may be hired to operate your program.

Financing facility construction (see Chapter 6 for greater detail) has been a greatly debated topic among civic leaders with serious questions and concerns about the economic value of sport facilities. The most common ways to finance sport facilities have been by using taxes, private investment, federal grants, luxury seat fees, guaranteed federal bonds, city bonds, county bonds, and/or state bonds. Many facilities today are financed by using multiple financing strategies as listed above rather than relying on only one source of revenue (Sawyer & Smith, 1999).

Safeguarding Revenue

It is very important that the sport manager develop and implement a plan for safeguarding the income generated by the organization. The first step that should be taken is requiring all employees who deal with money be bonded up to a certain amount of money. This is an insurance policy to protect the organization from employee embezzlement.

Further, measures must be established to ensure accountability for membership fees, admissions fees, and ticket sales. These measures should allow for daily sales reports or game attendance including, but not limited to, number of tickets sold, fees collected, complimentary tickets, press passes, team and coach passes, and VIP passes.

These same kinds of measures should be in place for the food concession, parking concession, and merchandise sales. If the concessions for food, merchandise sales, and parking are assigned through a contract to a vendor, a sound accounting process must be outlined in the agreement to guarantee the implementation of the financial aspects of the contract.

Expenditures

Expenditures are costs, or money paid out, that an organization encounters. Costs are those factors associated with producing, promoting, and distributing the sport's product (Shank, 2002). There are three types of costs: fixed, variable, and total.

> Expenditures are expenses (costs) that have been consumed in the process of producing income (revenue). Expenditures are often called expired costs or expenses.

Fixed costs are those that do not change or vary in regard to the quantity of product or service consumed. A fixed cost used in break-even analysis is that cost that remains constant regardless of the amount of variable costs. For example, fixed costs include insurance, taxes, etc.

Variable costs are those costs that are going to increase or decrease based on the increase or decrease in a product or service provided. For example, variable costs include advertising, utilities, postage, etc. If the facility will host a rock concert, a basketball game, and a beauty pageant this week, the cost for advertising events may increase. If only a basketball game is scheduled, the advertising needs may be less. Although an athletic team experiences very few variable costs in the total cost equation, a manufacturer of

Illustration 4.1

Sample Operating Budget

Hannibal State University

Expenditures		Revenue	
Personnel	2,750,000	Student Athletic Fees	2,200,000
Scholarships	2,250,000	Ticket Sales	1,500,000
Travel		Licensing Contract	750,000
Team	1,000,000	Sponsorships	1,000,000
Recruiting	100,000	Concessions	2,000,000
Guarantees	500,000	Parking	500,000
Advertising	1,000,000	Guarantees	725,000
Operations		University Allocation	1,000,000
Telephone	20,000	Donations	600,000
Printing	300,000	Total Revenue	10,300,000
Duplication	20,000		
Office Supplies	50,000		
Athletic Supplies	700,000		
Sport Medicine Supplies	125,000		
Awards and Banquets	50,000		
Computer Maintenance	10,000		
Association/League Fees	65,000		
Officials Fees	200,000		
Technology Upgrades	100,000		
Insurance	30,000		
Contingency	30,000		
Capital Projects	1,000,000		
Total Expenses	10,300,000		

pure sport goods would encounter a significantly greater number of variable costs (Shank, 2002). As the number of units sold increases, the costs for packing and shipping the product also increase.

The total costs for operations is arrived at when the fixed costs (expenses) and variable costs (expenses) are added together. Costs are considered to be internal factors that can be largely controlled by the organization; however, they can have an external or uncontrollable factor. The cost of raw materials, league imposed salary minimums, and shipping of products is controlled by external factors. When establishing a budget, the sport manager must review the total operating expenses considering both internal and external factors to forecast the expenditures for the upcoming year.

The common expenditures found in sport enterprise budgets include personnel, guarantees (i.e., dollars paid to visiting teams), advertising, team travel, recruiting travel, scholarships, costs of operation (i.e., postage, utilities, telephone, duplication, printing, office supplies, athletic supplies, sports medicine supplies, computer maintenance, etc.), association/league fees, officials fees, technology upgrades, capital projects, awards and banquets, insurance, and facility lease agreements.

Break-Even Analysis

The point in the operation of an organization at which revenues and expenses are exactly equal is called the break-even point. At this level of operations an organization will neither realize an operating revenue nor incur an operating loss. Break-even analysis can be applied to past periods, but it is most useful when applied to future periods as a guide to business planning, particularly if either an expansion or a curtailment of operation is anticipated. In such cases, it is concerned with future prospects and future operations and thus relies upon estimates. The reliability of the analysis is

greatly influenced by the accuracy of the estimates.

The data required to complete a break-even analysis includes (1) total estimated fixed costs and expenses for a future period such as a year, and (2) the total estimated variable expenses for the same period, stated as a percent of net sales. To illustrate, assume that fixed expenses are estimated at \$90,000 and that variable expenses are expected to amount to 60 percent of sales. The break-even point is \$225,000 of sales revenue, computed as follows:

Break-Even Sales (in \$)=Fixed Costs (in \$) + Variable Expenses (as % of Break-Even Sales)

$$S = \$90,000 + 60\%S$$
$$40\% \quad S = \$90,000$$
$$S = \$225,000$$

Break-even analysis may also be employed in estimating the sales volume required to yield a specified amount of operating revenue. The previous formula can be modified for use in this computation by the addition at the end of the equation of the desired amount of operating revenue. For example, the sales volume required to yield operating income of \$40,000 for the enterprise assumed above would be \$325,000, computed as follows:

Sales = Fixed Expenses + Variable Expenses + Operating Revenue

$$S = \$90,000 + 60\%S + \$40,000$$
$$40\% \quad S = \$130,000$$
$$S = \$325,000$$

Operating revenue is the amount of dollars necessary to maintain business operations.

Summary

Establishing a budget is a necessary process to help an organization keep sight of its mission, goals, and objectives. There are five frequently used budget types: the line-item, program, performance, zero-based, and entrepreneurial budgeting systems. A combination of two or more of these types is often used to effectively handle an organization's budgeting needs.

When collecting data for budget preparation, sport managers should use a variety of resources. A manager may need various statistics to aid in developing a budget. These statistics include how income and expenses compare for a given period of time (variance analysis), usage and participation data, program evaluation reports, inventory levels, and other sources as appropriate.

Effective budget management is the result of continuous long-range planning, review, evaluation, and preparation. Before one can begin to plan for the future of the organization, a budget must be prepared. Total costs are determined by reviewing fixed and variable costs, which will aid in determining expenses for a given budget cycle.

The task of the future sport manager is to seek out new resources that can help an organization achieve its goals. The unprecedented prosperity of sport in the 1970s and 1980s are gone and traditional revenue resources can no longer cover rising costs (Howard & Crompton, 2003).

Without adequate financial planning, organizations with continued limited resources will not be able to sustain economic stress. This stress can come from short-term issues such as cash flow, or long-term problems such as litigation or national and international economic downturns. It is the responsibility of the manager to prepare for future financial stability of the organization.

References

Crompton, J.L. (1999). *Financing and acquiring park and recreation resources.* Champaign, IL: Human Kinetics.

Farmer, P.J., Mulrooney, A.L., & Ammon, Jr., R. (1996). *Sport facility planning and management.* Morgantown, WV: Fitness Information Technology, Inc.

Horine, L. & Stotlar, D. (2003). *Administration of physical education and sport.* (6th Ed) Dubuque, IA: Wm. C. Brown Company.

Howard, D.R. & Crompton, J.L. (2003). *Financing sport.* (2nd Ed) Morgantown, WV: Fitness Information Technology.

Jensen, C.R. (1988). *Administrative management of physical education and athletic programs.* Philadelphia, PA: Lea & Febiger.

Sawyer, T.H., & Smith, O. (1999). *The management of clubs, recreation and sport: Concepts and applications.* Champaign, IL: Sagamore Publishing.

Shank, M.D. (2002). *Sports marketing: A strategic perspective.* Upper Saddle River, NJ: Prentice Hall.

Suggested Reading

Fried, G., Shapiro, S.J., & Deschriver, T.D. (2003). *Sport finance.* Champaign, IL: Human Kinetics.

Miller, L.K. (1997). *Sport business management.* Gaithersburg, MD: Aspen.

Purchasing

Introduction

The purchase of sports equipment and supplies involves an intricate process that is generally controlled by institutional or organizational policies and regulations. The ultimate goal of the purchasing process is to provide the organization with the best product at the best price. Purchasing may be controlled through a central purchasing office or by independent agencies.

The purchasing process involves: 1) the selection process, 2) needs assessment, and 3) procurement. The selection of sport equipment and supplies is one of the most important responsibilities of a sport manager. The selection process is an integral component for the organization to provide quality programs and facilities.

Walker and Seidler (1993) identified the needs assessment as a simple determination of the needs of the program that begins with a simple overview of the situation. Is the program new or pre-existing? Is the program educational, recreational or competitive? In each circumstance, it is important to understand the scope, variety and nature of the program(s) to be offered.

The procurement process provides a means to provide consistency in the selection and purchase of equipment and supplies. The procurement process usually begins with a purchase request and ends with a purchase order, delivery and payment of the invoice.

The institution or organization should establish a process that ensures that equipment and supplies that are purchased will: 1) meet program needs, 2) provide quality, 3) be acquired following an organizational established procedure, 4) be properly accounted for, and 5) be maintained for future safe use.

Equipment is identified as items that are non-consumable, which implies they will be used over a period of years. Supplies, on the other hand, are consumable materials such as paper, pens, and athletic tape.

Instructional Objectives

After reading this chapter, the student will be able to:

- Develop guidelines for the selection and purchase of equipment,
- Describe how to evaluate equipment before purchase,
- Explain the procurement process,
- Compare and contrast different types of bid processes, and
- Write effective ordering specifications.

What is the Role of Purchasing?

No matter what type of purchasing system is used, there are common principles and guidelines which apply. Horine (1999) identified the following as being common components of any purchasing program:

- Standardize
- Quality
- Prompt Payment
- Early-bird Ordering
- Professional and Personal Relationships with Vendors
- Businesslike Approach

Standardization of ordering equipment and supplies should be based upon conservative items that would be well received when personnel change. The sport manager does not want to incur additional costs by reordering equipment or supplies because new personnel feel it is necessary to have a different brand or style. The selected products chosen to standardize should be somewhat generic in nature and provide effective use for any personnel.

Purchasing quality equipment can be very economical in the long run even though the organization may have to pay higher initial costs. Proper security, storage, and maintenance along with initial high quality can increase the longevity of many products.

An organization should only order items that can be afforded and should be able to pay bills in a timely fashion. Failure to do so can result in damage to the professional reputation of the organization.

Early-bird ordering provides a means of having inventory available when it is needed. In many cases, there are discounts available when ordering early or prepaying.

Develop both a professional and personal relationship with the vendors that are most commonly used. A good working relationship allows both parties to provide assistance for the other. For the organization, there are opportunities for discounts, information on new products, trial use, group rates, and the possibility to expedite orders. The vendor has the opportunity to improve image, get repeat orders, and have a valuable reference.

Regardless of the vendor or order, purchasing should be done in a professional, businesslike manner following organizational procedures with checks and balances. Ultimately, the sport manager is striving to get the highest quality for the best price.

Walker and Seidler (1993) developed the following factors to be considered in developing the needs assessment for the selection and purchase of equipment and supplies. These factors include:

- Available Space and Facilities—Some equipment is limited to indoor use. Safety and circulation around equipment should be considered before purchase.
- Desired Activities—Certain activities cannot be properly conducted without unique equipment.
- Safety and Health of the Participants—Attempts to reduce costs through reduced safety is unjustifiable.
- Number of Participants – The number of participants who will use the equipment greatly affects the amount required.

- Cost—Will the equipment purchased fulfill the needs of the organization?
- Staff and Supervision—The personnel required to safely supervise the use of the equipment should be considered during the selection process.
- Instructor/Coach Input—Consultation with those individuals directly involved with the administering of programs provides thorough feedback in the selection of equipment.
- Continual Learning – Technological advances occur every day. Up-to-date knowledge of what equipment functions well under given circumstances, what vendors are currently available, and the drive to get better products should influence the selection process.
- Storage—Proper storage can enhance the longevity of the products. Obtain storage requirements from the manufacturer to ensure the life of the product (temperature control, humidity, orientation).
- Age of Participants—The equipment provided for a group should be appropriate for that age group.
- Gender of Participants—All male, all female, and coed teams provide unique challenges for the equipment manager. Selections will be based in part on the rules developed by the governing body (size of basketball to be used by men and women).
- Skill of Participants—The skill level of the participants has a major impact on the equipment selected.
- Physical and Mental Abilities
- Type of Organization—If the organization purchasing the equipment is a school, there may be league or conference requirements on what equipment can be used.
- Length of Season—The number of days per year that the equipment can be used may prohibit the purchase of large amounts.

- Geographical Location—The location, climate, and local environment are major factors in determining program needs.
- Fit—Properly fitted equipment, especially protective equipment, is essential.
- Inventory—Comparison of current needs of an existing program should be made first. An inventory should not just include the number of items but also sizes and condition of the existing products.
- Prioritizing—Prioritize your wish list from the "must haves" to the "nice to haves." Participant and spectator safety should be top priority.

The program should be the determining factor in selecting the equipment and supplies needed. As previously stated, it is much better (and economical) in the long run to purchase high-quality equipment.

Guidelines for Selecting Equipment and Supplies

In addition to the selection variables identified above, specific standards have been developed regarding sport and fitness equipment. The National Operating Committee on Standards for Athletic Equipment (NOCSAE) and the American College of Sports Medicine have established standards that should be of first considerations made when considering the purchase of athletic equipment. NOCSAE was formed to meet the need for nationally approved and accepted standards for activity and sport. Sawyer and Smith (1999) identified other guidelines for the selection of equipment and supplies. These guidelines include:

- Determine purchasing power (how much money is available),
- Begin and maintain a "wish list" of needed and wanted equipment,
- Determine organization needs,
- Determine quality desired,
- Consider whether the product is both budget and maintenance

friendly, and is manufactured by reputable companies,

- Consider whether old equipment can be reconditioned successfully or whether new equipment should be purchased,
- Purchase must be based on program goals, objectives, and budget,
- Determine the priority need and amount of funds available for purchase,
- Consider those persons with disabilities,
- Consider only equipment that meets safety standards,
- Obtain product information from various and diverse vendors, organizing the information by category and type, and each specific company,
- Consider the guarantee, whether or not replacement parts are accessible, the ease of maintenance, and whether or not it fits properly,
- Evaluate the usability of the equipment, making certain that it is adjustable, is state of the art in terms of both design and safety, and is user friendly for all persons,
- Evaluate companies in terms of service record, scientific merit of claims, dependability record, amenities offered, and price, and
- Consider trends in equipment and supplies.

Guidelines for Purchasing Equipment and Supplies

It is important for managers to develop specific guidelines for the purchasing of equipment and supplies. These guidelines enable the manager to standardize equipment and supplies, supervise the entire process of selection and purchase, maintain an inventory, secure bids for larger ticket items, test the items received, and decide on a plan for distribution. Sawyer and Smith (1999) identified specific guidelines that should be implemented by any organization when considering the purchase of equipment and supplies. These guidelines include:

- All purchases should meet the organization's requirements and have management approval,
- Purchasing should be done in advance of need,
- Specifications should be clear,
- Cost should be kept as low as possible without compromising quality,
- Purchases should be made from reputable business firms,
- Central purchasing can result in greater economy,
- All requests must have purchase requisitions,
- Local firms should be considered,
- Competitive bids should be obtained (for large purchases), and
- All purchases must be accompanied by a purchase order.

Purchase requisitions are requests to purchase items. The purchase request is a check measure that allows the manager to determine if funding is available from the desired budget line and to ensure that there is not unnecessary replication of items to be purchased.

The purchase order (PO) is an official request from the organization to the vendor to deliver a specific item at a specific price. The purchase order is usually synonymous with voucher.

Both the purchase request and the purchase order should contain the following:

- Name, and contact information for person submitting request (return address)
- Name and contact information of the vendor
- Date
- Account number
- Department
- Amount
- Quantity
- Unit
- Description
- Unit price

- Special terms: date for delivery, substitutions, discount
- Requestor's signature
- Supervisor's signature

The formal purchase order will also contain a purchase order number for tracking and bookkeeping purposes. Once the purchase order is approved, it will be sent to the vendor for filling the order. Upon receipt of the merchandise, the accounting office will approve payment to the vendor. Figure 5.1 provides a sample purchase order. The organization/agency should provide a blank purchase order form in the policy and procedures manual.

Figure 5.1

To:	Ship/Bill To:
FlagHouse Physical Education & Recreation 601 FlagHouse Drive Hasbrouck Hts., NJ 07604-3116	Julia Ann Hypes Dept. of Health, Physical Education and Sport Sciences Morehead State University 201 Laughlin Health Building Morehead, KY 40351

Purchase Order Number 014325

Account Number 10-15320-201   Date June 4, 2003

QUANTITY	ITEM	UNITS	DESCRIPTION	UNIT PRICE	TOTAL
5	G11655	Ea.	Wilson Impact Rubber Basketball Size 7	14.00	70.00
10	G5786	Ea.	Rawlings RWW Leather Basketball Size 6	56.00	560.00
3	G5976	Pr.	Thera-Brand Dumbbell Roller	20.00	60.00
10	G11970	Doz.	Spalding Top Flight Series X-Out Golf Balls	10.00	100.00
				Subtotal	790.00
				Shipping	$40.00
				Balance Due	$830.00

Requestor _____   Approved by _____

Special Delivery Instructions: Ship via UPS Ground for arrival by August 1, 2003.

Evaluating Equipment Before Purchase

Every organization should have a plan for a comprehensive evaluation of equipment before purchasing. Before the final selection is made, the manager should ask the following questions regarding the equipment to be purchased.

What are the safety issues relevant to the equipment?

Is the equipment safe to be used or are there obvious design flaws that increase the risk to the user? Are there backup electronic circuits? Does the nature of the use of the equipment require putting body parts in a position where they may go beyond the normal range of motion? Can more than one person safely use the equipment at one time?

Are there special considerations for using the equipment?

Is the equipment self-instructing? Does the use of the equipment necessitate the assistance of a spotter? Is the equipment easy to use? Easy to learn? Does the equipment provide a means to motivate the user through a feedback system? Does the equipment have capabilities to accommodate individuals of different body types? Does the equipment have capabilities to accommodate individuals of differing ability levels? Does the equipment have capabilities to accommodate for individuals with disabilities? Is a comprehensive ownership manual provided with the equipment? Is the product aesthetically pleasing? Is the product space efficient and appropriate for your facility?

Does the product meet your needs?

Does the product perform the task for which it was intended? Does it operate quietly and with precision? Is the product built to last? Is the product composed of high-quality components? Does the product possess surface treatments that are durable?

What is the warranty?

How long is the product warranty? Does it include parts and labor? Are parts kept in stock by the dealer? Will the manufacturer provide replacements? Is there an option to purchase an extended warranty?

What do you know about the manufacturer?

How long has the product been available? What is the past history of the manufacturer? Is the manufacturer likely to be around in the next three to five years? Will the manufacturer provide instruction? Does the manufacturer or dealer provide setup/installation?

Miscellaneous questions to ask yourself.

Have your participants requested the product? Is it desirable? Is the product a fad? Will the product become obsolete quickly? Do you have first-hand experience with the product? Will the manufacturer provide a list of users to be contacted as references for the product?

The manufacturer will, in many cases, provide written documentation regarding the product, covering everything from maintenance procedures to safety features and warranty information. You may have to request this information from the manufacturer. Trade journals and magazine articles also can be a source of valuable information during the purchasing process.

The Procurement Process

The procurement process is that part of the purchasing process that begins with the purchase request and ends with the purchase order and payment of the invoice. Sawyer and Smith (1999) cited the primary goal of the procurement process to be "to obtain the desired, high-quality equipment and supplies, on time, and at the lowest possible price" (p. 160). The most common steps involved in the procurement process include:

- Need established
- Management consultation
- Initial request submitted
- Request reviewed
- Determine if funds are available
- Preparation of specifications
- Receipt of bids
- Comparison of bids
- Recommendation of appropriate bid for purchase
- Purchase order to supplier
- Follow-up, receipt of goods
- Payment authorized

The Bid Process

Most governmental units, such as schools and universities, restrict direct purchasing. The school system, college/university, or agency places a dollar limit ($500) on direct purchases. Many managers do not have a choice whether to direct purchase or bid. There may be regulations or laws that prohibit direct purchasing over a certain amount and require the use of a bid process. The bidding process usually involves the intention to purchase, identification of specifications, vendors deciding upon cheapest price at which to sell, and the submission of this figure as an official bid on the product.

Horine (1999) identified the following disadvantages and advantages of the bid process:

Disadvantages
- Quality can suffer.
- The bid system sometimes adds to equipment costs if the item is rather inexpensive but the process is complex.
- The system is slow.
- The process can discourage purchasing from local vendors.
- The process can generate competition among vendors to see who can "cut the most corners."
- Many times the product delivered does not meet the specifications but is used because it is needed immediately.

Advantages
- Can result in lower costs through honest competitive selling.
- Can result in on-time deliveries.
- It can stimulate the vendor to include warranty information and reliable service.
- Shares the wealth. Purchases are spread across a number of vendors.
- It will ensure favoritism and friendship is not the basis of the purchase.
- Reduces the chance of mistakes regarding the technical quality of the product.

There are different types of bid systems available. The competitive sealed bid is the most frequently used system. The specifications are advertised for a set time, usually seven to 21 days, for open bidding. Competitive negotiation is similar to sealed bidding but is not as specific. Rather than provide technical specifications, the competitive negotiation describes what the product is to accomplish. Competitive negotiation after competitive sealed bidding is a method that can be used if the product bids are expected to exceed available funds. The purchasing agent can negotiate with the vendors once it is determined that all bids exceed available funds. Noncompetitive negotiation is used when there is not time to bid. This could be utilized for replacement parts or if the product is needed to match existing products.

The typical bidding process as described by Sawyer and Smith (1999) includes:
- Write specifications for approved items to be purchased,
- Advertise for bids from vendors,
- Receive bids,
- Evaluate bids to ensure all specifications have been met,
- Choose vendors,
- Submit the purchase order,
- Receive equipment, and
- Pay invoice after equipment or supplies are verified.

Writing Specifications

Writing a clear, well-defined, and complete set of specifications is the most important step in assuring what is ordered is in fact what is delivered. Developing written specifications helps to guarantee fair comparisons of bids when alternatives are proposed. The specifications need to be stated clearly and concisely and should be well defined so that the burden of responsibility for providing the product that meets the user's needs falls on the shoulders of vendor. In general, written specifications include clear descriptions of the product being ordered, quantity, quality, size, color, material, brand, model number, catalog number, performance characteristics, any assembly or installation requirements, delivery requirements, and acceptable alternatives, if any. Sawyer and Smith (1999) identified the following specific suggestions that should be considered when writing accurate specifications.

Clothing

It is important to include the following when ordering clothing:
- Manufacturer or name brand
- Style number
- Fabric content
- Shrinkage factor
- Color
- Colorfastness
- Sizing
- Special cuts
- Lettering
- Numbering

Shoes

The purchaser needs to include the following:
- Manufacturer or name brand
- Style number
- Shoe material
- Color

Protective Equipment

When purchasing protective equipment the following should be considered:
- Manufacturer or brand name
- Material content
- Certification standards
- Accurate sizing

Playing Equipment

The purchaser needs to consider the following:
- Manufacturer or brand name
- Equipment model number

Figure 5.2

Incomplete	Worth BW8 Powercell Baseball Bat or equivalent (does not specify length requested and allows vendor to make judgment on substitution)
Complete (without substitutions)	Worth BW8 Powercell Baseball Bat, 35" Length, 32 ounce weight, 2 5/8" diameter – No substitutions or alternatives
Complete (with substitutions)	Worth BW8 Powercell Baseball Bat, 35" Length, 32 ounce weight, 2 5/8" diameter Or Easton LK8 Magnum Bat, 35" Length, 32 ounces weight, 2 5/8" diameter Or Louisville Slugger "YB-17" Baseball Bat, 35" Length, 32 ounce weight, 2 5/8" diameter

- Material content
- Size
- Weight

Scheduling the Purchase of Equipment and Supplies

If the organization is involved in purchasing sport equipment and supplies it needs to be understood that the bidding process can take between four and six weeks before the purchase order is released. Add on to this the possibility that another six to eight weeks can pass before the product is delivered. Therefore, it is necessary to plan ahead. It is recommended to allow six to 12 weeks for the product to be delivered onsite.

Sawyer and Smith (1999) provided the following recommendations regarding a purchase schedule for sports equipment:

Sport Season	Order Date	Delivery Date
Early Spring	October 1	February 1
Late Spring	December 1	March 15
Fall	May 1	August 1
Winter	July 1	October 15

Summary

Purchasing is a process that is generally controlled by institutional or organizational policies and regulations. The purchase process includes the election process, needs assessment, and procurement.

Purchasing has as its main goal to obtain the highest quality product at the lowest possible price. This process involves developing guidelines for selection and the evaluation of equipment before purchase.

The bid process typically involves writing specs, advertising, receiving the bids, evaluation, selection of vendors and submitting the purchase order. It is important to understand that state laws and regulations may restrict direct purchasing thereby forcing you to bid out the product.

References

Horine, L. (1999). *Administration of physical education and sport programs* (4th ed.). Boston, MA: McGraw-Hill.

Sawyer, T.H., & Smith, O. (1999). *The management of clubs, recreation and sport. Concepts and Applications.* Champaign, IL: Sagamore.

Walker, M.L., & Seidler, T.L. (1993). *Sports equipment management.* Boston: Jones and Bartlett.

Suggested Readings

Bucher, C.A., & Krotee, M.L. (2001). *Management of physical education and sport* (12th ed.). Boston, MA: McGraw-Hill

Athletic Business

Athletic Management

Part III

Financial Development

Understanding the Revenue Streams

Introduction

Since 1961 professional sport venues for Major League Baseball, the National Basketball Association, the National Football Association, and the National Hockey League franchises have cost, in 2003 dollars, approximately $24 billion (Crompton, 2004; Crompton, Howard and Var, 2003). The public sector's share of this amount has been approximately $15 billion, which represents 64% of the total (Crompton 2004). Prior to 1950 the venues were almost totally built by use of private dollars.

Venue development has passed through four recognizable joint private and public funding eras (Crompton, et al., 2003). Table 6.0 depicts the four eras and shows that there has been a substantial shift over time in responsibility for funding these types of facilities (Crompton, et al., 2003). It is clear that the public is growing weary of supporting venue construction for billionaire owners and multi-millionaire players. The future funding for facility construction will require substantially more private funding and in some cases 100% private funding (e.g., According to Solomon, a New York City based journalist, the St. Louis Cardinals new $400 million stadium will be almost entirely privately funded).

Table 6.0

Comparison of Public and Private Sector Financing by Funding Era

Combined Costs for Stadiums and Areas

Era	% Public	% Private
Gestation (1961-69)	88	12
Public Subsidy (1970-84)	93	07
Transitional Public-Private Partnerships 1985-94	64	36
Fully-Loaded Public-Private Partnership 1995-2003	51	49
Future Partnership (2004-2015)	33	67

Modified from Crompton, J. (2004). Beyond Economic Impact: An Alternative Rationale for the Public Subsidy of Major League Sports Facilities. *Journal of Sport Management, 18*(1), 41.

Sport entities that are successful year after year have a variety of revenue streams. The good manager understands how to develop new revenue streams, manage the revenue streams, and retain all the revenue streams that have been secured. The revenue is generated through three common sources, including public sources, private sources, and joint public and private ventures. This chapter will focus on understanding the revenue streams available to sport managers.

Learning Objectives

After reading this chapter, the student will be able to:
- Understand how taxes can be used to finance sport entities,
- Describe how tax abatements work in financing sport entities,
- Describe the use of non-taxable bonds in financing sport entities,
- Outline the value of taxable bonds in financing sport entities,
- Understand how a TIF works,
- Describe the use of luxury suites, club (premium) seating, and personal seat licenses to finance sport entities,
- Outline the value of naming rights in financing sport entities, and
- Understand the use of broadcasting rights in financing sport entities.

Public Revenue Streams

Local, county, and state governments for over 50 years have played a major role in constructing and operating sport facilities for many programs including youth, interscholastic, community golf courses, community swimming pools, and professional ballparks, stadiums, and/or arenas. The financing often includes construction costs, infrastructure development (i.e. roads, sewers, water, and other utilities), equipment, and operations. (See Table 6.1 for a listing of sport stadiums/arenas constructed in the United States.)

Table 6.1

Stadiums/Arenas in U.S.

Stadium/Arena	Team	Capacity	Opened	Cost (millions) In 1995 $	% Publicly Financed	State	Sport Authority	League
Bank One Ballpark	Arizona Diamondbacks	48,500	1998	338	75	Arizona	Yes	MLB
Arizona Cardinals Stadium	Arizona Cardinals	73,000	2004	335	100	Arizona	No	NFL
American West Arena	Phoenix Suns	16,000	1992	97.7	39	Arizona	No	NBA
Coyotes Arena	Phoenix Coyotes	16,210	2004	210	85	Arizona	No	NHL
Anaheim Stadium	California Angels	64,593	1966	112.6	100	California	No	MLB
Dodger Stadium	Los Angeles Dodgers	56,000	1962	116	0	California	No	MLB
Network Associate Coliseum	Oakland Athletics	47,313	1966	120	100	California	No	MLB
	Oakland Raiders	62,000				California		NFL
The New Arena	Golden State Warriors	15,025	1966	120	100	California	No	NBA
PETCO Park	San Diego Padres	46,000	2004	456.8	49	California	No	MLB
Qualcomm Stadium	San Diego Chargers	71,294	1968	105	100	California	No	NFL
3 Com Park	San Francisco Giants	62,000	1960	126.5	100	California	Yes	MLB
	San Francisco 49ers	70,207				California		NFL
Staples Center	LA Lakers	18,500	1999	330	18	California	No	NBA
	Los Angeles Kings	16,005				California		NHL
Arrowhead Pond Arena	LA Clippers	17,250	1993	84.3	100	California	No	NBA
Arrowhead Pond Arena	Mighty Ducks	17,250	1993	84.3	100	California	No	NHL
ARCO Arena	Sacramento Kings	17,317	1988	90.15	0	California	No	NBA
HP Pavillion	San Jose Sharks	17,190	1993	179	82	California	No	NHL
Coors Field	Colorado Rockies	50,100	1995	215	75	Colorado	Yes	MLB
Invesco Field	Denver Broncos	76,125	2001	364.2	100	Colorado	No	NFL
The Pepsi Center	Denver Nuggets	19,309	1999	160	20	Colorado	No	NBA
	Colorado Avalanche	18,129				Colorado		NHL
Civic Center Coliseum	Hartford Whalers	15,100	1975	86.4	100	Connecticut	No	NHL
RFK Stadium	Washington Redskins	56,454	1961	96.7	100	D.C.	No	NFL
MCI Center	Washington Bullets	20,674	1997	260		D.C.	No	NBA
	Washington Capitals	19,700						NHL
Pro Player Stadium	Florida Marlins	47,662	1987	154.2	3	Florida	No	MLB
	Miami Dolphins	74,916						NFL
ThunderDome	Tampa Bay Devil Rays	46,000	1990	171	100	Florida	Yes	MLB
Raymond James Stadium	Tampa Bay Buccaneers	65,647	1998	168.5	100	Florida	No	NFL
ICE Palace	Tampa Bay Lightning	19,500	1996	153	66	Florida	Yes	NHL
Jacksonville Stadium	Jacksonville Jaguars	73,000	1995	135	90	Florida	No	NFL
Miami Arena	Miami Heat	15,200	1988	68.3	75	Florida	Yes	NBA
Office Depot Center	Florida Panthers	15,200	1998	182	100	Florida	Yes	NHL
TD Waterhouse Centre	Orlando Magic	17,248	1989	125	100	Florida	No	NBA
Turner Field	Atlanta Braves	49,831	2000	235	100	Georgia	Yes	MLB
Georgia Dome	Atlanta Falcons	71,594	1992	232.4	100	Georgia	Yes	NFL
Phillips Arena	Atlanta Hawks	18,750	1999	213.5	100	Georgia	Yes	NBA
Wrigley Field	Chicago Cubs	38,765	1914	3.8		Illinois	No	MLB
U.S. Cellular Field	Chicago White Sox	44,321	1991	167.8	100	Illinois	Yes	MLB
Soldier Field	Chicago Bears	66,950	1924	20	100	Illinois	No	NFL
United Center	Chicago Bulls	21,711	1994	179.9	9	Illinois	No	NBA
	Chicago Blackhawks	20,500						NHL

Continued

Table 6.1 Continued

RCA Dome	Indianapolis Colts	60,127	1984	139.3	50 Indiana	Yes	NFL
Conseco Field House	Indiana Pacers	19,200	1999	183	70 Indiana	Yes	NBA
Kauffman Stadium	Kansas City Royals	40,625	1973	73.7	100 Kansas	Yes	MLB
Arrowhead Stadium	Kansas City Chiefs	77,872	1972	78.3	100 Kansas	Yes	NFL
Superdome	New Orleans Saints	76,791	1975	379	100 Louisana	Yes	NFL
Camden Yards	Baltimore Orioles	48,000	1992	228	96 Maryland	Yes	MLB
Ravens Stadium	Baltimore Ravens	68,900	1998	200	100 Maryland	Yes	NFL
FedEx Field	Washington Redskins	80,116	1997	250.5	70 Maryland	No	NFL
USAir Arena	Washington Bullets	18,756	1973	61.7	Maryland	No	NBA
	Washington Capitals	18,130					NHL
Fenway Park	Boston Red Sox	33,871	1912	6.5	Massachusetts	No	MLB
Gillette Stadium	New England Patriots	68,000	2002	325	Massachusetts	No	NFL
FleetCenter	Boston Celtics	18,624	1995	160	Massachusetts	No	NBA
	Boston Bruins	17,565					NHL
Comerica Park	Detroit Tigers	40,000	2000	300	38 Michigan	Yes	MLB
Ford Field	Detroit Lions	68,000	2002	300	50 Michigan	No	NFL
Palace of Auburn Heights	Detroit Pistons	21,454	1988	103	Michigan	No	NBA
Joe Louis Arena	Detroit Red Wings	18,227	1979	71.3	100 Michigan	No	NHL
H. Humphrey Metrodome	Minnesota Twins	56,144	1982	118.4	91 Minnesota	Yes	MLB
	Minnesota Vikings	63,000					NFL
Target Center	Minnesota Timberwolves	19,000	1990	136.3	72 Minnesota	Yes	NBA
Xcel Energy Center	Minnesota Wild	18,834	2000	130	100 Minnesota	No	NHL
Cardinals Ballpark	St. Louis Cardinals	47,900	2004	370	100 Missouri	Yes	MLB
Trans World Dome	St. Louis Rams	65,300	1995	299	96 Missouri	No	NFL
Savvis Center	St. Louis Blues	18,500	1994	138.8	46 Missouri	Yes	NHL
Giant Stadium	New York Giants	78,124	1976	200.8	100 New Jersey	Yes	NFL
	New York Jets						NFL
Continental Airline Arena	New Jersey Nets	20,039	1981	142.5	100 New Jersey	Yes	NBA
	New Jersey Devils	19,040					NHL
Shea Stadium	New York Mets	55,601	1964	117.8	100 New York	No	MLB
Yankee Stadium	New York Yankees	57,545	1923	28.3	21 New York	No	MLB
Ralph Wilson Stadium	Buffalo Bills	80,290	1973	75.5	100 New York	No	NFL
HSBC Arena	Buffalo Sabres	21,000	1996	125	45 New York	No	NHL
Madison Square Garden	New York Knicks	19,763	1925	200	New York	No	NBA
	New York Rangers	18,200					NHL
Nassau Vet Mem Coliseum	New York Islanders	16,297	1972	114	100 New York	No	NHL
Ericsson Stadium	Carolina Panthers	72,350	1996	247.7	20 No Carolina	No	NFL
Charlotte Coliseum	Charlotte Hornets	24,042	1988	67	100 No Carolina	Yes	NBA
RBC Center	Carolina Hurricanes	18,763	1999	158	88 No Carolina	Yes	NHL
Great American Ball Park	Cincinnati Reds	42,036	2003	297	100 Ohio	No	MLB
Paul Brown Stadium	Cincinnati Bengals	65,000	2000	400	100 Ohio	No	NFL
Jacobs Field	Cleveland Indians	42,400	1994	177.8	88 Ohio	No	MLB
Gund Arena	Cleveland Cavaliers	20,562	1994	159.3	97 Ohio	No	NBA
Nationwide Arena	Columbus Blue Jackets	18,138	2000	200	Ohio	No	NHL
Rose Garden	Portland Trail Blazers	21,401	1995	94	14 Oregon	No	NBA
Veterans Stadium	Philadelphia Phillies	62,382	1971	188	100 Pennsylvania	No	MLB

Continued

Table 6.1 Continued

Facility	Team	Capacity	Year	Cost	State		League
Philles Ballpark	Philadelphia Phillies	43,000	2004	346	50	Pennsylvania	No	MLB
First Union Spectrum	Philadelphia 76ers	21,000	1996	206		Pennsylvania	No	NBA
First Union Center	Philadelphia Flyers	19,519	1996	206	100	Pennsylvania	No	NHL
Lincoln Financial Field	Philadelphia Eagles	62,000	2003	285	50	Pennsylvania	No	NFL
PNC Park	Pittsburgh Pirates	38,365	2001	262	100	Pennsylvania	Yes	MLB
Heinz Field	Pittsburgh Steelers	65,000	2001	230	67	Pennsylvania	Yes	NFL
Mellon Arena	Pittsburgh Penguins	17,537	1961	112	100	Pennsylvania	No	NHL
Cumberland Stadium	Nashville Oilers	76,000	1998	292	100	Tennessee	Yes	NFL
The Coliseum	Tennessee Titans	67,000	1999	290	1000	Tennessee	No	NFL
Gaylord Entertainment Center	Nashville Predators	17,500	1997	144	100	Tennessee	No	NHL
The Memphis Pyramid	Memphis Grizzlies	20,142	1991	65	100	Tennessee	No	NBA
The Ballpark @ Arlington	Texas Rangers	49,292	1994	196	71	Texas	Yes	MLB
Minute Maid Park	Houston Astros	42,000	2000	250	68	Texas	Yes	MLB
The Summit Arena	Houston Rockets	16,311	1975	51	100	Texas	No	NBA
Reliant Stadium	Houston Texans	69,500	2002	400	100	Texas	No	NFL
Texas Stadium	Dallas Cowboys	65,846	1971	131.6	100	Texas	No	NFL
American Airlines Center	Dallas Mavericks	19,500	2001	420	50	Texas	No	NBA
	Dallas Stars	18,000						NHL
SBC Center	San Antonio Spurs	18,500	2002	186	100	Texas	Yes	NBA
Delta Center	Salt Lake City	19,911	1991	100.6	26	Utah	No	NBA
Safeco Field	Seattle Mariners	46,621	1999	517.6	85	Washington	Yes	MLB
Seahawks Stadium	Seattle Seahawks	67,000	2002	430	100	Washington	Yes	NFL
Key Arena	Seattle SuperSonics	17,102	1995	114	82	Washington	No	NBA
Miller Park	Milwaukee Brewers	43,000	2001	400	78	Wisconsin	Yes	MLB
Bradley Center	Milwaukee Bucks	18,633	1988	116	42	Wisconsin	No	NBA
Lambeau Field	Green Bay Packers	60,789	1957	6.5	100	Wisconsin	No	NFL

Taxes

There are a variety of taxes that can be levied by local governments including so-called hard taxes and soft taxes. All of these taxes provide revenues to pay the public's share of costs for sport entities.

Hard Taxes

Hard taxes include real estate, personal property, general sales, and local income tax. The burden of the hard taxes falls on all (sales tax) and a significant portion (local income, real estate, and personal property taxes) on the taxpayers. The hard taxes often require voter approval.

Local Income Tax

Over the past two decades, local income taxes have been levied for economic development and other good reasons. The assessment ranges generally from .5 percent to 2.0 percent. In some jurisdictions, these taxes require voter approval.

Real Estate Tax

Local government (i.e., cities, counties, school districts, and in some states community college districts) for generations has been dependent on real estate tax revenue to cover operational and capital costs. Real estate taxes are based on the value of land and improvements (i.e., buildings and infrastructure). The current value (100 percent of market value) increases annually, but generally is only reassessed every three to five years. Every time the owner improves the land or buildings, he/she is required to report the improvements to the local tax assessor.

All property owners are required to pay the real estate tax except for churches, charitable organizations, educational institutions, and other government agencies. Some states exclude cemeteries, hospitals, and historical properties. The real estate tax serves as a benefit tax since its revenues are used primarily to finance local government expenditures for services that benefit property owners and increases the value of the property.

Personal Property Tax

The personal property tax includes tangible property (e.g., furniture, machinery, automobiles, jewelry, artwork, etc.) and intangible property (e.g., stocks, taxable bonds, and insurance). Many states have repealed the personal property tax for homeowners and collect taxes for motor vehicles through an annual licensing tax. Some states have eliminated all personal property taxes to encourage more businesses and manufacturing development within the state borders.

General Sales Tax

Sales taxes are the largest single source of state tax revenues and the second largest source of tax revenues for local governments after the real estate and local income tax. If a community is small but has a large retail center, the sales tax will very likely exceed real estate tax revenues. A sales tax is considered a user's tax and all taxpayers are taxed equally. However, it is also considered a regressive tax, which bears more heavily on lower income groups than on higher income groups. Many states reduce the regressive nature of the sales tax by exempting at home food items and prescription drugs.

The combined local and state general sales tax rates generally range from three to 10 percent. However, the portion most commonly collected by cities and/or counties ranges from one percent to two percent. It is not uncommon to find in a few northern states a general sales tax of 10 percent with seven percent going to the state, two percent to the county, and one percent to the city.

The general sales tax has been used, in part, to finance sport entities and facilities since the early 90s. The largest increases for sport facilities have been 0.5 percent (for Lambeau Field, Great America Ballpark, Seattle Seahawks Stadium, Paul Brown Stadium, Safeco Field, and Raymond James Stadium), and the lowest was 0.1 percent (for Invesco Field at Mile High, Miller Park, and Coors Field). In most jurisdictions a voter referendum is required since the burden is borne by all residents.

Soft Taxes

The soft taxes include car rental, hotel-motel, player, restaurant, sin, and taxi. The soft taxes are borne by a select and relatively smaller portion (i.e., tourists generally) of taxpayers and are easier to levy.

Tourist Development Taxes

These are taxes imposed primarily on tourists. They include the cost of occupying a hotel or motel room and the cost of renting a motor vehicle. These taxes are easy to impose, and cities are always ready to tax people who will not be there to take advantage of the taxes paid. Some might view this, like our forefathers did in Boston, as "taxation without representation."

Car Rental and Taxi Taxes

Many local governments have instituted a car rental tax to finance sport entities and recreational facilities. This mechanism has increased in popularity since the early nineties. The average tax rate nationwide according to the American Automobile Association is eight percent. Some communities have developed surcharges to be added to the base for a specific number of years to cover the cost construction of a sport facility (e.g., Atlanta three percent for the Phillips Arena, Dallas five percent for the American Airlines Center). The AAA and the car

rental industry indicate that greater than 50 percent of the rentals are booked by tourists.

The taxi tax is similar to the car rental tax. The tax is calculated into the final fare the rider pays to the cab driver, limo driver, shuttle driver, or bus driver. The tax ranges from two to five percent. Approximately 30 percent of the taxes are collected from tourists.

Hotel-Motel and Restaurant Taxes

These taxes have been in existence for a long time and are the most commonly applied tourist taxes by local government. Many communities use a portion of this revenue to support the development and operations of sport venues. The tax rate ranges from six percent to 15 percent of which two to five percent is used to retire bond issues. The hotel-motel tax was originally called a bed tax.

Sin Taxes

There are three common sin taxes imposed on the sale of alcohol and cigarettes and gambling and prostitution (Nevada only). These taxes have partially been used to assist in financing the development and operations of sport facilities. Generally, the revenue is guaranteed for 15-20 years. In states where gambling has been legalized since the early nineties, a portion of the tax revenue has been directed toward the development and operation of sport facilities.

Player Tax

In the early 90s, state and local governments began to impose a tax on income earned by visiting players. Currently there are 43 states that have imposed player taxes. The press has referred to this tax as the "jock tax." The tax is based on the right of states to tax

Applebee's Park Facade   *Photo by M.G. Hypes*

Nashville Coliseum Ticket Office   *Photo by M.G. Hypes*

Nashville Coliseum Pro Shop   *Photo by M.G. Hypes*

Nashville Coliseum Scoreboard   *Photo by M.G. Hypes*

non-residents on income received for services performed within their boundaries. Many employees who live near state borders are taxed by the state they work in and again by the state they live in. For athletes, the tax is generally based on the number of days they performed in the state times their average per-game salary. However, there are states that define "duty days" as game days, practice days, days spent in team meetings, preseason training camps, and promotional caravans. In some jurisdictions, the player is taxed by the state and the local government. Players have challenged this taxation but have failed to gain any ground. The real issue should be fairness. The question that should be asked and answered is, "Do other performers who enter the state pay taxes such as actors, musicians, dancers, singers, and other entertainers?" If the answer is no, then maybe the player tax is unfair and taxation without representation.

Tax Abatement

Another tax strategy used by governments to stimulate private sector investment and create employment in the community is to offer property tax abatements (Howard & Crompton, 2004). Abatement programs exist in approximately two-thirds of the states (Severn, 1992). Typically, they are awarded whenever they are requested (Wolkoff, 1985) therefore, they often are part of a city's incentive package in negotiations with professional franchises (Howard & Crompton, 2004). A tax abatement will exempt an organization's assets from property taxation for a given period of time. It may be for all or a portion of the tax. The length of time varies according to the state enabling legislation.

Grants

Additional sources beyond taxes and bonding available from the public sector include state and federal appropriations and public grants. (See Chapter 16 for greater detail.)

Private Funding Sources

Private sector investment is preferred by most stakeholders as a result of declining public monies and questionable economic impacts (Miller, 1997). Private sector investments take on a variety of forms and degrees of contribution. The private sector regularly contributes to financing of sport facilities, in ways such as the following:

Donation of Cash: Cash is donated to the organization for a general or specific use in return for a personal tax deduction.

In-kind Contributions: An organization, business, or craftsman donates equipment or time to the project in return for a tax deduction.

Naming Rights: Corporations vie for the right to place their name on the facility for a specific sum of money for a specific number of years (e.g., RCA Dome in Indianapolis, $2 million a year for 10 years; Conseco Fieldhouse in Indianapolis, $2.5 million a year for 10 years; Raymond James (Financial Inc.) Stadium in Tampa, $3.8 million a year for 10 years; Pacific Teleis Corporation - Pacific Bell Park, $50 million over 24 years) (see Table 6.2a and 6.2b).

The key elements of a naming rights agreement include term or length of contract, consideration, signage rights and limitations, installation costs, marketing rights, termination upon default, reimbursement, and renewal option (Howard & Crompton, 2004).

Concessionaire Exclusivity: Companies purchase the exclusive rights for all concessions within a spectator facility for a specific number of dollars over a specific time period.

Food and Beverage Serving Rights: Companies purchase exclusive rights to soft drink, beer, and foods sold to spectators (see Chapter 11 Retail Operations for greater details).

Table 6.2a

Stadium Financing

Stadium/Arena/year	Public Financing	Private Financing	Total in Millions
Raymond James Stadium/1998	.5% sales tax		$168.50
The Coliseum/1999	$149.5 million thru hotel/motel taxes		$290
	$70 million from State		
	$55 million in bonds repaid by sales tax		
	$12 million for infrastructure		
	$2 million land donations		
MCI Center/1997	$60 million for infrastructure	Private loans	$260
Office Depot Center	$184.7 million thru 2% tourism tax	$42 million naming rights over 20 years	$212
RBC Center/1999	$22 million City and County	$20 million franchise	$158
	$48 million thru hotel tax	$80 million naming rights $4 million per year/20	
	$22 million NC State		
	$18 million State of N.C.		
Phillips Arena/1999	$130.75 million revenue bonds/arenas	$20 million from Turner Broadcasting	$213.50
	$62.5 million from 3% car rental tax		
American Airlines Center/2001	50% public financing	50% private financing	$420
America West Arena/1992	City bonds	private debt	
	City debt service	$26 million naming rights for 30 years	$90
Gaylord Entertainment Center/1997	General obligation bonds		$144
Nationwide Arena/2000		Private financing	$200
United Center/1994	City contributed infrastructure	Private financing	$175
SBC Center/2002	City sales tax		$186
49ers new stadium		100% privately finaced	$100
New Fenway Park	$50 million for traffic and infrastructure	$350 million design and construction	$545
	$80 million for parking garages (2)	$65 million for land	
Gillette Stadium/2002		$325 million	$325
Miller Park/2001	$310 million from a five county .10% sales tax	$90 million	$400
FedEx Filed/1997	$70.5 million by state	$180 million private financing	$250.50
Philles Park/2004	$174 million	$172 million	$346
Safeco Field	$340 million .5% food tax and rental car tax	$75 million Mariners owners	$517.60
Minute Maid Park/2000	$180 million from 2% hotel tax and 5% rental-car tax	$52 million from Astros Owners	$250
		$33 million no-interest loan	
Heinz Field/2001	$96.5 million	$76.5 million by Steelers	
		$57 million for naming rights over 20 years	
PNC Park/2001	$262 million		$262
PETCO Park/2000	$225 million hotel-tax reveune	$153 private financing	$456.80
	$57.8 million project-gnerated redevelopment bonds		
	$21 million San Deigo Unified Port Dist		
Great American Ball Park	$297 million		$297

Table 6.2b

College Corporate Naming Rights

Venue	School	Total Value In Millions	Length of Contract
Save Mart Center	Fresno State Univ	40	23 years
Comcast Center	Univ of Maryland	20	25 years
Value City Arena	Ohio State Univ	12.5	Indefinite
Cox Arena	San Diego State Univ	12	Indefinite
United Spirited Ctr	Texas Tech Univ	10	20 years
Bank of America	Univ of Washington	5.1	10 years
Cox Pavilion	Nevada-Las Vegas	5	10 years
Wells Fargo Arena	Arizona State Univ	5	Indefinite
Papa John's Cardinal Std	Univ of Louisville	5	15 years
Coors Event Ctr	Univ of Colorado	5	Indefinite
Carrier Dome	Syracuse Univ	2.75	Indefinite
Alltel Arena	Virginia Commonwealth	2	10 years
Rawlings Stadium	Georgetown College (KY)	.2	4 years
Midwest Wireless Ctr	Univ of Minnesota-Mankato	6	20 years
U.S. Cellular Arena	Marquette Univ	2	6 years
First National Bank Ctr	North Dakota Univ	7.2	20 years
Reser Stadium	Oregon State Univ	5	10 years
Ryder Ctr	University of Miami (FL)	9	NA

Source: Modified from Howard and Crompton (2004), 277.

Premium Restaurant Rights: Corporations purchase exclusive rights for all the restaurants within a spectator facility.

Sponsorship Packages: Large local and international firms are solicited to supply goods and services to a sporting organization at no cost or at substantial reduction in the wholesale prices in return for visibility for the corporation (see Chapter 7 Sponsorships for greater details).

Life Insurance Packages: These programs solicit the proceeds from a life insurance policy purchased by a supporter to specifically benefit the organization upon the death of the supporter (see Chapter 14 Fundamentals of Fundraising for greater details).

Lease Agreements: These programs lease facilities to other organizations during the off-season or lease additional spaces within the facility not used for the sporting activity such as office space or retail space.

Luxury Suites (i.e., skyboxes): Luxury suites are a dominant and universal feature in every new or remodeled stadium or arena. Luxury seating was first included in stadium and arena designs in the early 90s. The luxury suite generally includes amenities such as carpeting, wet bar, restroom, seating for 12 to 24 guests, computer hook-ups, cable television, telephones, and an intercom. Table 6.3 depicts the number of suites as of 2001.

Premium Seating (i.e., club seating): This is VIP seating located within the luxury suites or in the club areas of the stadium, which are the most expensive seats in the facility (see Table 6.4 depicting club seat breakdowns for a number of facilities.).

Personal Seat Licenses (PSL): Personal seating licenses became a widespread practice in sport venues in the early 90s. The seat license is to the individual as the luxury suite is to a corporation. A seat license requires an individual to make an advance payment to purchase the right to secure a particular seat in the venue. After making the one-time payment, the buyer is provided with the opportunity to purchase a season ticket to that seat for a specified period of time (see Table 6.5 for average cost of a PSL in the professional leagues).

Parking Fees: These fees are generated from parking lots that surround the

Table 6.3

Luxury Seats in Sport Facilities

League	# suites 2001	# Teams	Annual Lease Price
MLB	2,286	30	$ 85,000
NBA	2,533	29	$113,000
NFL	4,294	31	$100,000
NHL	2,813	30	$ 77,000
Total	11,926	120	$ 93,750 average price

Source: Modified from Howard and Crompton, (2004), 265, 266.

Note: NBA / NHL Shared Arena annual lease price = $199,000.

Table 6.4

Sampling of the Number of Club Seats at Various Venues and the Prices Charged by Teams

for their Occupancy

Team	Facility	Number of Club Seats	Price Range/year
Lakers (NBA)	Staples Ctr	4,500	$12,995 to 14,995/season
TrailBlazers (NBA)	Rose Garden	2,500	$7,500 to 11,500/season
Nuggets (NBA)	Pepsi Ctr	1,854	$65 to 100/game
Knicks (NBA)	Madison Square	3,000	$175 to 1,350/game
Coyotes (NHL)	American West	1,651	$72/game; $3,250/season
Bengals (NFL)	Paul Brown	7,700	$995 to 1,900/season
Bucs (NFL)	Raymond James	12,000	$950 to 2,500/season
Ravens (NFL)	PSINet	3,196	$108 to 298/game
Indians (MLB)	Jacobs Field	2,064	$32/game; $1,905/season
Rockies (MLB)	Coors Field	4,400	$30 to 32/game
Rangers (MLB)	Arlington	5,700	$2,00 to 3,000/season

Source: Modified from Howard and Crompton (2004), 270.

Table 6.5

PSLs Average Cost by League

League	Average Price Range
MLB	$3,615 – 14,600
NBA	$ 900 – 5,000
NFL	$ 600 – 3,350
NHL	$ 750 – 4,000

spectator facilities (see Chapter 11 Retail Operations for greater details.).

Merchandise Revenues: This income is generated by the sale of shirts, shorts, hats, pants, t-shirts, sweatshirts, key rings, glassware, dishware, luggage, sports cards, balls, bats, and other licensed goods (see Chapter 8 Licensing and Chapter 11 Retail Operations for greater details.).

Advertising Rights: Rights are sold to various entities that wish to advertise to the spectators within the sport facility.

Vendor or Contractor Equity: The vendor or contractor returns to the owner a specific percentage of the profit generated by the firms during the construction process.

Bequests and Trusts: Agreements are made with specific individuals that upon their deaths a certain amount of their estates will be given to the organization (see Chapter 14 Fundamentals of Fundraising for greater details.).

Real Estate Gifts, Endowments, and Securities: Agreements are made with specific individuals to give to an organization real estate, stocks, or mutual funds to support an endowment for a specific project. Only the annual income returned by the endowment would be used, not the principal (see Chapter 14 Fundamentals of Fundraising for greater detail).

Project Finance: In 1993 the Rose Garden (Portland, OR) was the first facility financed using a new mechanisms called project finance. Project finance is the Wall Street term that refers to the type of financing used to build arenas such as the Rose Garden, Delta Center, SBC Park, American Airlines Arena, and recently the St. Louis Cardinals' pending new home.

The word "project" is used because traditionally this type of loan has been used to finance utility plants, factories, and other large enterprises. These entities have guaranteed revenues that provide comfort to the insurance companies and pension funds that lend the money. The recent Rose Garden bankruptcy case may leave insurance companies and pension funds reluctant to finance in sport venues in the future.

Lexus Lots: Atlanta's Turner Field and Miami's Office Depot Center , with the backing of area Lexus dealers, are craving out sections of preferred parking reserved for those fans who drive a Lexus. A new twist on sponsorship which may be called exclusionary or elitist, but in the competitive marketplace it should be classified as creative thinking.

Joint Public-Private Funding

Over the past decade, public-private partnerships have been developed to construct large public sport facilities. Typically, the public sector lends its authority to implement project funding mechanisms while the private partner contributes project-related or other revenue sources. The expanded revenues generated by the facilities and their tenants have resulted in increases in the level of private funding (Regan, 1997). Recent examples of partnerships include the Alamodome (San Antonio), Coors Stadium (Denver), and Big Stadium (Saint Denis, France) (Regan, 1997). (See Table 6.6 for some examples of joint funding efforts.)

Broadcast Rights

There are 10 common types of broadcast media including networks as outlined in Table 6.7.

The sale of broadcast rights is a major revenue source for professional sports, Division I intercollegiate sports, and many interscholastic tournaments. Television contracts are multi-year contracts worth millions of dollars to leagues and teams. For example, the National Football League has a seven-year deal with ABC, CBS, ESPN, and FOX worth $17.6 billion; Major League Baseball has a five-year agreement with ESPN and FOX for $3.35 billion; National Basketball Association has a five-year contract with ESPN, ABC, and Time Warner for $4.6 billion; National Hockey League has a five-year contract with ABC and ESPN for $600 million; NCAA Men's Basketball has an 11-year contract with CBS for $6 billion; NCAA Football has a five-year contract with ABC for $500 million; and Professional Golf Association has a four-year contract with ABC, CBS, ESPN, and NBC for $107 million (Schlosser & Carter, 2001).

Table 6.6

Summary of Naming Rights Deals

Park	Location	Cost for Rights in Millions	Contract Length in Years
3 Com Park	San Francisco	4	5
Adelphia Coliseum	Nashville	30	15
Air Canada Centre	Toronto	40	20
American West Arena	Phoenix	26	30
American Airlines Arena	Miami	42	20
American Airlines Center	Dallas	195	30
Arco Arena	Sacramento	7	10
Arrowhead Pond	Anaheim	19.5	13
Bank One Ballpark	Phoenix	33.1	30
Cinergy Field	Cincinnati	6	5
Comerica Park	Detroit	66	30
Compaq Center	San Jose	72	18
Compaq Center	Houston	5.4	6
Conseco Fieldhouse	Indianapolis	40	20
Continental Airlines Arena	East Rutherford	29	12
Coors Field	Denver	15	10
Corel Centre	Ottawa	26	20
Edison International Field	Anaheim	50	20
Enron Field	Houston	100	20
Ericsson Stadium	Charlotte	20	10
FedEx Field	Landover	205	27
First Union Center	Philadelphia	40	31
Fleet Center	Boston	30	15
Gaylord Entertainment Center	Nashville	80	20
General Motors Place	Vancouver	25	20
Great Western Forum	Los Angeles	20	15
HSBC Arena	Buffalo	24	30
Invesco Field @ Mile High	Denver	120	20
Key Arena	Seattle	15	15
Lowe's Motor Speedway	Charlotte	35	10
MCI Center	Washington, D.C.	44	13
Mellon Arena	Pittsburgh	18	10
Miller Park	Milwaukee	41	20
Network Associates Coliseum	Oakland	13.7	5
PNC Park	Pittsburgh	30	20
PSINet Stadium	Baltimore	105.5	20
Pacific Bell Park	San Francisco	50	24
Pengrowth Saddledome	Calgary	20	20
Pepsi Center	Denver	68	20
Philips Arena	Atlanta	168	20
Pro Player Stadium	Miami	20	10
Qualcomm Stadium	San Diego	18	20
RCA Dome	Indianapolis	10	10
Raymond James Stadium	Tampa	32.5	13
Reliant Stadium	Houston	300	30
Safeco Field	Seattle	40	20
Savvis Center	St. Louis	70	20
Skyreach Center	Edmonton	3.037	5
Staples Center	Los Angeles	100	20
TD Waterhouse Centre	Orlando	7.8	5
Target Center	Minneapolis	1.875	15
Tropicana Field	St. Petersburg	30	30
United Center	Chicago	25	20
Xcel Energy Arena	St. Paul	75	25

Table 6.7

10 Common Types of Broadcast Media

- ABC, CBS, NBC, FOX, Westinghouse Broadcasting, and Public Broadcasting Service,
- Ultra High Frequency (UHF) Channels,
- Superstations (namely, WGN in Chicago, and WTBS in Atlanta),
- Cable Channels (i.e., TNT in Atlanta, and USA Network in New York City),
- Sports Channels (i.e., Entertainment and Sports Programming Network [ESPN], Sportsvision and Sports Channels in Chicago, St. Louis, Ohio, and Orlando, Prime Network in Houston, Prism in Philadelphia, and Sunshine Network in Orlando),
- Independent Producers,
- Local TV Stations (local Very High Frequency [VHF]),
- Cable Franchises,
- Pay-For-View, and

- Local AM and FM Radio.

Broadcasting executives link audience size and revenue together when making decisions whether or not to broadcast a sporting event. The larger the audience size, the higher the potential for revenue production from advertising. Broadcasters seek programming that will appeal to larger, more valuable audiences. The contract for broadcasting rights is based on the potential for generating advertising and gaining high TV ratings. The greater the advertising revenue and the higher the average TV rating (i.e., the average five-year TV ratings for the NFL was 11.2; MLB was 2.8 for season 12.4 for World Series; NBA was 2.75; and NHL was 1.1) (Schlosser & Carter, 2001), the greater the value will be for the short-term contract for the sporting entity.

Financial Team

All building projects need to assemble a proper financial team in order to design, organize, and finance a public, private, or public/private facility. A successful financial team should include the owner, facility manager, feasibility consultant, examination accountant, business plan consultant, financial adviser, facility consultant, architect, cost estimator, contractor, construction manager, senior underwriter, bond council, and owner's legal counsel (Regan, 1997). The financial team must work together to develop the goals and objectives of the community and/or owner. Successful facility financing is a partnership among the regional community, the owner, government, the financial institutions, and the investors.

Essential Points of a Financial Plan

The following are essentials in financial plan. These points should be broken down for each year of the financial plan.
- The mission, goals, and objectives for the overall plan,
- An analysis of the organization's

current financial situation,

- An analysis of revenue projections versus expense projections, including dollars obtained through private fundraising and government resources,
- An analysis of capital projections throughout the time period of the plan broken down into needs versus ideals, and
- Specific information regarding the intended financial state at the end of the time period.

Mechanisms for Financing Debt

Cities, counties, and states invest in capital projects by borrowing substantial amounts of money over an extended period of time. The loans or bond issues secured are backed by tax revenue streams such as real estate, personal property, personal income taxes, general sales tax, hotel-motel and restaurant taxes, sin taxes, and others. The downside, like personal loans to individuals, to spreading out payments over a 15- to 30-year period is the amount of interest incurred. However, politically, debt financing is a desirable approach and, from an equity perspective, long-term debt financing makes good sense. The primary source for governments to secure long-term financing is through bonds. Bank loans are used for short-term loans of less than five years.

Bonds

The issuing of bonds is the most common way for a city or county to generate the needed money for recreation and sport facilities (Miller, 1997). A bond is defined as "an interest-bearing certificate issued by a government or corporation, promising to pay interest and to repay a sum of money (the principal) at a specified date in the future" (Samuelson & Nordhaus, 1985, 828). According to

Howard and Crompton (1995), a bond is "a promise by the borrower (bond issuer) to pay back to the lender (bond holder) a specified amount of money, with interest, within a specified period of time" (58). Bonds issued by a government or a subdivision of a state are referred to as municipal bonds. Municipal bonds are typically exempt from federal, state, and local taxes on earned interest. Bond buyers can include individuals, organizations, institutions, or groups desiring to lend money at a predetermined interest rate. However, according to Miller (1997), bonds are not a panacea for recreation and sport facility development for two primary reasons — debt ceiling or capacity and tax-exemption concerns by the public.

Tax Exempt Bonds Issued by Government Entities

There are basically two types of government bonds — full-faith and credit obligations, and non-guaranteed. A general obligation bond is a full-faith and credit obligation bond. The general obligation bond refers to bonds that are repaid with a portion of the general property taxes. There are two key disadvantages to issuing general obligation bonds — it requires voter approval and it increases local debt.

The second type of full-faith and credit obligation bond is a certificate of obligation. The certificate(s) is secured by unlimited claim on tax revenue and carries a low interest rate. Its greatest advantage to politicians is that the certificate(s) does not require a voter referendum.

Non-guaranteed bonds including revenue bonds, tax increment bonds, and certificates of participation have been the most common type of bonds used in funding sport facilities construction and operations (Howard & Crompton, 2004). These bonds are sold on the basis of repayment from other designated revenue

Gaylord Entertainment Center, Marquee   *Photo by M. G. Hypes*

Gaylord Entertainment Center, Concourse Area   *Photo by M. G. Hypes*

sources. If revenue falls short of what is required to make debt payments, the government entity does not have to make up the difference. There are three main advantages for using this funding mechanism: voter approval generally is not required, debt is not considered statutory debt, and those who benefit the most from the facility pay for it.

Revenue bonds can be backed exclusively by the revenue accruing from the project or from a designated revenue source such as hotel/motel tax, restaurant tax, auto rental tax, or a combination of these taxes and others. Revenue bonds normally carry a higher interest rate compared to general obligation bonds (i.e., approximately two percent).

Certificates of participation are third-party transactions. It involves a non-profit public benefit organization or government agency borrowing funds from a lending institution or a group of lending institutions to construct a new facility. Once the facility is completed, the organization/agency leases the facility to a public or private operator. This operator, in turn, makes leases payments to retire the certificates. There is no need for a voter referendum.

Taxable Bonds Issued by Private Entities

There are two types of taxable bonds: private-placement bonds and asset-backed securitizations. Private-placement bonds are sold by the sporting entity. The security for these bonds is provided by a lien on all future revenues generated by the sport entity. The asset-backed securitizations are also sold by the sporting entity. Its security is provided by selected assets, which are held by a bankruptcy proof trust.

In the mid- to late 90s, local governments were inclined to provide less and less support for the construction and operation of sport facilities. Therefore, the private sector began developing a number of other financial strategies, including luxury suites, premium or club seating, premier restaurants (i.e., high-class restaurants), naming rights, and private-placement bonds. Facilities initially using the private-placement bonds included the Fleet Center (Boston) for $160 million, First Union Center (Philadelphia) for $142 million, and the Rose Garden (Portland) for $155 million. These private-placement bonds were issued for a long term (20-30 years) with a fixed interest rate (six to nine percent) bond certificates to a large number of private lenders (i.e., insurance companies and venture capitalists). The private-placement bonds are secured by revenues generated from premium seating, advertising, concessions, parking, and lease agreements.

The asset-backed securitizations (ABS) are a variation of the private-placement bonds. The ABS is the newest debt financing mechanism in the private sector. It is secured by selling future cash flow through bundling such revenue streams as long-term naming rights agreements, luxury suite leases, concession contracts, and long-term corporate sponsorship deals. The following sport facilities have used ABS as the financing mechanism: Pepsi Center (Denver) and Staples Center (Los Angeles).

Tax-Increment Bonds

"Over half the states now have enabling legislation authorizing tax increment financing (TIF)" (Howard & Crompton, 1995, 102). TIF is available when an urban area has been identified for renewal or redevelopment. Real estate developed with the use of TIF is attractive to stakeholders as tax increases are not necessary (Miller, 1997). The tax base of the defined area is frozen, and any increases in the tax base are used to repay the TIF bonds. The economics of any TIF are dependent on the development potential of a chosen site and its surrounding land (Regan, 1997).

Special Bonding Authority

Special authority bonds have been used to finance stadiums or arenas by special public authorities, which are entities with public powers (e.g., Niagara Power Authority, New York State Turnpike Authority, or the Tennessee Valley Authority) that are able to operate outside normal constraints placed on governments. Primarily, this has been used as a way to circumvent public resistance to new sports projects (i.e., Georgia Dome, Oriole Park at Camden Yards, or Stadium Authority of Pittsburgh Three Rivers Stadium) and construct them without receiving public consent through a referendum. Without having to pass a voter referendum, the authorities float the bonds that are sometimes guaranteed or accepted as a moral obligation by the state (Howard & Crompton, 2004).

Summary

Successful sport entities have a variety of stable revenue sources to meet increasing expenses. There are three major categories of revenue sources, including public, private, and a combination of public and private sources. It is extremely important for the sport manager to ensure that all varieties of revenue streams are maintained.

The public sources of revenue primarily include hard and soft taxes, tax abatement, non-taxable and taxable bonds, tax incremental financing, and special bonding authorities.

The private sources include grants, donations, in-kind contributions, naming rights, concessionaire exclusivity agreements, premium restaurant rights, sponsorship packages, leases agreements, luxury suites, premium (club) seating, personal seating licenses, parking, merchandise revenues, food and beverage serving rights, advertising rights, broadcast rights, vendor or contractor equity, real estate gifts, and bequests and trusts. The value of private sector funding is best illustrated by the amount of revenue generated from private sources in the construction of The Ball Park in Arlington, Texas, which included $12.7 million from the ballpark's concessionaires, $6 million from first-year luxury suite revenues, $17.1 million from preferred-seat licenses totaling $35.8 million (Brady & Howlett, 1996).

All sport entities should have a financial team in place to develop and implement a multi-year financial plan. The financial team is essential to bring together a partnership among the regional community, the owner, government, financial institutions, and the investors. Through these partnerships, the financial team will develop the goals and objectives of the community at large and the owner(s). It is a team effort to develop a sound financial plan to construct and operate sport facilities.

References

Ammon, R. Jr., Southall, R.M., & Blair, D.A. (2004). *Sport facility management: Organizing events and mitigating risks.* Morgantown, WV: Fitness Information Technology, Inc.

Brady, E., & Howlett, D. (1996, September 6). Economics, fan ask if benefits of building park outweigh costs. *USA Today,* pp. C13-C14.

Crompton, J. L. (2004). Beyond Economic Impact: An Alternative Rationale for the Public Subsidy of Major League Sports Facilities. *Journal of Sport Management, 18*(1), 41.

Crompton, J.L., Howard, D.R., & Var, T. (2003). Financing Major League facilities: Status, evolution and conflicting forces. *Journal of Sport Management, 17*(2), 156-184.

Howard, D.R., & Crompton, J.L. (1995). *Financing sport.* Morgantown, WV: Fitness Information Technology, Inc.

Howard, D.R., & Crompton, J.L. (2004). *Financing sport* (2nd ed.). Morgantown, WV: Fitness Information Technology, Inc.

Kaplan, D. (1998). ABS: A new way to pay. *Sport Business Journal, 1*(1), 3.

Miller, L.K. (1997). *Sport business management.* Gaithersburg, MD: Aspen Publishers, Inc.

Regan, T. (1997). Financing facilities. In M.L. Walker, & D.K. Stotlar, (Eds.), *Sport facility management.* Sudbury, MA: Jones and Bartlett Publishers.

Samuelson, P.A., & Nordhaus, W.D. (1985). *Economics.* New York: McGraw-Hill.

Schlosser, J., & Carter, D. (April 2, 2001). TV sports: A numbers game. *Broadcast & Cable,* 32-33.

Severn, A.K. (1992). Building-tax abatements: An approximation to land value taxation. *American Journal of Economics and Sociology, 51*(2), 237-245.

Solomon, J. D. (2004) Public Wises up, balks at paying for new stadiums. *USA Today,* April 1, 2004, 13A.

Stadiums & Arenas: Club Seat Breakdown. (2003). Street & Smith's *Sport Business Journal,* July 17-23, 10-11

Wolkoff, M.J. (1985). Chasing a dream: The use of tax abatements to spur urban economic development. *Urban Studies, 22,* 305-315.

Sponsorships

Sport offers many characteristics and opportunities that are attractive to businesses. The business may seek to associate with a winning program or be looking for an effective addition to their marketing program. Sponsorship has been defined as "the acquisition of rights to affiliate or directly associate with a product or event for the purpose of deriving benefits related to that affiliation" (Mullin, Hardy & Sutton, 2000). Another view of sponsorships is that they are a partnership with corporate entities to assist financially with a particular project or sport event in order to gain a higher public profile (Sawyer & Smith, 1999).

The key to corporate connection has as its foundation three main concepts for the successful production and sale of a product:

Corporations are not involved in organization marketing but rather they're involved in communication and sport organizations provide the communication medium,

Sport organizations can provide access to ready-made consumer segments, and

Sport organizations provide marketers the opportunity to attach an image to their product that differentiates them in the marketplace (Sawyer & Smith, 1999).

A sponsorship is business. It must serve the interests of four constituent groups, including:
- The business interest of the sponsoring company,
- The best interests of the event and participants,
- Serve as a positive influence on the sponsor's direct customers, and
- Benefit the customer who buys the products.

For sport organizations, sponsorships are a way to obtain funding to operate their programs and events. For the corporations, sponsorships provide a means to get their product in the minds of the consumers.

Instructional Objectives

After reading this chapter, the student will be able to:
- Identify the role of sponsorships,
- Identify and describe the components of the sponsorship proposal,
- Explain the philosophical basis of sponsorships,
- Describe the various levels of involvement for a sponsorship,
- Customize a sponsorship package,
- Price a sponsorship,
- Identify and explain the benefits of a sponsorship, and
- Develop a sponsorship agreement.

What is the Role of Sponsorships?

The role of sponsorship in sport has changed over the last decade. Early sponsorships were primarily philanthropic in nature and provided CEOs a vehicle through which to associate with elite athletes and provide entertainment for clients. Today's sponsorship packages are designed to provide benefits for both the sponsoring organization and the sporting event or program. Sponsorships are now driven by sound business practices that are designed to meet the needs of the four constituent groups identified above. The goal is to develop a win-win strategy that benefits both the sponsoring corporation and the sport organization. It has been considered that sport has become too dependent upon corporate sponsorship in order to cover expenses of the organization. Sport managers are continually looking for ways to increase revenues and to broaden exposure of their programs. The sponsors want to increase their revenues and the exposure of their products. The corporate sponsorship is a way to enhance both groups' desires. However, not everyone agrees with the idea of having corporate sponsorship in sport. The sport organization needs to be aware of community reaction to involvement with certain corporate sponsors whose products may not be well received in the local marketplace. Alcohol and tobacco sponsorships are two that the sport manager must carefully consider the impact on the constituent groups prior to entering into an agreement. Some governmental agencies and governing bodies of various sports have attempted to restrict alcohol and tobacco advertising in sport settings.

Another area of concern has been the overt commercialization of sport. The NCAA, for example, found the need to impose rules governing the size of corporate logos that can be displayed on team uniforms and equipment (Stotlar, 2001).

Ultimately, the role of a sponsorship is to provide benefits for both the sponsoring business and the sport organization. The sport manager must remember to consider the effect of the sponsorship on not only the sport organization but the greater community as a whole.

Philosophical Basis for Sponsorships

The sport manager must develop a philosophical base for the incorporation of sponsorships in their program. The key elements involved in developing their philosophy include:
- The exchange process,
- Philanthropy,
- Advertising cost and value,
- Return on investment, and
- Market research.

The exchange process involved in the corporate sponsorship of sport provides for the return of something for the involvement of sponsor. In other words, "You give me something and I'll give you something." The sport sponsorship grants the right of association to a corporate entity.

Gaylord Entertainment Center, Concourse Area   *Photo by M G. Hypes*

Gaylord Entertainment Center, Predators Ice   *Photo by M G. Hypes*

As stated earlier, previous sponsorships were made as a philanthropic venture on the part of the sponsor. It is important to determine if the parties involved in the sponsorship agreement are seeking an equal exchange. It would be very difficult to guarantee equal exchange when considering a sponsorship for a high school or similar entity. However, in the sponsoring of a racing team, the corporate entity may well receive benefits beyond those of the initial investment due to the world-wide coverage.

The sport organization needs to be able to show the sponsor how the package will benefit the business in relation to regular advertising costs and value. The sponsor is involved in a number of different marketing campaigns and the sport organization needs to provide evidence of being a viable method through which the corporation can reap benefits.

The key is to provide evidence of return on investment. The better prepared the sport organization is and the more data readily available to show this potential, the better the chance the corporation will enter into a sponsorship agreement.

Sponsorship Objectives

Sport programs and events can provide opportunities that extend well beyond simple advertising. The ability to reach consumers at the point of experience is what makes the sponsorship so appealing.

There has been extensive research conducted regarding the objectives of sponsorship. Lough (2000) identified the objectives that most often are utilized in decisions to enter into a sport sponsorship agreement. These objectives include:

- To achieve sales objectives,
- To generate media benefits,
- To secure entitlement or naming rights,
- To increase public awareness of the company, the product, or both,
- To alter or reinforce public perception of the company,
- To identify the company with the particular market segments,
- To involve the company in the community,
- To build good will among decision makers,
- To create an advantage over competitors, through association or exclusivity, and
- To gain unique opportunities in terms of hospitality and entertainment.

Corporate Sponsorships

Shank (1999) identified the Sport Event Pyramid, which can be used to describe the scope of a corporate sponsorship. The Pyramid consists of five levels. Each level classifies events on the basis of width and depth of interest in the event.

As the name implies, *global events* have the broadest coverage and generate a great deal of interest among consumers. *International events* are international in scope. These events might have high levels of interest but not in global capacities or they may be global in scope with lower levels of interest in certain countries or regions. *National events* such as the World Series, NCAA Final Four, and the Super Bowl have high interest among consumers in a single country or two countries. A *regional event* has a narrow geographic focus but has high interest within that region. The lowest level of the Pyramid are *local events*. Local events are the most narrow in geographical focus and attract a small segment with a high level of interest in the event.

Another aspect of the corporate sponsorship is determining the athletic platform. Brooks (1994) defines the athletic platform for sponsorships as being either:

- The team,
- The sport,

Applebee's Park, Makers Mark Ad   *Photo by M G. Hypes*

Applebee's Park, Outfield Signage   *Photo by M G. Hypes*

- The event, or
- The athlete.

Athletic platform can be further defined by the level of competition:

- Professional,
- Collegiate,
- High school, or
- Recreational.

The selection of athletic platform should be based upon the sponsorship objectives.

Sponsorship Proposal and Agreement

There is no absolute model or format for a sponsorship proposal or agreement. The format to be utilized should be creative and neat. The information in the proposal or agreement should include:

- Objectives of the sponsorship program,
- Profile and background of sponsoree,
- Promotional opportunities available,
- Levels of sponsorship,
- Sponsor benefits,
- Fee structure,
- Contract length and renewal options, and
- Evaluation methodology.

Sawyer and Smith (1999) identified the following questions that the planner should be able to answer before drafting a proposal.

- How would you describe the organization?
- What is the event to be sponsored?
- What impact do you have on the local economy?
- What is the purpose of your event?
- How will the organization involve the community?
- Will the event heighten public awareness about the organization or activity?
- How does the event allow sponsors to reach their consumers?
- Is the event based on a similar successful event?

- Why is the event unique?
- What are the advantages for sponsors associated with the event?

Sport managers should be aware that the law as it pertains to sponsorship agreements is not well defined. The manager should be very careful when constructing such an agreement and legal counsel should be consulted before entering into the contract to ensure that it is stated in clear language and provides for mutual understanding.

Levels of Sponsorship

There are four common levels of involvement in sponsorships. These levels include:

- Exclusive sponsorship,
- Primary sponsorship,
- Subsidiary sponsorship, and
- Official supplier.

An exclusive sponsor has the sole financial commitment for an event. The sponsor may even own the event. In most cases, however, the sponsor usually has a major say in the event.

A primary sponsor makes a major financial commitment but shares the commitment with one or more companies that provide a smaller financial commitment. The primary sponsor has the opportunity to maximize exposure opportunities with minimal effort and financial risk. The primary sponsor tends to have a major say in the organization and management of the event.

A subsidiary sponsor is a company that is providing a smaller financial commitment behind a primary sponsor. These sponsors generally have exclusivity within a particular product category. The product category is frequently essential to the event.

An official supplier is on the same level as a subsidiary sponsor except the product is not crucial to the event. The official supplier has exclusivity within the product category.

Customizing a Sponsorship Package

Once the level of sponsorship has been established the next step is to customize the package to fit the needs of the sponsor. Brooks (1994) suggests the following when considering the customized sponsorship package:

- Official status,
- Sponsorship fee,
- Title rights,
- Television exposure,
- Public relations and media exposure,
- Logo use,
- Signage,
- Advertising rights,
- Hospitality rights,
- Point-of-sale promotions,
- Direct-mail lists,
- Product sampling,
- Legal liabilities,
- Future options, and
- Clientele use.

Figure 7.1 provides a sample sponsorship agreement.

Sponsor Benefits

Sawyer and Smith (1999) identified the following as possible opportunities and benefits of a sponsorship package:

- Season tickets for events,
- Yearbook, program, media guide, and scoreboard advertisement,
- Scoreboard/PA exposure,
- Special events nights,
- Arena signage, and
- Special items (VIP room, luxury box, parking passes).

It is important to sell the above as benefits to the potential sponsor. Keep in mind the level of sponsorship when providing benefits. Do not "sell the farm." In other words, do not provide benefits that equate to substantially more than what the sponsor is providing.

Pricing a Sponsorship

Sponsorships are dynamic entities. Sponsorship agreements change due to:

- Increased competition,
- Changing economy, and
- A volatile marketplace.

There are three basic approaches to sponsorship pricing. These include:

- Cost-plus strategy,
- Competitive market strategy, and
- Relative-value strategy.

The cost-plus strategy involves calculating the real cost of the sponsorship package and then adding a predetermined percentage for profit. The determining of the appropriate percentage factor is tricky. It is important not to neglect the needs of the sponsoring company.

Competitive market strategy is at the opposite end of the continuum. It is based on what managers think the market will bear given the competitive environment. The sport manager should review the following before establishing a price:

- Degree of primary consumer match with company's target market,
- Size of the primary consumer base,
- Potential media publicity,
- Sales opportunity,
- psychological association, and
- Exposure opportunity.

Relative value is the final strategy. In this strategy, the sport manager shows the prospective company the value of a sponsorship package. For this to be an effective strategy, the sport manager must have an excellent knowledge of the market value of what is being offered as well as its value to the sponsor.

Summary

Corporate sponsorships are everywhere in sport. From professional sport to the local high school, sponsorships play a key role in the financing of programs.

When developing sponsorship agreements, the sport manager must have a clearly defined set of objectives. Why

Figure 7.1

Sample Sponsorship Agreement
Intercollegiate Sponsorship 2003–2004

Memorial State University (MSU) enters into this sponsorship agreement with Rick's Sporting Goods, Inc. (Rick's, Inc.)

Rick's, Inc. Objectives for Its MSU Sponsorship

There are two major objectives for Rick's, Inc. in the MSU sponsorship agreement:
1. Increase market share and sales volume.
2. Enhance image in sporting goods market.

Rick's, Inc. Purchase of Sponsorship Rights from MSU

By purchasing sponsorship rights, Rick's, Inc. was trying to prevent avenues for its competitors—Jones Sports, Lerner's Sporting Goods, etc. from ambushing its MSU sponsorship. For example, if Jones Sports became a sponsor of MSU Athletics, this company could easily fool the public into thinking it was also a MSU sponsor.

Rick's, Inc. Sponsorship of All MSU Teams

Rick's, Inc. selected sports with high media exposure where it could maximize its MSU sponsorship bond and keep out competitors. It sponsored 16 different MSU teams.

Rick's, Inc. Use of MSU Symbols

Rick's, Inc. has exclusive use of MSU symbols, slogans, and mascot and informed all retailers that this was the preferred logo use. Rick's, Inc. used the MSU logos to create MSU-themed packaging, special-edition Rick's, Inc. decals for merchants, MSU pin giveaways, posters, and merchandise premium offers, and to generally enhance the image of Rick's, Inc. MSU-themed packaging promotions were used to set the MSU Tigers program apart from competitors.

Rick's, Inc. Reason for Using MSU Symbols

The MSU symbols stand for dedication, quality, and excellence. Rick's, Inc. hoped that the public image of MSU would become associated with Rick's, Inc. products. This could give Rick's, Inc. a competitive advantage in the marketplace.

Continued

Figure 7.1 Continued

Rick's, Inc. Fundraising Activities for the MSU Teams

Among Rick's, Inc. merchants, fundraising is the one most common promotional activity used. Merchants could use the following fundraising activities:

"Pull for the Team" donation-per-transaction program.

Customer-direct donations via MSU provided statement inserts.

Donations to MSU from annual special sales.

Pre-transactions matching donations.

Fundraising from sales of MSU premium merchandise items.

Other client/customer-direct donations.

Rick's, Inc. Rights to the MSU basketball team

One of the specific teams to which Rick's, Inc. purchased rights was the basketball team, the most highly televised team in the MSU stable. This established a direct association with a highly publicized team, giving Rick's, Inc. the exposure it wanted on television, magazines, and radio. Everywhere the MSU basketball team competed, Rick's, Inc. was there displaying banners and maximizing its high-profile association with basketball and MSU athletics.

Rick's, Inc. Public Awareness Activities

Rick's, Inc. is prepared to promote public awareness of MSU and Rick's, Inc. in the following ways:

Rick's, Inc. arranged ("Win the Conference") sweepstakes,

Ex-MSU athletes used for speeches or demonstrations in employee events, public exhibitions, and advertising,

MSU public service announcements to local television stations,

Participation in MSU reunions for fundraising,

MSU radio contests,

MSU promotions at local retailers,

Fifty special MSU athletes selected to be Rick's, Inc. hosts at the various high profile MSU sporting events. News releases were sent to the hometown newspapers of these MSU athletes.

Rick's, Inc. Sponsorship Guide

Rick's, Inc. will publish the Rick's, Inc. MSU Sponsorship Manual which was designed to guide Rick's, Inc. merchants on how to use the MSU sponsorship.

Rick's, Inc. will also support its MSU sponsorship with regular bulletins and kits illustrating Rick's, Inc. programs and an extensive communications effort.

have a sponsor? What benefits do the organization and the sponsor receive? The sponsorship arrangement needs to be a win-win situation.

There are various levels of sponsorship with each affecting the financial commitment as well as control of the event.

Sponsorship packages should be customized to meet the needs of the organization and the needs of the sponsor. Pricing of the sponsorship and benefits will vary based on the objectives of the agreement.

References

Brooks, C.M. (1994). *Sports marketing: Competitive business strategies for sports*. Englewood Cliffs, NJ: Prentice-Hall.

Lough, N.L. Corporate sponsorship of sport. In Appenzeller, H., & Lewis, G. (2000). *Successful sport management* (2nd ed.). Durham, NC: Carolina Academic Press.

Mullin, B., Hardy, S., & Sutton, W. (2000). *Sport marketing* (2nd ed.). Champaign, IL: Human Kinetics.

Sawyer, T.H., & Smith, O. (1999). *The management of clubs, recreation and sport: Concepts and applications*. Champaign, IL: Sagamore.

Shank, M.D. (1999). *Sports marketing: A strategic perspective*. Englewood Cliffs, NJ: Prentice-Hall.

Stotlar, D. Sponsorship. (2001). In Parkhouse, B.L. *The management of sport: Its foundation and application* (3rd ed.). Boston, MA: McGraw-Hill.

Stotlar, D. (2001). *Developing successful sport sponsorship plans*. Morgantown, WV: Fitness Information Technology.

Licensing

Licensing has become a very lucrative endeavor for many for many sport organizations. The use of brand, brand name, brand mark, or trademark in exchange for royalties provides another source of revenue for the organization. Through licensing agreements, the organization's logo can show up on apparel, collectibles, furniture, and novelties to name a few items. The organization can also enter into collaborative contracts where teams and leagues act together in the licensing process.

Licensing is defined as a contractual agreement whereby a company may use another company's trademark in exchange for a royalty or fee. Since the emergence of NFL Properties in 1963, licensing has become one of the most prevalent sports product strategies (Shank, 1999).

Irwin (2001) cited the following four factors as contributing to the growth in sales of licensed products:
- The increasing popularity of American sports and resulting media coverage,
- Significant developments in imprinting technology,
- The maturation of licensing as an industry, and
- The financial challenges facing sport managers.

Instructional Objectives

After reading this chapter, the student will be able to:
- Develop a licensing agreement,
- Identify the benefits of a licensing agreement,
- Explain licensee exclusivity, and
- Identify and explain trademark issues.

Why Licensing?

Consumer demand for logoed apparel has allowed sport programs to financially benefit through licensing. In addition to financial gains, exposure for the program is created through the availability of logoed products in the marketplace.

Licensed Apparel from Morehead State University   *Photos by M G. Hypes*

Licensing also allows for protection under the law. The organization is able to exercise control over the use of name, likeness, symbol, logo, or other mark associated with the organization (Irwin, Sutton & McCarthy, 2002). Trademarks are not limited to just the organization. Events, leagues, teams, and individual athletes can apply for and receive trademarks. Once marked, the organization is covered under the Lanham Act, which levees severe penalties for unauthorized use of the mark.

Licensee Recruitment

Sawyer and Smith (1999) suggest to actively recruit licensees and screen all manufacturers expressing an interest in obtaining a license to produce logoed products through an application process. Typically, a manufacturer is asked to supply information regarding financial stability, marketing and distribution channels, production capabilities, projected sales performance, and a list of current licensing references.

Some of the most common tactics in the recruitment of licensees have been through personal contact, direct mail, and tradeshow networking. The licensing agent should provide the prospective licensee with operational policy and procedure material.

Licensing Application Process

"The first step in the registering of trademarks at the federal level is a search to determine whether anyone has previously registered the mark in question" (Howard & Compton, 1995). Many organizations may have the same mascot or initials. Trademarks can be allowed based on a geographical basis if both parties agree. Howard & Compton (1995) identify the use of the capital letter "T" as an example. Both the University of Texas and the University of Tennessee recognize the "T" as an important symbol of the institution.

The next step is to select the appropriate class once it is determined the mark or name is to be registered. The mark must be registered in each class that covers the product category for any product that will bear the mark. Howard and Compton (1995) identified the following classes for marks:

Class 6 – Metal Goods,
Class 16 – Paper Goods and Printed Matter,
Class 18 – Leather Goods,
Class 21 – Housewares and Glass,
Class 24 – Fabrics (pennants and banners),
Class 25 – Clothing,
Class 26 – Fancy Goods (patches for clothing, buttons),
Class 28 – Toys and Sporting Goods, and
Class 41 – Education and Entertainment Services.

The following marks indicate ownership:

TM – Trademark notification,
® - Federally registered mark, and
© - Copyright notification.

In addition to the mark, many sport organizations require that goods be labeled or tagged as "Officially Licensed." These labels and tags help to ensure the authenticity of the product as well as provide a means to police or control the marketplace.

Licensing Program Public Relations

For a licensing program to run smoothly, there must be good communication between the organization and the company licensed to sell the product. The licensing organization can facilitate a network of communication between the organization, the licensee, and retailers. Irwin (2001) suggests that the organizations recognize the manufacturer and retailers of licensed products through the use of certificates of appreciation and point-of-purchase displays. Organizational representatives should make the commitment to visit the retailers of the licensed products.

Licensing Program Product Promotions

An integrated promotional mix will help to enhance the general awareness of licensed products. Irwin (2001) cites the most popular promotional media employed as:

- Direct mail,
- Broadcast media, and
- Trade publications.

The organization can reduce costs by mandating in the license agreement that the licensee must provide advertising of the product. The licensor should, however, compile and distribute a product catalog.

In-house or Outsourced

Once it is determined that the organization wants to enter into a licensing program, it should be decided whether to handle operations in-house or outsource. In-house licensing involves the appointment of staff to oversee the program. Outsourced licensing involves the procurement of the services of an outside licensing agent or management company (Howard & Compton, 1995). The decision on whether to operate in-house or outsource the licensing program depends on the:

- Scope of the licensing program,
- Potential for the sale of the product,
- Budget, and
- Availability of specialized expertise.

Organizations with limited personnel or modest expectations may prefer to outsource. Organizations may require more comprehensive services and thus require outsourcing. Ultimately, the decision should be based on the organization's need and resources that are available.

Operating Procedures

Sawyer and Smith (1999) identified the following operating procedures for new entries in the sport licensing industry:

- Initial procedure should be to examine all available descriptive marks and determine which may be commercially attractive,
- Actively recruit licensees and screen all manufacturers,
- Decide whether the licenses executed are to be on an exclusive or non-exclusive basis,
- Establish a policy for license revocation or non-renewal if the agreement is compromised,
- Request an actual product sample for approval prior to distribution. This helps to protect the organization from possible product liability issues,
- Schedule regular compliance reviews and conduct audits,
- Develop policies regarding the unauthorized use of the trademarked item,
- To detect unlicensed merchandise, use some type of identification such as "officially licensed product of..." tags,
- Federal and state trademark laws have traditionally provided the legal foundations for licensing activities,
- Familiarize the public with the licensing program operations and the intent to enforce legal protection, and
- Promoting the availability of licensed products should have a significant effect on revenue production.

Royalty Audits

Irwin (2001) identified royalty audits as a means of verifying the accuracy of royalty reports. The royalty audit can be conducted by a member of the organization or by an external auditing specialist. The benefit of periodic royalty auditing is the identification of underpayments.

Royalty Exemptions

Exemptions may be granted from royalty payments at the discretion of the licensing organization. Most sport organizations utilize a nonexempt policy; however, colleges and universities commonly exempt the institution's departments from paying a royalty on items that are consumed internally such as office supplies. A compulsory nonexempt policy provides the best avenue for record-keeping purposes.

Licensee Exclusivity

The manager must decide whether the license executed should be on an exclusive or non-exclusive basis. The non-exclusive agreement enables numerous manufacturers to produce merchandise in the same product category. The exclusive agreement restricts the number of manufacturers for each product category to one. While each method has certain advantages, the exclusive agreement provides the licensor greater leverage in negotiating fees, expedites communication between the parties, and helps combat unauthorized use of logos.

International Distribution

International opportunities in licensing continue to grow. The increased popularity of American sport and the influx of international players into the NBA, MLB, and NHL provides golden opportunities in the licensing of products. While these endeavors seem very lucrative in nature, the sport manager must be aware of trademark law in the country where the product will be distributed. A licensing agency familiar with international trademark issues provides a vital resource for the organization entering into an international licensing program.

Trademark Issues

A trademark is a word, symbol, or device used by a manufacturer or merchant to identify its goods and distinguish them from those manufactured or sold by others (Irwin, 2001). A "common law" right to the mark means that the organization has been using the mark for a long period of time and thus has control over the mark. If other organizations also use the mark and the sport organization has not officially registered the mark to protect it from use by others, the sport organization may lose the right to use the mark. Trademark infringement is the reproduction, counterfeiting, copying, or imitating in commerce of a registered trademark (Irwin, 2001). The sport organization who owns the right to the mark must decide how to pursue cases of trademark infringement

The Black Market-Counterfeit Detection and Reduction

An effective means of controlling and reducing counterfeit products is through the development of an enforcement strategy for the licensing program. This strategy involves taking action to make sure that companies using the organization's marks are doing so in authorized manner. If the company is using the mark without permission or in an unauthorized manner, it is eliminated.

Enforcement strategies involve efforts at the local, regional, and national levels. Locally, an effort to identify all local retailers that sell merchandise bearing the licensed mark is needed. In the event that the retailer is not a licensed vendor, appropriate legal action then needs to take place. Regional and national efforts are best done through the collaborative actions of leagues, licensees, and the organizations to curtail the unlawful use of marks. This group approach allows for shared costs and provides collective clout. Through "sweeps" of unauthorized retailers, the products are confiscated and legal action can be taken if needed. National counterfeit rings are usually well organized and it is recommended that the organization operate in conjunction with legal counsel when attempting to dismantle these rings.

chandise bearing their logos for a royalty fee. The organization has the option to handle the licensing program in-house or by outsourcing the program to independent firms.

Once marks have been identified, the organization should officially register the marks. In addition, a policy regarding the recruitment of licensees, enforcement, royalty options, and auditing should be developed.

Summary

Customer demand for logoed apparel has afforded professional and amateur sport programs the ability to financially benefit through licensing, which grants a second party the right to produce mer-

International licensing programs provide expanded opportunities for the sport organization. Careful attention should be paid to the trademark laws of the specific countries being targeted.

References

Graham, S., Neirotti, L.D., & Goldbatt, J.J. (2001). *The ultimate guide to sports marketing*. New York, NY: McGraw-Hill.

Howard, D.R., & Compton, J.L. (1995). *Financing sport*. Morgantown, WV: Fitness Information Technology.

Irwin, R.L., Sutton, W.A., & McCarthy, L.M. (2002). *Sport promotion and sales management*. Champaign, IL: Human Kinetics.

Irwin, R.L. (2001). Sport licensing. In Parkhouse, B.L. (Ed.), *The management of sport: Its foundation and application* (3rd ed.). Boston, MA: McGraw-Hill.

Sawyer, T.H., & Smith, O. (1999). *The management of clubs, recreation and sport: Concepts and applications*. Champaign, IL: Sagamore.

Shank, M.D. (1999). *Sports marketing: A strategic perspective*. Upper Saddle River, NJ: Prentice-Hall.

The Franchise Game

A franchise is defined as a tool for marketing goods and services. The basic features of a typical financial arrangement include:

- The franchiser allowing the franchisee to see its name or brand,
- The franchiser exercising continuing control over the franchisee,
- The franchiser providing assistance to the franchisee, and
- The franchisee making periodical payments to the franchiser (www.franchise.org).

There are advantages and disadvantages associated with franchising. One advantage is it provides an opportunity for the franchiser's business to grow through the capital and manpower provided by the franchisee. In this manner, the franchiser is able to expand its business in a short period of time (www.franchise.org). This expansion has been evident through expansion efforts in professional sport.

A major disadvantage of franchising is loss of control over day-to-day operations.

There are also financial risks involved in franchising. The franchisee may not be capable of running the business effectively, or there may not be sufficient capital to sustain the operation.

DeBolt (www.franchise1.com) identified important questions that need to be carefully and thoughtfully answered before buying a franchise. These questions include:

- Are you willing and able to take on the responsibilities of managing your own business?
- Will you enjoy the franchise?
- Are you willing to completely follow the franchise system?
- Do you have a history of success in dealing and interacting with people?
- Can you afford the franchise?
- Have you carefully studied the legal documents?
- Does the franchise you are considering have a track record of success?
- Are the franchisees generally happy and successful? and

•Do you like the franchise's staff with whom you will be working?

Instructional Objectives

After reading this chapter, the student will be able to:
- •Define franchise,
- •Describe how a team becomes a member of a league,
- •Explain the financial impact of a franchise on a community, and
- •Describe various tax options available for subsidizing a sport franchise and/or facility.

What is a sport franchise?

A sport franchise can be a team franchise in the case of a professional sport team, or it can be a product manufacturer such as an apparel company entering into a licensing agreement. For the purposes of this chapter, emphasis will be placed on the team franchise and how it affects the league and the local economy.

Franchising is a strategic alliance between groups of people who have specific relationships and responsibilities with a common goal to dominate markets (www.entremkt.com). It is a common misconception that entering into a franchise agreement, you are "buying a franchise." In reality, you are entering into an agreement to invest assets in a system to utilize the brand name, operating system and ongoing support.

How does a sport franchise get admitted into a league?

The sport league has been described as a unique form of organization (Weiler, 2000). League rules are carefully designed in order to define the nature of the product being provided. Weiler (2000) explains that the Sherman Act bars only combinations in restraint of trade. The leagues have been able to define their rules in terms of operating as a single entity designed to create a single product.

A sport franchise gains admittance into a league in one of three primary ways. The first is the development of a new franchise through the expansion of a league. In the expansion process, the proposed franchise has to provide evidence of substantial capital assets, the existence of or ability to provide adequate facilities, and the existence of demographic data to support the franchise.

A second means of gaining admittance is through the relocation of the sport franchise. While this scenario might suggest that the franchise already exists, it may constitute the reorganization of a league or leagues based on geographical regions or population demographics. The restructuring of Major League Baseball during the last round of expansion greatly changed the structure of both the National and American Leagues as well as the divisions within the leagues.

The third method of admittance is through the sale of an existing franchise. While the organization may not change name or location, it must be understood that the owners of the franchise are a significantly different group than the previous owners and they must be willing to comply with the policies established and enforced by the franchiser (league).

How does a sport franchise relocate from one location to another?

The move to relocate a sport franchise may represent an opportunity to remove the franchise from a market that has been unprofitable. The league, functioning in the role of the franchiser, has the right to approve or disprove the proposed move.

Antitrust legislation will be considered when addressing complaints or desires to move the franchise. Complaints that may need to be resolved by the courts include:

- A league disapproving an owner's request to move the franchise to another city,
- Objections raised by a competing league,
- Perpetuating or achieving monopoly control of the particular sports market, and
- The city's opposition to having the franchise move away.

What is the role of a sport franchise in the local economy?

A professional sport franchise may increase media coverage for the city in which it is located (Howard & Compton, 1995). Along with more media attention, politicians see attracting a sport franchise as a means to enhance their image and to show their leadership capabilities. Franchises and their accompanying facilities are enthusiastically recruited by banks, real estate developers, insurance companies, construction firms, and elements of the tourism industry such as restaurants and hotels (Howard & Compton, 1995).

A common side effect of attracting a sport franchise is the need to build new stadiums and arenas to house the franchise. Many individuals are under the assumption that these construction projects generate jobs in the local area. Fried et. al. (2003) addressed the issue by stating that, "Although stadium proponents claim building a stadium creates jobs, the cost of creating a stadium-related job is over $100,000 per job versus a job at a retail shop or supermarket, which often costs under $10,000." Another aspect of stadiums and income growth identified by Fried was that 27 of 30 cities that had facility changes in the last 10 years showed no significant relationship between income growth and the building of the facility. In fact, three areas experienced reduced income.

While there may be an increase in tourism dollars, there is not significant income growth to balance the cost of publicly subsidizing the franchise and facility. In addition, the public may be encumbered with the burden of funding the new facilities without reaping any of the financial rewards. The municipality may have bonds to repay, but tax revenues may have been an incentive for the franchise to relocate in the city. The taxpayers are under the burden of both paying off the bonds and also providing additional revenue for the franchise.

It must be decided early in the recruitment/planning phase as to whether the community's cost of investment will create economic benefits. Public scrutiny over how tax dollars are spent make it very important to show a positive economic impact analysis.

How does a sport franchise impact the local taxes?

The public sector investment in the sport franchise usually occurs through subsidization and construction of facilities. Property taxes may be increased to help provide the funding for a new facility. Other tax dollars that may be used to subsidize the sport franchise and facility include:

- Sales tax,
- Hotel-motel tax,
- Utility tax,
- Car rental tax,
- Restaurant tax,
- Taxi or limousine tax,
- "Sin" tax (liquor, tobacco),
- Road tax, and
- Capital improvement tax.

The most popular of these taxes are the hotel/motel, restaurant, and auto rental taxes (Sawyer & Smith, 1999). These taxes are most frequently paid by tourists and fans, thereby not applying additional financial requirements on the permanent citizens in the community.

Summary

Keup (1995) describes the franchise as a contract or agreement by which:
- A franchisee is granted the right to engage in the business of offering, selling, or distributing goods or services under a marketing plan or system prescribed in substantial part by the franchiser,
- The operation of the franchisee's business pursuant to that plan or system is substantially associated with the franchiser's trademark, service mark, trade name, logotype, advertising, or other commercial symbol designating the franchiser or its affiliates, and
- The franchisee is required to pay, directly or indirectly, a franchise fee.

The sport franchise can impact local economies either positively or negatively. Local tax dollars are usually invoked to help subsidize the sport franchise and its facility.

References

DeBolt, D. *Ten questions to ask before buying a franchise.* www.franchise1.com/articles/article.asp?articleid=78

Fried, G., Shapiro, S.J., & Deschriver, T.D. (2003). *Sport finance.* Champaign, IL: Human Kinetics.

Hong Kong General Chamber of Commerce. *Advantages and disadvantages of franchising.* www.franchise.org.hk/advant.asp

Hong Kong General Chamber of Commerce. *What is franchising?* www.franchise.org.hk/whatis.asp

Howard, D.R., & Crompton, J.L. (1995). *Financing sport.* Morgantown, WV: Fitness Information Technology.

Keup, E.J. (1995). *Franchise bible: How to buy a franchise or franchise your own business.* Grants Pass, OR: Oasis Press/PSI Research.

Sawyer, T.H., & Smith, O. (1999). *The management of clubs, recreation and sport: Concepts and applications.* Champaign, IL: Sagamore.

Weiler, P.C. (2000). *Leveling the playing field: How the law can make sports better for fans.* Cambridge, MA: Harvard University Press.

Part IV

Sales Operations

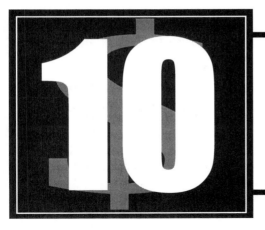

Box Office Operations

Introduction

The box/ticket office is the heart of a sport enterprise that fields teams. Its management is the key to financial success. Selling tickets to events is a major financial resource for any sporting team whether at the interscholastic, intercollegiate, or professional level. It is vital for sport managers to book a well-rounded schedule of events to satisfy the desires of the market and to ensure a major portion of the annual operating revenue.

This chapter is designed to assist the future sport manager in understanding how to manage box or ticket office operations.

Instructional Objectives

After reading this chapter, the student should be able to:
- Understand the function and operation of a box/ticket office.

Box Office Operations

For sport organizations that depend on fan participation to generate revenue, the box office becomes a vital operation. If the box/ticket office is not operated efficiently and effectively, it could cause a serious financial dilemma for the organization. The box office is also the point of entry for your new and older, reliable fans. The impression the ticket personnel leave with the customer is like a first impression at a job interview. Return purchases by fans can and will be influenced by the box office staff.

The Importance of Ticket Sales or Memberships

The importance of ticket sales varies greatly from one professional league to another and from one collegiate division to another (i.e., Division I-A to Division III). The media-rich NFL (i.e., long-term contracts with ABC, Fox, NBC, ESPN, and TNT) is the only professional league that ticket sales is not the most prominent revenue source. The amount of ticket revenue generated by sport organizations is dependent on two interrelated factors: the number of tickets sold and the unit cost of each ticket sold. The mission of the sport manager relating to ticket sales is to determine the optimal ticket prices that will maximize total cash flow per seat (i.e., general admission, club or premium seats, and luxury box seats). Pricing, in the past, has been based on the best, informed guesses of management. In the future, a successful sport manager must establish ticket prices based on market research, which provides an understanding of sport consumers' expected price threshold or their willingness to pay. The manager must be knowledgeable about marketing techniques and strategies to effectively sell the product(s) to the general public.

While the mission of managers in club settings (i.e., golf, racquet, health and fitness, and multi-sport) focuses on developing optimal membership programs, selling and retaining memberships is the lifeblood of the sport club sector. The key challenge facing sport club managers is to sustain membership levels in the face of growing competition such as watching television, including cable and satellite, internet access, renting a videotape or DVD, renting a PlayStation 2 game, attending a movie, purchasing a CD, going out to dinner, attending a rock concert or Broadway play, or going to your child's sporting or other event. In the future, sport club performance will be based on how effectively clubs recruit and retain members as well as their ability to maximize income return from each member.

The challenges of selling tickets to sporting events for the athletic director at any level or president of a professional sport enterprise are very similar to those faced by the sport club manager mentioned above. Both groups of managers must sell their products to the general public more effectively then the competitors. Further, they must retain the customer from year to year or event to event, in order to be successful.

The Product of a Box Office

The primary product of the box office is the ticket. When selecting a ticket and the method by which the ticket will be sold, there are a number of factors to consider, including the physical characteristics of the facility, seating plans, ticket system, ticketing software (e.g., BOCS, Data Factors, Haven Systems, Folio Box Office Management, Nortech Software, Smart Box Office, Software4Sport, and Tickets.com), outsourcing ticketing (e.g., TicketMaster, TicketWeb, 800BuyTickets), online ticketing, pricing structure, credit card service, group sales, discounted prices, advanced sales, and sales incentive plans utilized.

The ticket is a product. It is a souvenir for the patron. It can also be used to notify patrons of dangers by the inclusion of a warning on the backside of the ticket. Further, the backside of the ticket could include a safe harmless clause with the warning. This alerts the patrons to known dangers (i.e., when purchasing a ticket for a hockey contest, it could warn patrons seated in rows 10 and higher of the possibility of being hit by a puck).

Printing of Tickets

Tickets can either be purchased from an outside organization or printed internally in the ticket office through a computerized system. General admission tickets are easily controlled and can be purchased at any print shop, Wal-Mart, or K-Mart. Reserved tickets are more complicated.

If the box office is not computerized, tickets must then be purchased for every seat for each event. If the tickets are not sold, the remaining tickets must be

Gaylord Entertainment Center Ticket Offices   *Photo by M G. Hypes*

Gaylord Entertainment Center Ticket Prices   *Photo by M G. Hypes*

Applebee's Park Ticket Offices   *Photo by M G. Hypes*

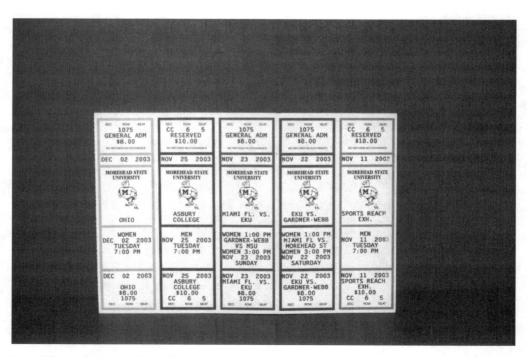

Event Tickets at the Morehead State University   *Photo by M G. Hypes*

destroyed. If there are 10,000 seats in the sporting facility and there are 15 home games, the box office then needs to store 150,000 tickets for the season. The tickets need to be stored by each event and seat. This requires a large area and a number of cabinets with appropriate shelving to secure the tickets. Once tickets are received from the printer, they all need to be checked and inventoried. The tickets sold must be checked off the master-seating chart to avoid duplicating sales. This system is labor intensive, costly, time-consuming, and exposes the box office to seating errors.

In a computerized box office, there is no need for ticket storage and purchase of tickets from an outside vendor. The computer will generate the tickets and automatically record the sale. The manager will need to purchase ticket stock on a regular bases. Internal printing also enables the ticket manager to control how many tickets are printed for each event. This reduces waste and the need for storage space. Further, the computer will allow box office personnel to print complete season-ticket packages with mailing labels. The tickets are separated for each season order, placed into envelopes for mailing, and mailing labels are attached. Printing tickets internally and in packages is preferable for the organization than buying a computerized system. Many organizations cannot afford this cost and continue to use the manual reserved system or sell all seats as general admission.

Types of Tickets

Typically sport organizations use one or more of the following types: reserved, general admission, season ticket, mini-season plans, individual event, complimentary, student, or raincheck. What tickets are available depends on the organization (e.g., interscholastic, intercollegiate, or professional sports). The larger, more established organizations will offer all types of tickets.

The season ticket provides a guaranteed source of income before the season starts and does not depend on variable factors including weather, quality of opponents, or team record. The season ticket involves the sale of a particular seat and location in the stadium or arena for an entire season for a one-time fee.

The mini-season plans allow fans to purchase tickets for a portion of the season. These plans offer a lower financial commitment to individual game ticket holders who wish to become more active fans but are not ready to purchase season tickets. The plans are designed to encourage individual event purchasers to move up to a multi-plan with hopes of making them season-ticket holders.

Individual tickets are tickets that are available for walk-in purchases the day of the event. The purchasers are generally in town for a convention, a business meeting, or visiting friends or relatives, and want to experience a game.

Complimentary tickets (comps) are those given to individuals (e.g., visiting dignitary, politician, local hero, donor, key clients, family and friends of players and coaches, etc.) or groups (e.g., Boy Scouts, Girl Scouts, youth sport teams, elementary school teams, etc.). There are two key strategies behind complimentary tickets: (a) to increase crowd size and (b) the organization hopes the "free" experience will be so positive that fans will want to return as paying customers.

Universities and colleges generally allocate seats for students. These tickets are often discounted, but not always. Many institutions require students to pick up their tickets early to control crowd size and to allow the athletic department to sell unclaimed student tickets.

Rain checks are tickets given to patrons when an event is cancelled due to weather or other reasons. The patron can return to the next event without paying an admission fee. Some organizations require the patrons to notify the box office one week prior to the event to control crowd size and to determine what additional tickets can be sold.

The Event

Before an event goes on sale, the ticket manager gathers important information about the venue, the organization, and the event itself and provides this information to all points of sale, including individuals selling tickets on consignment. The ticket manager should be familiar with all aspects of the event that affect the patron. The ticket manager should visit the venue ahead of time, sit in different locations in the house, attend a rehearsal or performance, and be ready to offer feedback on the event based on first-hand experience.

Event Information

You will need to give the following information to box office managers and ticket outlets so that they are able to answer patron inquiries.

Information obtained from the producer:

- A description of the event including featured performers, and
- Number and length of intermission(s).

Will any of the performances be ASL (American Sign Language) interpreted?

Instructions for writing checks

When running an independent ticket operation, checks should probably be written to the producing organization. If you are selling tickets through an established Box Office or ticket outlet, they will instruct the patron.

- Your organization's tax ID number.
- Any information regarding connected events such as a black tie opening, pre- or postevent receptions, or lectures.
- Web sites with information about the event or producing organization.

- A statement from the producer regarding the suitability of the event for children.
- Description of the event. At the point of sale, the ticket seller may be asked to volunteer information about the performance or the performing group to aid the patron in their decision-making process.

Information obtained from the representative of the venue

- Directions to the venue both by car and public transportation.
- Parking options.
- Information for patrons in wheelchairs regarding parking, access to building, the house, the box office, restrooms, and location of wheelchair seating in the house.
- Is there a TTY phone line at the box office? Does the venue have assisted listening devices?
- The seating capacity and seating chart of the house.

If you are using an established Box Office, they may already have this information.

- Web sites with information about the venue.
- Information obtained from the stage manager.
- An estimated running time for the event.

Setting Policies and Parameters

The following guidelines should be established in consultation with the producer, ideally two months in advance of the event.

Seating Configuration

- General Admission (unreserved) tickets are easier to sell and account for. They also make house management simpler. Remember to inform patrons that seating is on a first-come, first-served basis.

• Reserved Seating is used in special circumstances. It restricts seating options for patrons and house management, requires more work for the box office and usher staff working the event, and often delays the start time of an event.

Discounting Ticket Prices

Discounting tickets for special groups of people (e.g., students, seniors, disabled, etc.) can assist in filling the house and provide a nice community service. The discounted tickets can be used as a means of penetration marketing into a new customer base or to fill seats that may not be filled for the event. It is important for the manager to determine what number of individuals constitutes a "group." Further, it is important to decide prior to the season whether or not there will be discounted preseason games for all patrons.

It is the producer's responsibility to consider both the positive and negative impact of any special offers on the overall event budget. Special deals should be geared toward people who would not otherwise attend the event and for performances that would otherwise be undersold.

On Sale Date

Tickets for undergraduate events generally go on sale one month before the event. Do not publicize or advertise an event before tickets are on sale. If necessary, the On Sale Date should be included in press releases, brochures, and "save the date" postcards.

Tickets to be Held

Before tickets are on sale to the public, the ticket manager and producer should discuss how many and which tickets should be withheld from sale. This is a good time to determine the best and worst places to sit. If an event is reserved seating, sit in several different seats to determine what the view of the stage is like from different sections of the house. Reasons for holding tickets include:

• House Seats/Trouble Seats

These are seats that are kept off-line for last-minute problems. The house manager may need to use these seats if an error leads to a show being oversold or, in a reserved seating house, a seat being "double sold." They may also be needed if there is damage or a spill that makes another seat in the house unusable. House seats are also kept available so that the producer can accommodate last-minute ticket requests from VIPs.

• Usher Seats

Consult with the house manager on how many and which seats need to be held for ushers.

• Obstructed Seats

The placement of lighting and sound equipment or the need for cameras and other video equipment in the house often necessitates removing seats from the capacity because the equipment is placed in the seating area. These decisions need to be made early so that the appropriate number of tickets can be pulled. In the case of a reserved seating house, the exact placement of such equipment must be established before a show can go on sale.

• Obstructed View Seats

Some seats may offer particularly bad sight lines to the stage or have views that are obstructed by architectural elements or production equipment. The producer and ticket manager should use their discretion in deciding whether to pull these seats or to sell them at a reduced price. Patrons must be informed, by the ticket seller and by the text on the ticket, they are purchasing an obstructed view seat.

•Seats Required for Performers

A performer may need a seat if s/he is being "planted" in the house. Events with multiple performing groups may allow performers to sit in the audience for part of the performance.

•VIP Seats

A producer will often decide to make complimentary tickets available to performers, production crew and VIPs such as college staff and faculty, donors, and other special guests. The ticket manager should have a list of such individuals.

The producer and ticket manager should be very selective in offering complimentary tickets. If you offer someone a free ticket to one event, they are likely to expect free tickets to your next event.

Set a policy as to when unclaimed complimentary tickets will be released for sale. Inform all recipients that their tickets will be released at the door for sale if these tickets are not picked up 30 minutes prior to the advertised start time.

VIPs should be given a special invitation by the producer and asked to RSVP. The ticket manager can develop a list of VIPs for whom tickets should be held ahead of time and submit it to the Box Office.

Producers and ticket managers may offer performers and production crew a certain number of complimentary tickets. Since the core audience for most student shows is comprised of friends and family of the performers and production crew, be aware that a generous complimentary ticket policy will diminish your primary income source.

It is recommended that you create and use a complimentary ticket voucher that cannot be easily duplicated for cast and crew. Complimentary ticket vouchers simplify the process of complimentary ticket distribution for the ticket manager, especially for multi-performance events.

Complimentary tickets for cast and crew are usually offered on an "as available" basis, unlike VIP seats that are actually pulled from the pool of tickets put on sale.

Latecomer Seats

Think about latecomers before you put tickets on sale. If you decide that it is unsafe or impractical to admit latecomers at all, you need to include a "no latecomer policy" in your advertising and press releases. If you decide that latecomers can be admitted only to a particular area of the house, you'll need to pull those seats before an event goes on sale.

Waiting Line Policy

When an event sells out, the patrons should be informed by the ticket sellers that a waiting line will be established at the door. It is not recommended to start a waiting list either by phone or for friends who did not buy a ticket in time. A clearly established policy set ahead of time should clarify when and where the waiting line will begin and at what time tickets will be released. It should be well marked and be out of the way so that it does not interfere with other patron traffic. If tickets can be released, start releasing them at fifteen minutes before curtain.

People in the waiting line may be admitted only if:
- Complimentary tickets are unclaimed,
- Unpaid reservations are unclaimed,
- Standing room is available, and
- The producer and house manager decide to release house seats.

Preparing the Box Office for an Event

For each event there is a beginning and an end. The beginning commences after the event is scheduled and the tickets are offered for sale. The ending is after the books are closed and all sales are finished. The length of an events promotion depends on the promoter. It could be as few as two weeks or as long as six weeks.

Pre-event preparations

Each ticket seller is assigned a specific number of tickets and a small bank in order to make change. The seller confirms the number of tickets and the amount of money in the bank by signing in section of the ticket sellers audit sheet. Each organization has a different set of audit or reconciliation forms as directed by the organization's controller.

During the Event

There should be a will-call window for spectators to pick up prepaid tickets, complimentary tickets, press passes, and tickets being held for someone. The ticket seller at this window will not have separate tickets to be sold nor a bank. The seller should have a list with the names of the people assigned to the tickets. Once a person identifies him or herself with appropriate identification, tickets should be signed for on the master sheet. Finally, this seller would also be the trouble-shooter to assist other ticket sellers with questions or complaints.

Post Event

At the conclusion of the event, the ticket sellers will reconcile their banks and cash, checks, and credit card receipts received for the tickets they were assigned. The head ticket seller will verify everything is in order before allowing the ticket seller to leave. The head ticket seller will prepare a final event sales report and deposit the cash, checks, and credit card receipts in the bank. The final event report will include the total number of tickets sold, number of complimentary tickets provided, number of press passes provided, number of season patrons attending, total amount of income received, and the total number of people in the audience paid and non-paid.

The head ticket taker will confirm with the head ticket seller the total number of patrons present at the event. The ticket takers will collect the tickets and count all those that were collected or

scan them into a small computer. If tickets are collected, they should be torn in half with half being retained by the patron (for a souvenir). If the ticket is scanned, the entire ticket can be given to the patron.

Box Office Design

The box office is the initial contact office for most patrons. Sales windows should be located on all sides of the facility and a drive-up window should also be considered for customer convenience. The box office manager can decide which window areas should be open on a daily and event basis.

This space should be easily accessible to all patrons. It must be compliant with the Americans With Disabilities Act (ADA) sections dealing specially with facility accessibility.

The main box office space should be large enough to accommodate such areas as office spaces for personnel, sales windows (at least 10) for walk-in traffic and a drive-up facility, storage area for office supplies and ticket paper stock, a small conference room, and rest rooms. The smaller sales areas should have a minimum of six windows for sales and will-call tickets. These spaces should be protected from the elements and have a depth of at least 15 feet. All smaller auxiliary ticket sales areas should be facing the outside of the facility. The main ticket area should have inside and outside windows. The windows should be shatter-proof. All computers to all sites should be networked to each other and to the main office computer. The tickets spaces should have environmental controls and telephone communication. The main office should have a safe built into the wall to store funds safely.

Summary

Booking outstanding events does not guarantee high-volume ticket sales. The key to selling tickets is good information and easy, convenient access for the tickets. The personnel in the box/ticket office must be user-friendly who provide sales services and serve as public relation folks. As a result of the service, audience and performer are brought together with the dollars generated from the sale of tickets held by the box/ticket office until distribution of monies between those responsible for providing services (i.e., performer, promoter, agent, sponsor, and facility) is determined.

Retail
Operations

Introduction

Sport organizations have known for years that retail operations can generate a significant and consistent revenue stream. If the retail operations are run well and are selling the right products at competitive prices, they should be turning a handsome profit and saving the clientele money.

Successful retail operations accomplish the following: (1) feature prominent locations that require clientele to pass through the various sites, (2) offer personalized service and competitive pricing, (3) print catalogues for clients to share with friends, (4) merchandise their goods/products (i.e., displaying goods/products in an appealing way), (5) consider themselves retail outlets, (6) sell innovative goods/ products, (7) concentrate on apparel, accessories, beverages, and food, (8) stock regularly-needed convenience supplies, and (9) sell licensed merchandise.

The most dramatic change for the food and beverage concession industry came in 1987 with the opening of Joe Robbie stadium. Joe Robbie Stadium started the luxury suites and club seats era. The owners of Joe Robbie Stadium offered its customers a new level of service never before available in a sports facility: waiter and waitress service at their seats and a fully air-conditioned and carpeted private concourse featuring complete buffets from gourmet sandwiches to homemade pasta and freshly carved prime rib. A new level of culinary expertise would now be required of the concessionaire and the concessionaire's skill would be instrumental in the success of the customer's total entertainment experience at the sport's venue.

Instructional Objectives

After reading this chapter the student should be able to:
- Understand the function of the retail operations,

- Prepare an RFP for a retail operation,
- Understand a retail contract, and
- Appreciate the value of bonding personnel involved with collecting money and reduce theft.

Retail Operations

Retail operations within a sport organization can include concessions including beverage (i.e., alcoholic and non-alcoholic), fast food, and parking found when attending most sporting events, licensed and convenience products, and full-service restaurants. Some operations (i.e., state and national parks) extend their offerings beyond products to include services including rentals (e.g., bicycle, watercraft, ski equipment, golf equipment), downhill ski facilities and services, equestrian services, golf courses and services, photography services, marina services, shuttle bus services, theater productions, vending machine services, and aquatic facilities. Retail operations must stretch the discretionary income of the clientele. Some operations

provide the organization a source of operating revenue separate from, but in addition to, a subsidy provided by the media rights and ticket sales. Others operate on a break-even basis and serve strictly as a service to clientele.

Concession Operations

The food and beverage concessions can be a gold mine if handled appropriately. Many stadia and arenas are expanding their options from the traditional concession stand to include favorite fast food options (i.e., Burger King, McDonald's, Pizza Hut, Papa John's, Hardees, Taco Bell, Long John Silver's, Kentucky Fried Chicken, Ballpark Frank's, TCBY yogurt, Krispy Kreme donuts, TGI Friday's-Miller Park, Outback Steakhouse-PNC Park, Hard Rock Café-SkyDome, etc.), as well as the traditional hot dog, popcorn, peanuts, pretzels, and beer concession. All stadiums have added, along with their luxury suites and club seats, full-service premium restaurants. Numerous concession companies have added regional favorites including a microbrewery and Rocky

Waffle Cone	4.25	Candy	3.00
Ice Cream Cup	3.50	Fresh Baked Cookie	2.25
ICEE	3.50	Brownie	2.00
Ice Cream Cone	2.75	Coffee/Hot Chocolate	1.75

All Prices Include Sales Tax
Building Policy Dictates All Bottle Caps Mus

Gaylord Entertainment Center, Concessions Pricings   *Photo by M.G. Hypes*

Mountain oysters in Denver, fish tacos in San Diego, cheese steaks in Philadelphia, and dog bone-shaped chocolate chip cookies in Cleveland. The greatest amount of profit in the food concessions business is from soda drink sales followed by popcorn, hot dogs, tacos and cheese, candy, and beer. (See Chart 11.1 for listing of 2003 soda and beer pouring rights for NFL stadiums.)

A food concession open from dawn to dusk must be flexible, offering breakfast, lunch, and dinner favorites that are fast and convenient. People expect to pay more at a food concession than elsewhere because of the convenience factor. The food concession will be successful if the customers' needs and wants are known and a clean, fresh atmosphere with friendly, convenient and fast service is provided.

The food concession must be conveniently located to the customer. Many stadia and arenas are now using portable concession stands as well as the permanent locations to provide more convenient service to the customers. The food concession area should have plenty of counter space, hot and cold running water, adequate electricity to operate popcorn popper, microwave, refrigerator and freezer, a warming unit, and storage space. The floor and walls should be tile. The floor should have numerous drains for cleaning. On the customer side, there should be plenty of space to accommodate a large number of people quickly and efficiently.

The seven major concessionaires in the food service industry are:
- Aramark (largest concession company in North America),
- Compass (European, largest concession company in the world),
- Fine Hosts Corporation,
- Global Spectrum,
- Sodexho (European),
- Sportservice Corporation (Buffalo), and

- Volume Services America (VSA) now known as Centerplate (Spartanburg).

Food Concession Guidelines

It is important for any food concession system to have operation guidelines. The recommendations address and include employee appearance, training goals, maintenance goals, operation goals, regulations, inspections, safety certification and sanitation, patron comforts, guest relations, professional signs and pricing, decorations, and food handler's guidelines. The guidelines that follow have been established by the Outdoor Amusement Business Association (OABA). The OABA can be reached at http://www.oaba.org. The OABA have guidelines for food and game concessions.

National Organizations for Concessionaires

The sport manager should be aware of the two national organizations that deal with food and beverage concessions. The first is the National Association of Concessionaires, which can be found on the web at http://www.NAConline.org. This organization offers a concession manager certification course and an executive concession manager certification course. The programs for these courses include these topics: management, profit planning, cost control systems, menu planning/branding, and event planning. The basis of the course and the textbook it is based on are also part of the curriculum at the School of Hospitality Management at Florida International University in Miami and the School of Human Sciences, Department of Nutrition and Food Science at Auburn University in Alabama. The second organization is the National Association of Collegiate Concessionaires whose URL address is http://www.nacc-online.com.

Chart 11.1

Beverage Contracts for NFL Stadiums 2003

NFL Stadiums	Soda Exclusive Pouring Rights	Beer Pouring Rights
Arizona Cardinals Sun Devil Stadium	Coke	NA
Atlanta Falcons Georgia Dome	Coke	NA
Baltimore Ravens M&T Bank Stadium	Pepsi	Budweiser, Bud Light, Coors Light, Miller Lite, Sam Adams, Killian's, Michelob Amber Bock, Red Hook
Buffalo Bills Ralph Wilson Stadium	Pepsi	NA
Carolina Panthers Ericsson Stadium	Pepsi	Miller Lite, MGD, Icehouse, Sky Blue, Miller, Budweiser, Bud Light, Michelob Ultra, Michelob Light, Red Hook, Widmer, Amstel Light, Heineken, Carolina Blond, Harp, Bass, Pilsner Urquell, Newcastle Brown, Coors Light, Foster's Miller, Miller Lite, Leinenkugel Red, Honkers Ale, Bass, Guinness
Chicago Bears Soldier Field	Coke	Budweiser, Bud Light, Michelob Light, Michelob Ultra, Miller Lite, MGD, Sam Adams, Warstiener Dunkel, Warstiener Okloberfest, Coors Light~ Barrelhouse Red Leg Ale, Barrelhouse Vandermeer Strong Ale, Hudy Delight
Cincinnati Bengals Paul Brown Stadium	Coke	Miller Lite, MGD, Budweiser, Bud Light, Coors Light
Cleveland Browns Cleveland Stadium	Pepsi	Budweiser, Bud Light, Coors, Miller, Miller Lite
Dallas Cowboys Texas Stadium	Pepsi & Dr Pepper	Budweiser, Bud Light, Labatt, Labatt Light, Heineken, Amstel Light
Denver Broncos Invesco Field	Coke	Miller Lite, MGD, Miller High Life, Rolling Rock, Labatt Blue
Detroit Lions Ford Field	Pepsi	Miller Lite, Bud Light, Foster's, Michelob Ultra, Heineken, Shiner Bock, Sam Adams, Fat Tire
Green Bay Packers Lambeau Field	Coke	NA
Houston Texans Reliant Stadium	Coke	St. Arnold, Sierra Nevada
Indianapolis Colts RCA Dome	Coke	Budweiser, Bud Light, Miller, Miller Lite, Coors Light
Jacksonville Jaguars Alltel Stadium	Pepsi	Bud Light, Budweiser, Miller Lite, Coors Light, Amber Bock, Michelob Light, Foster's
Kansas City Chiefs Arrowhead Stadium	Coke	Budweiser, Bud Light, Coors Light, Miller Lite, MGD, Heineken, Boulevard
Miami Dolphins Pro Player Stadium	Coke	Budweiser, Bud Light, Miller Lite, Icehouse, Michelob Light, Michelob Ultra, Michelob Amber Bock, Foster's, Killian's, Yuengling, Heineken, Amstel, Bass, Beck's, Sam Adams, Coors Light
Minnesota Vikings Metrodome	Coke	Budweiser, Bud Light, Grain Belt Premium (contract requires a Minnesota brew) and lots of specialty beers Budweiser, Coors Light, Bud Light, Heineken, Amstel Light, Guinness, Bass Ale, Sam Adams
New England Patriots Gillette Stadium	Pepsi	Budweiser, Bud Light, Miller Lite, Coors Light, World Select, Heineken, Michelob Ultra, Red Dog

Continued

Chart 11.1 Continued

Venue	Soda	Beer
New Orleans Saints Superdome	Coke	Miller, MGD, Miller Lite, Coors Light, Heineken, Guinness, Budweiser, Bud Light
New York Giants and Jets Meadowlands	Pepsi	Bud Light, Coors Light, MGD, Heineken, Dos Equis, Tecate, Gordon Biersch, Pyramid, Deschutes, Guinness, Foster's
Oakland Raiders Network Associates Coliseum	Pepsi	Miller, Miller Lite, MGD, Budweiser, Bud Light, Coors Light, Pilsner Urquell, Labatt
Philadelphia Eagles Lincoln Financial Field	Pepsi	Michelob Amber Bock, Foster's
Pittsburgh Steelers Heinz Field	Coke	Rolling Rock, Green Light, Loyal Hanna, Iron City, Iron City Light, Coors Light, Budweiser, Bud Light, Miller Lite, Labatt Blue, Guinness, Bass Ale, Harp, Penn Pilsner, Yeungling, Michelob Ultra
St. Louis Rams Edward Jones Dome	Coke	Budweiser, Bud Light, Miller Lite
San Diego Chargers Qualcomm Stadium	Coke	Budweiser, Miller, Heineken, Corona and more
San Francisco 49ers 3Com Park	Coke	Miller, MGD, Miller Lite, Budweiser, Bud Light, Coors, Coors Light, Gordon Biersch, Red Hook, IPA, Sierra Nevada, Heineken, Foster's, Anchor Steam, Beck's
Seattle Seahawks Seahawks Stadium	Coke	Budweiser, Bud Light, Busch, Michelob Ultra, Miller Lite, MGD, Coors Light, Widmer's, Heffeweisen, Amber Bock, Heineken, Beck's, Pyramid
TB. Buccaneers Raymond James Stadium	Coke	Budweiser, Bud Light, Miller Lite and Icehouse, Coors Light
Tennessee Titans Coliseum	Coke	Budweiser, Bud Light, Michelob Ultra, Miller Lite, MGD, Michelob, Coors Light, Bohannnon
Washington Redskins FedExField	Coke	NA

Modified from Kaufman, G. (December 2003). *Venuestoday, 2*(12), 28.

Alcohol Management

The focus on patron safety relating to alcohol consumption began in 1983 with the Bearman v. University of Notre Dame. The Indiana Supreme Court determined that Notre Dame had a "duty" to its paid patrons. This was a landmark case because the court determined that intoxicated persons could pose a general danger to other patrons. This determination flew in the face of previous decisions that placed the responsibility of duty of care on the individual or group not on the event organizers. The Court determined that foreseeability dictated that Notre Dame had a duty to protect its patrons from the potential dangerous actions of intoxicated third parties. This case set the standard for duty of care for the management of alcohol at events.

In a number of states, there are dram shop statutes that allow injured plaintiffs to bring suit against restaurants, bars, and other establishments that allow the defendant to become drunk. In some states, the court allows recovery through common negligence actions. There are a few states that allow recovery using both methods.

In addition to the dram shop statutes, another liability to be aware exists known as the social host liability. This statute provides the injured plaintiff an opportunity to sue based on a social host knowingly serving alcohol to a minor who becomes intoxicated and causes injury or damage to property. In the jurisdiction where this line of thinking is embraced, the venue manager should be aware of this type of liability.

Alcohol Management Plan

Venue managers should have in their liability tool bags an alcohol management plan. This plan should be coordinated with the crowd control management plan. The plan should include procedures to check age restrictions, restrictions on the number of beers served, terminating beer sale at a specific point during the event (i.e., basketball, end of third period; football, beginning of third quarter; ice hockey, end of the second intermission; and baseball, end of the seventh inning), deploying trained personnel to watch for trouble, and incorporating a designated-driver program.

Alcohol Sales Strategies

In 1992, Miller Brewing Company, in combination with previous research and encouragement from its legal department, provided the following suggestions regarding an effective alcohol sales strategy:

1. Decide whether or not to sell alcohol and if the decision to sell alcohol is made, then an alcohol management plan must be developed.

2. Develop procedures to stop outside alcohol from entering the venue.

3. Establish crowd management procedures for alcohol management for day and evening events and for weather.

4. Install appropriate signage to enlighten patrons about responsible and irresponsible drinking and its consequences.

5. Establish a strong ejection policy.

6. Do not promote or advertise drinking during the event.

7. Make sure that security personnel are aware of the demographics of the crowd in each section of the venue (e.g., gender, white-collar, blue-collar, families, senior citizens, under 21, etc.).

8. All staff (not just security and servers) should complete regulate alcohol management training.

9. Establish consumption policies (e.g., number of beers per patron at one time, termination of sales prior to conclusion of the event).

10. Tailgating only permitted in parking lots under strict supervision of security personnel.

11. Establish non-alcohol sections within the venue (i.e., family sections).

12. Develop a designated-driver program (Modified from Ammon, Southall, & Blair, 2004, 188-189).

Parking Concession

The parking concession can be profitable, but it has liabilities. The manager, before charging for parking, must ensure that the following has been accomplished: (1) purchase adequate liability insurance, (2) provide adequate surfacing for the proposed traffic, (3) ensure safe entrance and exit areas, (4) provide adequate lighting, (5) plan for immediate snow and ice removal, (6) establish an emergency plan for the space, (7) ensure that adequate supervision and security is available, (8) provide for the safety of the pedestrians, (9) plan a graphic system that makes it easy to find customers' cars at the conclusion of the event, and (10) provide an adequate number of cashiers and attendants. After the manager has accomplished the above, it is time to decide how many spaces will be for the handicapped, VIPs, and regular customers. The greatest amount of money will be made from VIP parking.

According to Russo (2001), the following controls should be implemented to ensure a smooth operation: "(1) sensors or loops buried in each entrance line, (2) a single pass lane, (3) a cashier or checker watching the sellers and authorizing passes, (4) spot checks on sellers, (5) different colored tickets for different events, days, or hours, (6) cash registers, (7) TV monitors, and (8) clean graphics and signs indicating special entrances."

The parking operation is second only to the box office in terms of direct contact between the facility and the patron. A well-designed and managed parking operation will ease crowd tension and allow for sufficient time for patrons to buy a snack and still be in their seats on time. There is no question that the ease of access and parking is a major factor in increased public acceptance and attendance at events.

Retail Operations

These are the stadium or arena gift or souvenir shops. They deal with licensed products and convenience items needed by patrons while attending a sporting event.

Finding a Retail Niche

Finding customers who value what you offer is difficult at best. Achieving customer approval is especially demanding in these uncertain times. It takes regular and consistent cultivation on several fronts. Every community is overwhelmed with retail shopping locations and merchants offering everything imaginable. What makes your business emerge from the masses as distinctive? Developing a niche and working it could be the long-lost answer.

Rigsbee (1997) suggests that the following questions are crucial to your success. Record your answers and you are sure to hit pay dirt. The questions tell who your customers happen to be and, more importantly, who they should be:

- "How is my store special and unique?
- What groups of people would most benefit by what I offer?
- How have I physically set up my store to be user-friendly in a concerted effort to serve this group of people?
- Is my advertising targeted to the customers I desire to serve?
- What products do I like?"

In your efforts to add value, a pitfall to avoid is that of adding the value you desire, rather than the value your niche customers want (Rigsbee, 1997). Become market- driven, rather than product-driven, by listening to your customers' needs, wants, and desires. Do this, and they will reward you with greater profitability than you have ever enjoyed before.

Using Cutting-Edge Retail Strategies in Merchandising and Buying

The world of retailing is changing at breakneck speed. These changes are driven by busy people who have too little time to shop, consumers who have new economic priorities, and the fact that too many stores are selling the same merchandise. All this is having a profound impact on when, where, and how merchandise is sold.

Ensman (1999) suggests there are nine steps to being a good buyer. He has put these nine steps under the umbrella of B-U-Y W-I-S-E-L-Y:

- "**B**e specific in defining needs, identifying performance, and results.
- **U**nderstand the options that are available prior to purchasing the item(s).
- Tell the supplier, It's **Y**our move. Tell me why you can meet my needs better than anyone else.
- Aim for a **W**in-win situation between you and the seller.
- **I**mpose deadlines and conditions when necessary.
- **S**eek assistance from an outside consultant when in doubt about a purchase.
- **E**ducate the seller about your special needs.
- **L**ook for after-sale service.
- **Y**ell for help when necessary."

The Four M's in Retail

Shaffer (1999) indicates that "operating a successful retail establishment comes down to the four M's: merchandising, markups, marketing, and methodology." The basis for any success in a retail business comes down to merchandising the items placed on the shelves. Fail to carry what the customer wants and needs, and they will breeze right past on their way to their destination; but capture their interest, and you have won a dedicated customer.

Merchandise must be visible. If nobody sees what merchandise is available, the store manager is setting himself up to fail. The store should be positioned in a high-traffic area where the customers must pass by on their way to activities. If merchandise is not in the customers' line of sight, they will probably not be enticed to enter the store. Keeping goods in a high-traffic space will discourage shoplifting.

Tips for Enlivening the Retail Store

The following are tips that can be used to enliven the employee store environment and generate increased customer traffic:

- Celebrate holidays with decorations.
- Place a number of inexpensive products near the sales counter or check out area to encourage impulse purchasing.
- Use all of your available space, not just shelf space.
- Computerize the store.
- Reward frequent shoppers with special sales and discounts.
- Give customers shopping bags with the organization's logo in which to carry their merchandise home.

Basic Store Merchandise

The retail store does not require a great deal of space. Some of the most popular elements that will enable an organization to start even the most basic store are outlined in Table 11.1.

Table 11.1

The Building Blocks

Clothing

T-shirts	Shorts	Hats
Socks	Sweatshirts	Tank tops
Bike Shorts	Gore-Tex running suits	Coolmax singlets

Most retailers agree that you should promote your retail store by offering clothes with the organization's logo. Embroidered items go so much faster than anything else. People like to wear items that look good and are crisp, sharp, and classy. Even with a really nice t-shirt, embroidery dresses it up.

Tip—Music Can Influence Consumers to Buy

"Retailers have found a new way to put customers in the mood to shop and buy their products. Music, originally intended to provide a calming, productive atmosphere for workers, is now used in many of the leading stores (e.g., J. Crew, The Banana Republic, Sears, Wal-Mart, J.C. Penny) as a marketing tool. Research indicates that customers are comfortable when surrounded by music that is familiar to them. Store sound systems ooze soft piano music when retailers want to expose the customer to a feeling of elegance. Meanwhile, rock 'n roll is piped in loudly for young adult or teen shoppers" (Ewing, 1999).

When selecting music, programmers make a point of excluding any type of music that might offend the audience. Programmers also shy away from playing anything questionable or negative. Again, the music is intended to make the customers feel good not to agitate them.

If the manager decides to use music in the employee store, be aware that the company may need to purchase music designed for store use from a supplier such as BMI or ASCAP. The company will be required to pay a licensing fee that will protect the company from fines for misuse.

Retail Store Design

The retail manager needs to carefully plan the layout of the retail store. The store layout is as much a marketing tool as are the catalogues and merchandise on the shelves. The manager needs to work with a consultant and visit other employee stores before making the final decisions regarding store layout, space needs (including storage), and overall design.

Effective Store Layout

"When a customer enters an employee store, what do they see? Do they see a store that is cluttered and disorganized or one that is clean, attractive, and interesting? Do they see too much merchandise or too little? Do they see merchandise that is poorly displayed or do they see a well-designed store that shows off the merchandise at its best? Do they find it difficult to locate specific merchandise, brands, styles, sizes, and colors, or do they find a store with merchandise that is logically organized on racks and shelves so that it is easy to find and buy? Do they experience a dynamic shopping environment or just another store where they can occasionally buy a few items because it is convenient and the prices are pretty good?" (Whalin, 1998)

Whalin (1998) indicates that customers expect more from every kind of store, whether it is located in the mall or where they work. Influencing employee customers' buying decisions means knocking their socks off with a creative shopping environment where the merchandise is the star. Further, he suggests three main keys to an effective store layout— maximizing the space, controlling and directing traffic flow, and maximizing exposure.

Maximizing the space

The key is to create an exciting, comfortable, and dynamic retailing environment for customers by using innovative layout and design software tools. The well-designed store maximizes every square foot of selling space. The manager needs to fine-tune the layout to minimize or eliminate "dead spots" and maximize a store's "hot spots" where almost anything will sell.

Controlling and directing traffic flow

The customer's experience, according to Whalin (1998), starts in "The Decompression Zone." This is the all-important space at the very front of the store where customers first enter and sometimes stop for just a few moments to be acclimated. During the first few moments after customers enter, they begin to get a feeling for the store, even those who may have been in the store many times before. If everything stays the same month after month and year after year, the customer simply breezes in, buys what he wants, and leaves, never seeing all of the other merchandise. Therefore, it is important to re-merchandise and change the location of the merchandise frequently.

Further, it is important that the customers feel as though the store is comfortable, inviting, easy to shop, and they are welcome. While it is nice to showcase new merchandise in the front of the store, it is more important to give customers a little space when they first enter the store to begin to feel comfortable.

After years of observing customers, researchers have discovered that more than 70 percent of the time when people enter a store they will either look or walk to the right. The simple explanation is that we have become a "right-handed" society. Researchers say even left-handed people frequently look or turn to the right. "What merchandise will customers find in the store when they look or turn to the right? Is there merchandise on the left side that is being ignored? Are the displays in the front of the store changed frequently so customers do not just come in and look past the merchandise?" (Whalen, 1998)

Another important research finding is that customers prefer shopping in stores where the aisles are wide enough to easily accommodate two or three people going in opposite directions. A growing number of the nation's most successful retail chains are discovering that wider aisles mean more sales and more satisfied customers.

Maximizing exposure

Are departments easy to find and identified clearly with appropriate signs? Are the fixtures and displays arranged in nice, neat, symmetrical rows, or are they angled to create open spaces that allow customers to see most of the merchandise? It is recommended by many retailers to arrange fixtures and displays at 45 percent angles creating soft corners that maximize customer exposure to merchandise. Fixtures placed at 45 percent angles and rounded corners are being used to display all types of merchandise.

King (1998) suggests the proper use of fixtures will make your life easier and your bottom line bigger, especially if you keep four things in mind: flexibility, convertibility, ingenuity, and simple common sense. A totally inflexible fixture should be used only for products that are sold in fixed quantities throughout the entire year (e.g., greeting card cases).

Further, King (1998) suggests the use of slatwall panels, wall systems, and fixtures like spinners, four-ways, and A-frames permit the use of a seemingly endless array of slatwall accessories. In addition, using slatwall as a component in a fixture can totally change its function. Put a slatwall on the back of a window display and you have just created a two-sided fixture.

Steel shelving is found everywhere, usually with flat shelves. Yet, you can create entirely new departments by removing the flat shelves and replacing them with a wide variety of inserts. They range from simple peg hooks and hang bars to spinner displays, units with glass doors, computer demo shelves, and even inserts for such items as fishing poles.

Table 11.1

Effective Store Layout Checklist

- Would you answer yes, no, or needs improvement to these questions about the store?
- If I were one of your customers, would I enjoy shopping in the store?
- Is the store always clean and well maintained?
- Are the shelves always stocked with merchandise?
- Do the in-store signs clearly communicate the information the customers need and expect?
- Is the store laid out so that it is easy for customers to move around and find the merchandise they want?
- Are merchandise displays dynamic, attractive, fun, and interesting?
- Is the merchandise frequently rearranged to take advantage of seasonal events?
- Is the store regularly remodeled to keep it fresh and inviting for customers?
- Do display fixtures fit the overall decor of the store?
- Is the exterior of the store attractive and inviting?
- Has management done everything within the budget to make the interior and exterior of the store more attractive and inviting?
- Is the store bright and colorful?
- Are all the merchandise display possibilities taken advantage of in order to make the store a pleasant and enjoyable place to shop?
- Are the merchandise displays fresh and interesting, and are seasonal themes used to create excitement and keep customers coming back?
- Does the lighting in the store show merchandise at its best?

Adapted from Whalin's work on *Effective Store Layouts* in **Employee Services Management**, *41*(2), 26-28.

One of the simplest ways to incorporate flexibility into fixtures is to put them on casters. You can then alter traffic layout, move fixtures into position for seasonal promotions, or even take them out of the store for special sales. There are ready-to-assemble fixturing systems available that can be reconfigured depending on the need.

The following are a few useful tips to maximize sales dollars per square foot:

- Look at that empty space between the top of your wall fixtures and the ceiling.
- Use box displays of various sizes, stacking them in different configurations.
- Jamming as much as possible into a limited space may not always be wise.
- Gridwall is a simple and inexpensive way to add display capacity.
- If the customer cannot find it, they cannot buy it.
- The simplest way to maximize the use of space is just to clean up the store.
- Research what is successful in other stores.
- Use conservative numbers when estimating future sales.
- Use logic when estimating how much money will be made (Helson, 1998).

Finally, Whalin (1998) has developed 15 questions to be used as a checklist for store managers to answer when preparing store layouts. (See Table 11.2)

The Most Common Mistakes Made by Retailers

A successful retail store is the outcome of constant planning and setting realistic goals. Yet, many business people run their businesses without any direction. The following are the 10 most common mistakes that retailers should avoid (Azar. 1999):

- "No business plan.
- No marketing plan.
- No sales plan.
- No advisory board.
- No cash reserve or real cash flow.
- Ignoring the numbers.
- Not being automated.
- Not knowing your customer.
- Ignoring employees.
- Being a lone ranger."

The Vending Machine

What could be more low-maintenance than a retail effort that requires minimal staff? How about something that involves no store staff at all? Many facilities are finding that an effective way to sell small retail products such as convenience items, health foods, and beverages is by positioning at least one vending machine in a prominent spot in the employee services area.

There are two ways to become involved with the vending option—own or lease the machine, or contract with a vending company for a commission. The first option, that of owning or leasing a machine or a number of machines, is the most profitable and the ultimate way to go. However, it can become labor intensive and requires an up-front investment in merchandise; plus, merchandise can take up valuable storage space. In contrast, the second option requires no labor nor any investment in merchandise. The commission covers the cost of electricity, floor space, and the store's percentage of the net income.

A vending machine location is accessible and unattended 24 hours a day, seven days a week. Another benefit is that vending machines virtually eliminate theft and facilitate inventory control. It is possible to vend such items as vitamins, minerals, protein supplements, sport drinks, socks, shirts, headphones, and almost anything else that will fit in a vending machine.

Staffing the Retail Store or Concession Stand

The dwindling pool of candidates, especially for sales positions, is of grave concern to all retailers and concessionaires. Store or concession managers are looking for a special type of retail salesperson who can perform a variety of tasks and build relationships with revisiting customers. To attract this type of person, you should know that surveys of employees show that the opportunity to do meaningful work, the feeling of being appreciated, and a sense of job security are as important to workers as the hourly salary and benefits. Of course, you should check to see what other stores are paying and offer as much as you can afford in order to attract the best candidates; but, you must look beyond money and benefits to create jobs that people will enjoy.

Where To Find Valuable Employees

Traditionally, most applicants discover retail positions by reading the classified ads section of a newspaper. To attract applicants in today's labor market, ads must be larger (which can be quite expensive) and more enticing. An effective ad should romance the job and the

Gaylord Entertainment Center, Predators Pro Shop   *Photo by M.G. Hypes*

Gaylord Entertainment Center, Predators Pro Shop   *Photo by M.G. Hypes*

excitement of working in your store. Be sure to mention the salary and benefits, if they are attractive, and specify the experience and skills required for the position.

Colleges, technical schools, and local high schools often have placement offices that will post employment listings. Many schools even provide internship programs which allow students to earn credit hours for time on the job. Students placed with a store as part of a course in retailing business may be interested in permanent placement in the future.

The community may have a program for retirees looking for part-time work. Senior citizens often make excellent employees. Network with friends and co-workers for potential candidates.

One of the best ways to advertise a job opening is to post a notice on the store door or prominently within the store. Customers who have shown an interest in your store and its merchandise may know someone who would like to work in your store. Avoid broadcasting that you are short-staffed or that an employee just quit and, out of respect for your current staff, don't post an hourly wage on the job opening notice. This is a matter that can be discussed with applicants later or mentioned in a memo attached to the application form. Also including a job description and the hours required in this memo will help applicants understand what type of experience and availability are necessary for the position.

Job Sharing

Consider having employees job share all specialized job functions such as bookkeeping, stocking, and managing the store. The store and the employees will benefit from this flexible arrangement and essential store responsibilities will not come to a halt if someone is ill or on vacation. Staff members will have someone to share the workload while parents can enjoy being home when children return from school or if a child is sent home ill from school. Usually those sharing a job build a close rapport,

developing their own division of tasks, and even setting their own schedule.

Typical Payroll Costs

The following are the typical payroll costs associated with retail operations and food and/or beverage concessions:

Concession Stand Workers	8-12 percent of concession sales
Food and Beverage Vendors	15-20 percent of vending sales
Catering/ Restaurant Workers	18-30 percent of catering/ restaurant sales
Sports Souvenir Vendors	12-17 percent of sports souvenir sales

Financial Risk Management

An adverse event that is planned, or unplanned, can potentially impact an organization, operation, process, or project. It is usually defined, in negative terms, as an outcome. If a risk has a positive outcome, it will be an opportunity. However, if it has a negative outcome, it will be a problem or loss.

If the activity is planned (i.e., defined, analyzed, and controlled), countermeasures can then be put in place before the risk materializes. If unplanned, the risk can result from minor consequences to severe catastrophes. The probability of outcome is part of the analysis as well as the financial impact. (See Chapter 17 for a more detailed discussion of financial risk management.)

Bonding

Bonding is an insurance agreement guaranteeing repayment for financial loss caused to the covered organization by the act or failure to act of a third person. Bonding is used to protect the financial operations of organizations. For purposes of the sporting enterprises, bonding is intended to protect the organization from losses caused by acts of fraud or dishonesty by officers, employees, or other representatives.

To Catch a Thief

Shrinkage (theft) happens to retailers, large and small. Here are the top five ways of minimizing the damage: (1) Lock it up. Sounds obvious, but often at the end of the day, every item must be stored securely away behind a gate or glass. (2) Play traffic cop. Positioning the employee store in a high-traffic area not only encourages impulse shopping, it also discourages sticky fingers. (3) Watch who cleans up after the employee store closes. (4) Encourage employees. Establish an incentive program for employees that can financially reward them for low shrinkage. (5) Keep an eye on the future. Technology is constantly changing in both equipment and in security. For those willing to make an investment, new practices similar to ink tags and computer chips can help prevent merchandise from leaving the store.

Summary

The retail store can generate a significant consistent revenue stream. If the retail store is run well and sells the right products at competitive prices, it should turn a handsome profit and also save the customers money. Successful retail stores accomplish the following: (1) feature prominent locations that require members to pass through the store, (2) offer personalized service and competitive pricing, (3) print catalogues for employees to share with friends, (4) merchandise their goods/products (i.e., displaying goods/products in an appealing way), (5) consider themselves retail outlets, (6) sell innovative goods/ products, (7) concentrate on apparel and accessories, (8) stock regularly needed supplies, and (9) sell licensed merchandise.

In your efforts to add value, a pitfall you will want to avoid is that of adding the value you desire, rather than the value your niche customers want (Rigsbee, 1997). Become market driven, rather than product driven, by listening to your customers' needs, wants, and desires. Do this, and they will reward you with greater profitability than you have ever enjoyed before.

King (1998) suggests the proper use of fixturing will make your life easier and your bottom line bigger, especially if you keep these four points in mind: flexibility, convertibility, ingenuity, and simple common sense. A totally inflexible fixture should be used only for products that are sold in fixed quantities throughout the entire year.

Learning to improve negotiating skills is the best use of time. A person cannot make money any faster than when he is negotiating well. When negotiating to buy or sell something, a person could be making thousands of dollars per minute.

References

Ammon, R. Jr., Southall, R.M., & Blair, D.A. (2004). *Sport facility management: Organizing events and mitigating risks.* Morgantown, WV: Fitness Information Technology, Inc.

Azar, B. (1999). The top ten most common mistakes that retailers make. *Employee Services Management, 42*(3), 37-38.

Ewing, S. (1999). Music influences consumers to buy. *Employee Services Management, 42*(3), 5-6.

Helson, C.M. (1997). Keeping control when outsourcing your store. *Employee Services Management 40*(8), 30-31.

Helson, C.M. (1998). Employee stores keep growing. *Employee Services Management, 41*(3), 11-14.

King, A. (1998). Maximize your sales dollars per square foot. *Employee Services Management, 41* (3), 15-19.

Mula, R.M. (1998). Employee vendor fairs. *Employee Services Management, 41*(10),31-32.

Rigsbee, E.R. (1997). Finding your retail niche in the competitive '90s. *Employee Services Management, 40*(10), 30.

Russo, F. (2000). Marketing events and services for spectators, 151-162. In Appenzeller, H., & Lewis, G. *Successful sport management* (2nd ed.). Durham, NC: Carolina Academic Press.

Schroeder, C.L. (1999). Staffing your store. *Employee Services Management, 42*(8), 37- 39.

Schwabe, L.D. (2001). *Your Store: The Secret Weapon.* ESM Association Annual Conference and Exhibit, New Orleans, LA. April 8-12, 2001.

Shaffer, A.L. (1999). Taking stock. *Club Industry, 15*(7),49-51.

Whalin, G. (1997a). Fourteen questions to ask before you buy a point-of-sale system. *Employee Services Management, 40*(9), 30-31.

Whalin, G. (1997b). Using cutting-edge retail trends in employee stores. *Employee Services Management, 40*(1), 26-27.

Whalin, G. (1998). Effective store layouts. *Employee Services Management, 41*(2),. 26-28.

Wong, G.M. (2001). *Essentials of amateur sports law* (2nd ed.). Dover, MA: Auburn House Publishing Company.

Customer Retention: A Key to Financial Stability

Introduction

Customer (fan) retention is a key to overall financial stability for any sport enterprise. There are many competitors for the entertainment dollars on any given day in the United States. A number of years ago there was an unlimited supply of new fans for sporting events. As the price of going to a sporting event has increased and the availability of more convenient and less expensive television opportunities have increased, many sporting organizations have seen a decline in their fan base. It is estimated it costs six times more to attract new fans than to keep existing fans. Sporting organizations' profits come from retention, not replacement of fans. If the retention rate is improved, the organization can expect dramatic increases in profits due to the lower cost of retaining customers as opposed to recruiting new ones (Sawyer & Smith, 1999).

Sport managers at the interscholastic, intercollegiate, and professional levels understand how critical fan retention is in the real world. These sport enterprises, particularly minor league baseball and the continental basketball league, cannot be successful unless fans continue to purchase tickets. The successful sport managers have learned that the fan comes first and the fans are never wrong. This chapter will assist the reader in understanding how to successfully retain fans and increase the fan base in the very competitive entertainment field.

Instructional Objectives

After reading this chapter the student should be able to:
- Understand why customers (fans) decide not to renew season tickets or increase the number of tickets purchased,
- Describe how to gather knowledge from current customers to guide the renewal process,
- Outline the costs of recruiting new customers,

- Understand how to retain the customer,
- Describe how to interact with fans and deal with angry customers, and
- Describe how technology can connect with the customers.

Knowing the Customer

Wal-mart has greeters, which is nice, but they do not know you. They are polite, welcome you to Wal-mart, and provide you with a shopping cart. Ticket takers for the Colorado Rockies provide patrons with a souvenir Colorado Rockies pin in exchange for your ticket, which is nice; but, in most cases, they do not know you. Lynne Schwabe (2001) suggests customers (fans) want value, choices, the newest items, convenience, long open-for-business hours, one-stop shopping, a friendly personal touch in a clean, friendly place to shop, and they do not want hassles (the Wal-mart philosophy developed by Sam Walton). Schwabe (2001) suggests the retail manager should focus on four critical areas with their customers, including (a) identify the customers, (b) differentiate the customers from one another, (c) interact with the customers, and (d) customize items for the customers.

Identifying Customers

Identifying customers can be a challenge, but a necessary one. Customer surveys are good ways for the manager to determine who the customers are and customers' personal needs, wants, and feelings towards what is sold beyond the ticket to the contest. This is very helpful in determining how to mail or market only to those who want or need what is being sold. Surveys assist the manager in determining which customers are mailed to, frequency of those mailings, and what is offered to the customers. Finally, a dialogue develops naturally when the customers realize they are being contacted only about products and services they are interested in personally.

The customer is no different than the retail manager. The manager expects from other organizations such traits as a willingness to stand by their products, on-time delivery, knowing and remembering the customer, clearance racks, impulse items, size and selection, convenient and easy payment plans, speedy service, service with a smile, competent assistance, preferred customer notice, approachability, convenience, uncluttered and clean stores, and convenient refund policies (a hallmark at Wal-mart, the largest retailer in the world). Guess what? The customers of the sport organization's retail store expect the same as the manager does of other frequently used retailers.

Schwabe (2001) indicates the manager should consciously create a system (see Table 12.1) that enables the manager to identify customers as individuals each time the manager comes in contact with the customer.

Table 12.2 outlines the manager's customer identification task list that should be used by all managers to identify their customers.

Differentiate Customers

Schwabe (2001) suggests every manager should rank customers by their value to the store including "(1) prioritize efforts and gain most advantage with Most Valuable Customers (MVCs), (2) tailor behavior toward each customer based on needs, (3) develop ranking criteria or a customer profitability and valuation model, and (4) categorize customers by their differing needs." Table 12.3 describes how to differentiate customers.

Ranking by Value

The criteria for ranking value by managers might include: total dollars spent, frequency of purchase, profitability on sales, profits earned on referrals from customers, value of collaboration, and benefits of customer reputation with current or potential customers.

Table 12.1

Identifying Customers: A Store Information System

- Use drip irrigation: ask 1-2 questions every time you are in touch with them. The customers begin to think the retailer is interested in their needs and wants.
- Verify and update customer data and delete departed individuals. Have a "spring cleaning" day. Run the database through the National Change of Address (NCOA) file.
- Take inventory of all customer data already available in an electronic format. This should include not only the current database but also website, credit card information, etc.
- Locate customer-identifying information that is currently on file but not electronically compiled: customer books, files, special order file, etc.
- Devise strategies for collecting more information. Concentrate on identifying customers who are valuable and will be potentially valuable in the future.
- Sources of information to be gathered by an employee store information system includes, but is not limited to: name, mailing address, business phone, home phone, fax number, e-mail, position and title, account number, credit card number, birthdays, anniversaries, spouse or significant other's name, children's names, buying history, preferences (wants and needs), and frequencies of purchases.
- Other sources of information could include: billing and invoice records, sweepstakes and contest entry forms, warranty records, coupon redemption and rebate forms, customer comment and research data, sales force records, repairs and service records, loyalty user-card, frequency program with most valuable customers, user number groups, clubs and affinity groups involving the company or products, company newsletter, and list swaps.
- Verify information at least every two years. This means updating five percent of names in the database every month or so. Prepare sales associates to update automatically.

Source: Schwabe, L.D. (2001). *Your Store: The Secret Weapon.* ESM Association Annual Conference and Exhibit, New Orleans, LA. April 8-12, 2001.

Table 12.2

Customer 10 Task List

•Determine first how many customers are known.
•Devise programs or initiatives to increase the number of customers known.
•Special contests for monthly or weekly give-a-ways.
•Establish a common format for identifying customers.
•Determine how to link customer ID with all of that customer's contacts and transactions across all divisions, departments, products, and functions.
•Make it easier for employees and managers to capture customer information.
•Allow customers to enter and update identifying information themselves.
•Determine how to collect nontransactional data (e.g., phoned in inquiries that do not generate a sale).
•Develop a system to ensure that contact information is kept up to date.
•Track all "referred to" and "referred by" parameters for all prospects and customers.
•Consider programs to increase referrals by current customers.

Source: Schwabe, L.D. (2001). *Your Store: The Secret Weapon*. ESM Association Annual Conference and Exhibit, New Orleans, LA. April 8-12, 2001.

Table 12.3

Differentiating Customers

•Differentiate top customers. Take the best guess at the top five percent using sales.
•Add customers based on profitability, referrals, status in community, etc.
•Determine customers who cost money. Look for simple rules to isolate the bottom 20 percent of your customers and reduce mail currently sent to them by at least half.
•Find customers who have complained about the product or service more than once in the past year. Babysit them. Call and check up on how strategy is working. Get in touch with them as soon as possible.
•Look for last year's customers who have ordered half as much or less this year. Get in touch with them as soon as possible.
•Divide customers into A's, B's, and C's. Decrease activities with C's and increase with A's.

Source: Schwabe, L.D. (2001). *Your Store: The Secret Weapon*. ESM Association Annual Conference and Exhibit, New Orleans, LA. April 8-12, 2001.

Ranking by Need

The criteria to be considered for need might be for a community of purchasers needs (i.e., fiction and non-fiction readers) and individual needs. Ranking customers by value and need allows the retail manager to prioritize marketing and sales efforts and treat customers individually in more cost effective ways. Managers can and should rank their customers as follows:

- "Most Valuable Customers (MVCs) is the customer base that should be retained without question. The manager should reward the customers for their loyalty and make certain they receive the highest level of service.
- Most Growable Customers (MGCs) is the customer base that should be grown. The manager needs to recognize these as good customers and turn them into great ones.
- Below Zeros (BZs) is the customer who needs incentives to make it more profitable. The manager might want to consider encouraging them to shop elsewhere and become an unprofitable customer for another retailer" (Schwabe, 2001).

Finally, the employee store manager should invest more in MVCs and MGCs and less in BZs. Table 12.4 describes ways to reduce BZs.

Interact with Customers

Schwabe (2001) encourages managers to engage customers in an ongoing dialogue that ensures that the manager will learn more and more about their particular interests, needs, and priorities. Interaction with customers can be good as well as bad (e.g. conflict resolution . . . the angry customer). Interactions should minimize customers' inconvenience. The outcome of the interaction should be a real benefit for the customer. The employee store manager should adjust the behavior towards customers based on the interaction. Interactions should take place within the context of all previous interactions with that customer. Further, the general rules regarding interactions include: do no harm, treat each customer as a best friend, and never do anything to the customer that you would not do to a best friend. Table 12.5 suggests how the retail manager should interact with customers, and Table 12.6 outlines customer interaction opportunities. Finally, Schwabe (2001) suggests there are five objectives for interactions: strategic value, customer needs, customer satisfaction and complaint discovery, do not use customer satisfaction and complaint discovery to excess, and recognize interaction opportunities.

Table 12.4

Reducing BZs

There are several ways to reduce the energy and resources that you devote to your BZs:

- Reduced service. Provide fewer options, less choice, and slower methods of shipping.
- Alternative service. Use virtual representatives for sales, customer service or support.
- Charge for service. Charge for services that were once free.
- Reduce communication. Decrease the frequency of mailings to these customers or eliminate entirely.
- Encourage BZs to use the website. Seek opportunities to bill these customers less frequently, eliminate billing inserts, or identify other cost-saving avenues.

Source: Schwabe, L.D. (2001). *Your Store: The Secret Weapon*. ESM Association Annual Conference and Exhibit, New Orleans, LA. April 8-12, 2001.

Tables 12.5

How the Retail Manager
Should Interact with Customers

- Have each sales person call their top three customers. Say hello! Do not sell, just talk and make sure they are happy.
- Call the company. Ask questions. See how hard it is to get through and to obtain answers. Call competition. Find out same.
- Use technology to make doing business with the store easier. Gather customer e-mail addresses and follow up with them. Offer non-postal mail alternatives for all kinds of communication. Consider fax-back and fax-broadcast systems. Find ways to scan customer information into database.
- Improve complaint handling. Plot how many complaints you receive each day and work to improve ratio of complaints handled on the first call.

Source: Schwabe, L.D. (2001). *Your Store: The Secret Weapon.* ESM Association Annual Conference and Exhibit, New Orleans, LA. April 8-12, 2001

Customize

Schwabe (2001) indicates that the employee store manager should act on what is learned about the customer. The manager needs to use the knowledge about individual customers to customize the way they are treated. The goal is to treat a particular customer differently based on something learned about the customer during the previous interaction. Table 12.7 describes how-to-customize things for the MVCs.

- Involve the staff in the decision-making process.
- Take immediate action.
- Present a positive image and friendly atmosphere.
- Be interested in customers.
- Deliver more than you promise.
- Ask for the customer's opinion frequently, and do not fail to use these opinions after collecting them."

Tips on Maintaining the Customer Service Edge

Customers are the lifeblood of any business. Consider the following when developing strategies to regain or maintain the customer service edge (Brownell, 1999):

- "Employ friendly staff who see their work primarily as a service to others and not as a means of personal gain.
- Educate, educate, and educate again—employees can never have too much education for the job.
- Reinforce positive behavior.
- Empower the staff.
- Walk the talk—managers must set the example.

Why do Customers Fail to Renew their Season Tickets?

It is not hard to understand that the campaign to retain customers begins the day a person purchases the season ticket or sport product. The critical time period is the initial year or the first few games attended. This period of time is when most people decide whether they will stay and become a more frequent buyer or drop out. Table 12.8 outlines why sport teams lose fans. The information provided in Table 12.8 could be used by sport managers to develop strategies to eliminate the common barriers for not retaining customers.

Tables 12.6

How to Interact with Customers

- Direct sales calls. Determine frequency and substance of calls, what products or services, and what % of total sales are sold this way.
- E-mail and electronic data interchange. Determine what proportion of customers want to be connected electronically to the firm, what transactions and interactions can be accomplished online and which are online already, and what kinds of electronic commerce that can use profitably invoicing, fulfillment, delivery scheduling, etc..
- Fax messages. Determine what link fax communication has within other media interactions (e.g., print, direct mail, phone), whether outbound fax is effective for dissemination of any kind of information, and how inbound fax messages are received, routed, and managed.
- Mail (postage). Establish frequency of direct mail campaigns and tenor of the campaigns, track which customers are most frequent recipients of mail, and establish testing mechanisms.
- Point of Purchase. Determine what customer information is captured at cash registers and points of product or service delivery to customer.
- Telephone. Establish method for scheduling, executing and evaluating outbound calls, and method of routing, handling, and evaluating inbound calls and for escalating calls from MVCs.
- Website. See how easy it is to ask the company a question via the company website; determine what tools will be used to capture customer information through the website and how it can automatically be transferred to database; explore ways of tracking activities on the store site and observing behaviors of the customers; examine options for differentiating communications with the best customers so they are treated with special care; explore automated response options to frequently asked questions; be sure the customers can help themselves and are able to obtain all necessary information directly from the website; and ascertain how difficult it is for customers to update their own profiles, ascertain up-to-date product and service information, configure and order products or services directly, check status of order, and talk to other customers or users, perhaps with similar profiles or similar needs or problems.

Source: Schwabe, L.D. (2001). *Your Store: The Secret Weapon*. ESM Association Annual Conference and Exhibit, New Orleans, LA. April 8-12, 2001.

The Fan Comes First

Retaining sport fans is a challenging task in this day of high technology and multiple entertainment opportunities that can be enjoyed in one's own living room. What makes the sport fan want to return to the ballpark, stadium, arena, or rink contest after contest? What can be done to draw customers to the events? Table 12.9 outlines a sample of ways to draw customers to the events.

Sport teams are well-oiled entertainment businesses built by hard-driving sport entrepreneurs. The entrepreneurs have a deep respect for their customers. They offer amenities including changing tables in restrooms for mothers or fathers with young children, more restrooms for women to reduce the waiting, day-care centers for mothers or fathers with young children, non-smoking and non-drinking seating areas, handicapped areas, barbershops, beauty shops, specialty foods, full-

Table 12.7

Customizing

- •Customize paperwork to save customer time and the employee store money. Use regional versions of catalogues. Segment mailing lists.
- •Personalize direct mail. Use customer information to individualize orders.
- •Ask customer how and how often they want to hear from the employee store. Use fax, e-mail, postal mail, or in-person visits as the customer specifies.
- •Ascertain what the customers want. Use focus groups and customer surveys to solicit feedback.
- •Ask top 10 customers what the employee store can do differently to improve the product or service. The manager should do what the customer suggests. Follow up and do it again.

Source: Schwabe, L.D. (2001). *Your Store: The Secret Weapon.* ESM Association Annual Conference and Exhibit, New Orleans, LA. April 8-12, 2001.

Tables 12.8

Why Sport Teams Lose Fans

There are a number of reasons why sport teams lose fans. Sport managers need to be aware of these reasons so that strategies can be developed to eliminate these reasons. The reasons include:
- •They did not feel as though they were important,
- •Cost outweighs enjoyment,
- •Dirty facilities,
- •Boring food service,
- •Poor seating,
- •Inconvenient parking,
- •No luxury seating,
- •No picnic areas,
- •No non-smoking areas,
- •No non-drinking areas,
- •No place to change the young children,
- •No day care facilities,
- •No playground for young children,
- •Souvenirs too expensive,
- •No other entertainment but the game itself,
- •Team is not exciting,
- •Team fails to win consistently, and
- •No opportunities to meet the players.

Source: Sawyer, T.H., & Smith R. (1999). *The management of clubs, recreation, and sport: Concepts and applications.* Champaign: Sagamore Publishing, 137.

service restaurants, highly recognized fast food establishments (e.g., Arby's, Burger King, Hardees, McDonald's, Pizza Hut, Subway, Taco Bell, etc.), luxury boxes, club seats, mini-malls (e.g., clothing shops, shoe stores, souvenir shops, etc.), reasonably priced souvenirs and other licensed products, entertaining scoreboards, reasonable and accessible parking, health and fitness center, play-grounds and entertainment rides, free parking for season ticket holders, car detailing service, and picnic areas.

Further, the owners provide special entertaining promotions including fireworks, celebrities during opening ceremonies or halftime or the seventh-inning stretch, contests for fans prior to the game or during halftime, children wearing any kind of sport uniform gets in free, hat or bat night, team picture night, family picture with favorite player, and ladies' night. These are all examples of how a sport manager can encourage his or her fans to continue their loyalty to the team (Sawyer & Smith, 1999).

Technology and the Customer

Technology is one key to successful operations in almost every aspect of the company, including the employee store. Technology makes operations more efficient and user-friendly. The manager needs to be aware of how technology can improve operations.

Table 12.9

How Can the Audience be Increased?

The following listing is a sample of what can be done to draw customers to the events:
- Pre-event entertainment,
- Youth games at half-time,
- Special group promotions (e.g., Boy Scouts, Girl Scouts, mother and son outing, father and daughter outing),
- Special rates for groups (e.g., senior citizens, ladies' night, honor students, high school band members and families),
- Giveaways (e.g., miniature baseball bats, baseball caps, miniature basketballs, miniature footballs, t-shirts, pins),
- Scheduling doubleheaders,
- Reduced ticket fees,
- Shoot-out contests at half time,
- Event buses,
- Special days (e.g., hometown day, specific town day, specific school day),
- Student athletes visiting schools as role models,
- Clip-out coupons,
- Radio giveaways to listeners (e.g., tickets),
- Use of pep band at events,
- Team color night (i.e., offer half-price admission to anyone dressed in team colors), and
- Face-painting contest (i.e., encourage students to come early and face paint each other in an area separate from the event area, and judge the painting jobs providing prizes to the winners at halftime).

Source: Sawyer, T.H., & Smith R. (1999). *The management of clubs, recreation, and sport: Concepts and applications.* Champaign: Sagamore Publishing, 137.

Making the Connection to the Customer

Managers need to begin taking advantage of the uses of e-commerce to enhance sales. Start by developing new ways to connect with suppliers and interact with customers. An example of a new approach to connecting with suppliers is the Collaborative Forecasting and Replenishment (CFAR) system used by Wal-Mart. Wal-Mart and its suppliers have become on-line partners in inventory control at the store level.

An example of a new approach to interacting with customers is Amazon.com selling books and music over the Internet. The company had $17 million in sales in 1996 and is expected to reach $1.0 billion in the year 2003 and a projected growth rate of 34 percent per month (Penderghast, 1999).

Customer Needs

In 1998, the Georgia Institute of Technology conducted a survey that identified the average age of Internet users at 35 and stated that 81 percent of them had some college training. A significant 88 percent of those surveyed log on to the Internet daily and 63 percent are able to make the connection from their homes. An impressive finding by this survey was that 76 percent of those surveyed have already made purchases using e-commerce (Penderghast, 1999).

Customers have four basic needs when ordering products over the Internet:

- "Security —the trust that the transaction will be honest. An Ernst & Young study reports that 87 percent of those surveyed stated that they would use e-commerce if security were improved.
- Support —the belief that the sellers will stand behind the products they sell.
- Information —both about the items offered for sale and about the use of an item after the sale is completed.
- Privacy —the hope that the demographic data collected as a result of the transaction will not be sold to someone else" (Penderghast, 1999).

The manager can turn the facility into a virtual store with the application of e-commerce, particularly during the off season. Think of it as expanding offerings without the need to bring additional inventory into the facility and display it on shelves. Consider placing orders electronically and having the merchandise delivered either to the store or directly to the customer.

The provider can make agreements with suppliers to provide information about their goods and services online for the customers. When placing orders, customers can make their payments directly to the store and the provider can then forward the agreed wholesale price to the supplier.

Another aspect of the virtual store concept is that the store can offer goods for sale to employees who live and work in other geographic locations and to retirees who have moved away. The provider will be able to expand the employee customer base, as well as expand the scope of products offered for sale (Penderghast, 1999).

Customers may have other needs that the provider can fulfill by using e-commerce. For example, consider providing access to items that might be important to the members of a hobby club. Why should the employees go elsewhere to buy these items when they can purchase them through the store?

The provider may also consider providing access to recreational resources. Foster Research predicts that by the year 2000, 25 percent of retail e-commerce will be related to tourism. Customers can go through you to make travel and vacation plans. Every time a customer makes travel plans through the store, the store earns a commission (Penderghast, 1999).

Making Preparations

Penderghast (1999) strongly recommends that managers need to plan to make an investment of managerial time and store resources to make e-commerce an operational addition to your store. The first thing the provider must do is to develop a web site. This will require the contributions of personnel who are technically qualified to build your site and make it appealing to your customers.

The provider will also need to train the store personnel in the use of e-commerce. They should know how to search for and acquire information from the Internet. They must learn to advise customers for this purpose.

One managerial issue to consider is the extent to which the provider wants to rely on e-commerce software to handle transactions. This can range from a browser, which can be used to search for information, to a full-blown package that can handle all aspects of catalogue purchases. Depending on the needs and complexity of the computer network, this software could range from $15,000 to $100,000 (Penderghast, 1999).

Another concern is the trade-off between glitter and download speed. The use of color, graphics, sound, and animation on your Web page may be appealing, but it also could result in an inordinate amount of time to transmit the page to your customers' computers. This is especially true when customers access the web page at home on their PC through a telephone modem. Research the options and make the page as appealing as possible without making it too difficult to access.

E-commerce offers a challenge to all managers. There are significant advantages for the customers and a potential for increased profit, but to do it right will require an investment of both management time and store resources. E-commerce is a reality. The genie is out of the bottle and can no longer be ignored. The manager has an obligation to the organization served to meet the needs of its customers. If the manager does not, someone else will.

A Dozen Ways to Use the Web

Penderghast (1999) outlines 12 features the Internet/Intranet offers for increasing revenues, speeding customer service, and enhancing employee productivity at the retail store:

- "Allows employees to browse items, place orders on the web, and then pick them up at the store.
- Integrates and allows employees to manage decentralized mail, phone and e-mail orders, web site sales, and the physical store's sales.
- Uploads the store data economically via the web.
- Empowers the POS with company information by exchanging data with a corporate web site or Intranet site.
- Sends e-mail notification of overdue layaways and the arrival of back-ordered items.
- Facilitates inventory balancing. When one employee store runs low on an item or has a surplus of a product, the manager is able visit a web site to view the inventory of another store.
- Interfaces with suppliers' web sites to check availability, place orders, and verify delivery dates.
- Provides access to your catalogues to display, compare, and order items not carried in the store.
- Displays vendors' web sites to customers. This feature can be used to showcase the local attractions that offer discount tickets through the store.
- Shows event seating charts and allows customers to make online reservations.
- Provides access to the web sites of letter carriers for shipping and tracking packages.
- Broadcasts online advertising and promotions from the POS system."

Dealing with Angry Customers

Something has gone wrong. You can see it in the customer's face, which is turning beet red. She may be raising her voice or issuing veiled threats. Your knees feel weak at this verbal onslaught and you are frantically trying to compose a response while keeping your emotions in check.

Anyone could easily encounter this situation. In fact, you probably often do so. Handling it effectively is easier than many think if you develop and practice anger response skills. The following is offered by Ensman (1998) as a step-by-step guide to turning things around with an angry customer:

"First 30 Seconds
- First and foremost, listen. And listen immediately. No delays. Remember the triggers that can deepen customer anger—a seemingly uncaring attitude, argumentation, or officious bureaucratic behavior (see Table 12.10, Anger Triggers: What Sets Customers Off).

- What type of person is challenging you: a methodical inquisitor, an avenger, a bureaucrat anxious to catch someone breaking the rules, or a righteous victim? Try to understand the emotional type, and you will be able to gear your conversation accordingly.
- As the customer speaks, listen with your entire body. Arch forward a bit. Keep your head erect. Gaze at the customer and nod as she emphasizes key points.
- If you find yourself becoming defensive or angry, relax, and count to 10 or take a deep breath for a few seconds.
- After the customer gets the conversation going, signal your willingness to continue. Invite the person to sit down, step over to a more private location, or enter your office. This simple action on your part symbolizes your interest in the customer and sets the tone for a productive resolution of the problem.

Table 12.10

Anger Triggers: What Sets Customers Off

As you ponder this list, ask yourself, "What steps am I able to take to prevent these problems from occurring in the first place?"
- Long delays.
- Service or sales problems that result in serious customer problems or emergencies.
- Uncaring or sloppy attitude.
- Wasted time, such as excessive trips back and forth to a retailer's location.
- Failure to listen.
- Failure to follow customer's instructions.
- Broken promises.
- Financial losses which result from poor service.
- Inability to provide needed answers or information.
- Impolite salespersons.
- Feeling that you are a number and not an important customer.

Modified from Ensman, R.G., Jr. (1998). Angry customers: A step-by-step guide to turning things around. *Employee Services Management, 41*(1), 33.

The Conversation:
2-10 Minutes

- Allow the customer to blow off steam early in the conversation, and let the customer know you take all complaints seriously and you want to seek a resolution to the problem. Do not promise anything at this point.
- Let your customer know you are an impartial observer and that your immediate goal is to understand the problem as well as the circumstances that caused it. Then work with the customer to address it.
- When you must answer a question or respond to a comment, speak slowly and thoughtfully.
- When the customer raises her voice, nod and make a notation on your notepad. This is an expression of your attentiveness.
- Remember your customer's emotional profile; it is time to use this knowledge. If the customer is angry that some rule wasn't followed, for example, you might explore your procedures. If the customer feels her pride was insulted, you might praise and affirm the customer. Model your communication style in response to the customer.
- While you continue to actively listen, you can relax your body somewhat during this phase of the conversation. Here, you may put the customer at ease for the first time.
- Continue to acknowledge the legitimacy of his emotions and offer anecdotes about poor service or problems you have encountered in the past.
- Try to ascertain why the customer is bothered by the problem. A customer who encountered a late delivery, for example, actually might not be angry about the late delivery, but rather about having to change her plans as a result of the delay.

Attacking the Problem:
2-10 Minutes

- Up to this point you have said very little, preferring instead to let the customer speak. Apologize if that is appropriate. Outline in general terms how you will go about resolving the problem. If you can offer specifics, such as correcting the error, making an adjustment on the customer's account, or replacing merchandise, then do so; but be sure to underpromise rather than overpromise.
- If you cannot firmly resolve the problem, indicate your next step, such as asking another individual to look into it, investigating further, or writing a letter to the manufacturer.
- Give the customer options—two or three ways you can address the problem. This symbolizes power to the customer.
- If you have discretion in resolving problems, simply ask: "What can I do to make things right?" While you might not be able to meet the customer's exact terms, those few words can begin a fruitful negotiation.
- Finally, this stage of discussion is often frustrating and aggravating; but think of it as an opportunity to sell your responsiveness. If you can indeed make a "sale" here, you may end up with a grateful customer for years to come."

Summary

Customer/fan retention is the foundation for successful business operations in sport-related organizations. It is definitely important to maintain customers. The simplest way to complete this task is to treat each customer as if he/she were the most important person in the world.

Most often customers do not return because they not satisfied with the services or attention provided to them or their needs. A major key to maintaining customers is knowledgeable, reliable, friendly, and effective staff. The sport manager needs to work hard to continually train all staff in tactics to maintain customers. There are a number of customer strategies that need to be considered by all sport managers regarding customer retention. Not all will fit every situation or organization. The sport manager should make sure that all customers feel they are an integral part of the organization and important to the organization. The successful sport teams have loyal season ticket holders because they cater to the fan and his/her needs. The "fan comes first" attitude will make a sport franchise successful.

The manager and staff need to understand how to deal with customer complaints. The manager should be certain that strategies to deal with complaints are reviewed regularly. The complaints should be analyzed to determine the frequency of the common complaints and the resolutions practiced.

Finally, the manager must make technology an integral part of the customer relations strategy. The customer/fan of the future will be technically oriented and will expect to be able to use current technology to communicate with the organization. If the manager fails to keep abreast of the latest technology, the customers will migrate to where the technology is present.

References

Brownell, E.O. (1999). How to keep your service edge. *Employee Services Management, 41*(5), 39-40.

Ensman, R.G., Jr. (1998). Angry customers: A step-by-step guide to turning things around. *Employee Services Management, 41*(1),31-33.

Ensman, R.G., Jr. (1999). Nine steps to being a good buyer. *Employee Services Management, 42*(3), 39-40.

Penderghast,T.F. (1999). Is your store ready for e-commerce? *Employee Services Management, 42*(7), 33-34.

Sawyer,T.H., & Smith R. (1999). *The management of clubs, recreation, and sport: Concepts and applications.* Champaign, IL: Sagamore Publishing.

Schwabe, L.D. (2001). *Your Store:The Secret Weapon.* ESM Association Annual Conference and Exhibit, New Orleans, LA. April 8-12, 2001.

Outsourcing Services

Introduction

Outsourcing is big business. Successful, efficient, and rapidly growing firms like Dell and Cisco have built their businesses by outsourcing much of their manufacturing operations while retaining core managerial functions to organize their many suppliers. They have relied on outsourcers for innovation and concentrated on the few things they do best in the world. Dell, for example, focuses on a responsive customer-support system and relies on upstream suppliers for everything else, including technical innovation.

With the frontiers of innovation moving so rapidly, no one company alone can stay ahead of the rest of the world. Dominant firms have dipped into the knowledge bases of their suppliers to innovate, while entire industries from electronics to automobiles have reorganized in this way. Innovation is particularly rapid in messaging and communications-based collaborative technologies. Like the need for constant innovation,

these functions have become an integral aspect of the operations of knowledge-based firms; many are turning to outsourcers for help in keeping up.

Instructional Objectives

After reading this chapter, the students should be able to:
- Understand the nature of outsourcing,
- Describe the advantages and disadvantages of outsourcing,
- Identify the reasons for considering outsourcing, and
- Outline what a sport manager should consider for outsourcing.

The Nature of Outsourcing

Outsourcing is where a third-party service provider hosts a family of integrated applications and infrastructure services. It is a form of contractual relationship that involves transferring ownership of a business process to a supplier of the process. A key element of outsourcing revolves around the transfer of control over the outsourced process: the buyer does not tell the supplier of the outsourced process how to do the work, but focuses instead on what results the buyer wants to pay for, thereby leaving the process of accomplishing these results to the supplier. A Service Level Agreement, or SLA, defines important performance levels required by the buyer. Buyers do not lose control over the outsourced activity but their means of control have changed.

Why Should a Sport Manager Consider Outsourcing?

A sport manager should consider outsourcing for a variety of reasons including, but not limited to: a reduction in operating costs, an increase in controlling operating costs, changing management's focus for the organization to one of core business functions, accessing world-class expertise and capabilities, redirecting resources toward activities that have greater return on investment, improving production and eliminating backlogs, and accessing information and professional solutions to non-business core functions of the organization. Often, outsourcing to specialty organizations for certain tasks (i.e., concessions, software development, housekeeping, parking, etc.), even though some control maybe lost, is profitable to the organization. Further, it can, in many situations, reduce the organization's liabilities in areas that are considered auxiliary of non-core business functions.

What Should the Sport Manager Outsource?

The sport manager should consider outsourcing for activities including: accounting and bookkeeping services, financial services, pension record-keeping services, auditing and taxation services, data entry and processing, e-mail system, software development, web site development, head hunting, concessions, safety and security, risk management, and parking. These activities generally are not core functions of a sport entity and would be difficult to management without employing additional personnel increasing overhead tremendously. Sport managers need to focus on core business functions and seek outside specialists to focus on the non-core business functions. It is important for the organization to determine very early what are the core and non-core functions of the sporting entity. Once this task is completed, it is easy to determine what functions should be outsourced. Once the areas have been determined, a process needs to be developed for selecting the vendor. The case study (see page 169) established a process for the selection of an outside vendor of an e-mail system.

In-House vs. Outsourcing Operations

Russo (2000) suggests the following advantages of outsourcing include "(1) volume purchasing enables the vendor to provide quality products at reduced prices, (2) the concessionaire can return to the facility more revenue than would be possible with an in-house operation due to its supervisory experience, efficiency, expertise, and capacity, (3) capital outlays for equipment are avoided, (4) management, staff, purchasing, maintenance, inventory, storage, and vendor relations are eliminated, and (5) the concessionaire takes all the financial risks and the sport organization earns a percentage of the gross income."

The disadvantages of outsourcing are "(1) losing some or all control of the operation, (2) customers being dissatisfied with the merchandise and services offered, (3) vendor failing to recognize the needs of the customers, (4) scheduling part-time employees, (5) purchasing perishable foodstuffs or imported souvenirs, (6) determining what stands are open on a given day or night, (7) deciding whether or not the sanitation policies are enforced, and (8) determining who is stealing money, food, or merchandise" (Russo, 2000).

An in-house operation offers, according to Russo (2000), the following advantages: "(1) management has complete control of concessions which allows immediate response to the needs that may arise, (2) management controls pricing, (3) the quality of product is controlled, and (4) there is greater potential for generating revenue."

The following is the profile regarding outsourcing (contracted) and in-house (self-operated) services within the professional sport venues and major universities:

- Major League Baseball
  100 percent contracted
- National Football League
  89 percent contracted;
  11 percent self-operated
- National Basketball Association
  77 percent contracted;
  23 percent self-operated
- National Hockey League
  55 percent contracted;
  45 percent self-operated
- Major universities (estimated)
  75 percent contracted;
  25 percent self-operated

One reason many facility managers self-operate today is that they have had bad experiences with concessionaires in the past. "They were uncooperative," "they were penny-pinchers," "they were too interested in their bottom line and not the good of the facility," are often-quoted phrases heard by many who contract with concessionaires. These complaints can be eliminated, for the most part, by understanding the concessionaires' business philosophy and financial objectives. The real key to a successful concession operation, whether contracted or in-house, is the on-site concessions manager.

Before entering into any concessionaire contract, seek interested parties through a request for concessionaire proposal (RFCP). The RFCP should, according to Wong (2001), include the following components: "(1) date submitted, (2) name/address/phone and fax numbers/e-mail address, (3) principal contact, (4) historical background of company (i.e., date organized, state incorporated in, list of owners, partners, or officers, bank references, current clients), (5) full description of business philosophy, (6) full description of financial objectives (i.e., pricing strategies, quality of goods/products, payroll, operating costs, capitalization, and profit projections), (7) commission, (8) equipment to be provided for concession, (9) insurance coverage, (10) a full description of personnel training programs, and (11) advertising and promotional efforts (i.e., television, radio, print, point-of-purchase, out door, transportation, in-house, other)."

Those who decide to outsource need to be certain they have a sound contractual agreement with the vendor. The following should be included in the concessionaire contract: "(1) type of merchandise and product lines to be sold, (2) license to sell products with the company's logo, (3) where products sold are produced (i.e., in or out of the country), (4) option to renew contract, (5) right to terminate the contract with notice, (6) commission clause (i.e., percentage to company of net proceeds, reporting gross sales, schedule of commission payments), (7) insurance, (8) indemnification, (9) right to remove merchandise, (10) maintenance clause (i.e., daily cleaning, repairs, regular maintenance to facility), (11) establishment of a company-vendor merchandising committee, (12) store hours, (13) security, (14) vending machine contract, (15) monthly meeting with the manager and the vendor, (16) exclusions from the contract (i.e., luxury suites and club seats, open catering, etc.), (17) definition of gross versus net, (18) audit controls (i.e., annual audit, monthly profit and loss statements, daily event summaries, and unannounced audits), and (19) buyout provisions" (Wong, 2001).

The typical facility concessionaire commissions range as follows:
- Concession Sales
  35-55 percent
- Catering/Suite Sales
  15-35 percent
- Restaurant Sales
  0-15 percent
- Sports/Souvenir Sales
  30-45 percent
- Beverage Sales
  35-55 percent

Two Typical Contracts

According to the National Association of Concessionaires (NAC) and the National Association of Collegiate Concessionaires (NACC), there are two typical contracts used when outsourcing services — commission agreement and management fee agreement. The commission agreement provides for the concessionaire to pay the venue operator a percentage of the concessionaire's gross receipts. The concessionaire is responsible for operating the concession stands or retail store and retains all profits after the above costs are deducted.

The management fee agreement provides for the concessionaire to receive a management fee based on gross receipts. The agreement has a profit incentive clause based on the net profits. The concessionaire supplies all personnel, product, and operating supplies similar to the commission agreement. However, in the management fee agreement, the facility retains all profits after the above costs are deducted.

The advantages of these types of contracts are outlined below:

Commission agreement
- "It eliminates the risk of financial loss to the facility.
- It simplifies the auditing of the concessionaire's operation.
- It insulates the facility from daily operating decisions" (NAC, NACC, 2000).

Management fee agreement
- "It removes the typical adversarial relationships found in many concessionaire contracts.
- It provides for both the contractor and facility to share the costs of operation and in the profits.
- It encourages regular input from the facility manager on a regular basis.
- It develops a partnership of mutual interest between concessionaire and facility.
- It provides the potential for increased revenues to the facility.
- It provides the facility with greater control and flexibility for retail and food service operating decisions" (NAC, NACC, 2000).

Summary

In today's technological society it is imperative that the small- to medium-sized sport entity seriously consider outsourcing its technology needs to an outside specialty organization or organizations. Further, the sport manager should consider outsourcing many if not all of its non-core function business to outside organizations that specialize in these activities. Non-core business functions should not be allowed to overshadow core business functions for the organization.

A Case Study: Outsourcing E-mail Systems

E-mail outsourcing is where an organization turns some or all of the management, operation, and maintenance of its e-mail system over to a third party. Note that the outsourcing work does not necessarily have to be done off-site. For example, you might have an outsourcer's staff on your premises, running your messaging backbone. The hardware does not necessarily have to be on the service provider's premises; some of it might be located on your own premises.

The outsourcing industry has coined a number of terms related both to the providers of the service and to the manner in which services are provided. Outsourcing generally implies the provision of services off-site in the facilities of the service provider. Less widely used terms associated with outsourcing include "in-sourcing," "mid-sourcing," "co-sourcing," "smart sourcing," and "single-sourcing." Other "sourcing" terms have evolved to emphasize that outsourcing is not a description of a monolithic, all-or-nothing business relationship.

Reasons to Outsource

Reasons to outsource e-mail are, in order of priority:

Resource Focus

Handing off routine messaging functions permits limited IT staff to focus on core business problems.

Greater Reliability

Improved reliability in uptime of e-mail servers, redundancy, and quality of Internet connections leads to improved end-user satisfaction.

Cost Savings

At vendor rates of $1 to $25 per outsourced mailbox per month, companies can either save little by outsourcing, or as much as 90 percent of their current costs of internally supported e-mail.

Up-to-Date Content Filtering

An outsourcer should be able to do a substantially better job of controlling viruses, suppressing spam, and other message content management.

Access to Expertise

For problem solving, in view of the current scarcity of technical talent, outsourcers offer a way to tap into highly skilled messaging specialists.

Predictable Costs

Not having to budget for unforeseen service and maintenance costs makes IT planning easier.

Technical Superiority

Outsourced solutions tend to include automatic hardware and software upgrades. In addition, outsourcer staff are more likely to stay current with the latest messaging technology.

Reduced Administration Efforts

The outsourcer may have better tools than clients, helping it provide support more efficiently.

Superior Scalability and Flexibility

Outsourcing offers universal access to e-mail and makes it easier to quickly add new mailboxes across dispersed locations or to handle spikes in message traffic.

Access to New Services

Outsourced messaging specialists are more likely to offer wireless services and advanced security options than most clients.

Reasons Not to Outsource

The major reasons not to outsource are loss of control, the risk involved in the relationship, and security.

Loss of Control

Organizations that operate their own messaging system have the final say on when things get done. With an outsourced system, the customer's priorities compete with those of the outsourcer and those of other customers. Thus, for example, an important new capability may be put in place more slowly than it would be were a system not outsourced.

Risk

Outsourcing entails high switching costs. If the service provider fails to perform adequately or goes out of business, it will be necessary to migrate to another outsourcer or bring messaging back in house. In either case, user service would be disrupted and there would be substantial costs and a substantial sudden demand on company IT resources. Few if any outsourcing agreements contain a procedure for how the service provider will migrate customers systems back to the customer, or to a third party.

Security

An outsourcer's staff might read the customers' confidential e-mail or modify messages and directory entries in an undesirable or unauthorized fashion. Whenever corporate data moves across networks and resides on servers outside the corporation, customers need assurances that the data and any related account information or transactions will remain private and secure in the outsourced environment.

Other Disadvantages

Other disadvantages are:
- Administrative complexity. Outsourcing entails yet another layer of technical support with additional help desks.
- The lack of vendor understanding of company-specific problems and requirements.
- Difficult and complex integration with custom-built applications or collaboration tools, such as workflows running on top of a core-messaging infrastructure.
- Loss of in-house technical competencies.
- Negative perceptions among IT technical staff that outsiders are replacing them.
- Problems in migrating to the outsourcer's system and disruptions for end users.

Making the Decision

After drawing up a list of reasons both for and against outsourcing, company executives should rank the criteria most pertinent to their own situations and priorities. In some cases, the decision will be clear-cut; in others, those tasked with the investigation of the outsourcing option may need to delve deeper into costs and pricing to make the business case.

There are both quantifiable and qualitative factors for determining whether to outsource corporate messaging. Although cost is an important criterion in the business decision, it is not the only one. For most organizations, the ability to focus IT staff on other areas, and better reliability, are more important than cost savings.

Criteria for Evaluating E-Mail Outsourcers

We now will discuss important items that should be considered when evaluating and comparing e-mail outsourcers. The key items include competence of organization, preserved and improved functionality of the organization's internal messaging system, tailored solutions for the organization's needs, service level agreements, costs, help desk support, new applications, mobile users, security, and archiving and backup. Each of these items are reviewed, analyzed, compared with other proposals, and given a score. The proposal with the highest weighted score would theoretically be the selected vendor.

Competence of the Organization

The prospective service provider should demonstrate its operational competence. Ideally, it should have a long track record and good references from customers using the same messaging system as the prospective client. Buyers should ask about the provider's procedures for managing the overall operation with clearly documented processes for installations, backups, restorations, and new user or service provisioning.

Preserved and Improved Functionality of the Organization's Internal Messaging System

An outsourcer should preserve the functionality of a client's internal messaging system. For example, users should not have to learn a new interface, and directory synchronization processes with internal corporate systems should still operate. The new service should also bring with it new, useful features, such as improved virus and spam control.

A Tailored Solution for the Organization

Buyers should be able to have a solution that is tailored to their particular needs. For example, buyers should be able to decide which servers will run on their own premises and which will run on those of the outsourcer; which staff will use an internal help desk for Tier-1 support and which will use the outsourcer's support; and receive invoices meeting specific customer accounting requirements.

Service Level Agreements

Service Level Agreements (SLAs) for administration and support are one of the most important aspects of the outsourcing relationship. In addition to the widely used system-availability criteria of, for example, 99.6 percent up time (which equates to about three hours of downtime per month), SLA metrics should cover items like time-to-repair, system-wide performance, directory propagation, disaster recovery, and administration details of, for instance, time to add new sets of users.

The SLA should detail penalties for substandard performance, with at least quarterly, and preferably, monthly evaluations based upon a comprehensive reporting system for key e-mail performance parameters.

Costs

Service providers typically offer e-mail hosting on a per user/per month basis. When issuing requests for proposals, prospective customers should have the various respondents detail not only the features included in their base price but also charges for services above this base for such items as additional storage per user, secure socket layer (SSL) connections for encrypted sessions, virus or spam control, and disaster recovery.

Prospective customers should also determine the bandwidth costs for connecting to the provider: it is usually the customer's responsibility to provide the wide-area network (WAN) connectivity. Failure to ensure sufficient WAN throughout can degrade performance and discourage end users through no fault of the provider.

Help Desk Support

Potential customers should note the terms of the help-desk support in the SLA—the hours of support (often 24x7), the allowable number of calls, and who may be serviced—whether Tier-1 support for end users, Tier-2 for administrators doing user adds or removals, or Tier-3 for assistance to the corporate IT department. Many SLAs may just include one tier in their standard bundled service but offer the option of adding other tiers for additional fees.

New Applications

Beyond the standard offerings, customers should assess the provider's ability to support enhanced and future functionality such as instant messaging and presence detection, real-time collaboration, groupware, or other messaging-based applications that may be needed in the future.

Mobile Users

Although more complex, a prospective buyer may want to examine the SLA separately for its remote-access coverage and support to mobile workers who have special needs. The provider should have appropriate connectivity through its network partners and sufficient infrastructure of remote-access servers, dial-up modem banks, and virtual-private-network or dedicated connections to ensure the service level that is required.

Security

While SSL is the most commonly used security protocol, some companies require even more security. These organizations, in particular, should check whether their data will be stored on the same hosted server being used for other customer companies, since such shared arrangements increase the risk of unauthorized disclosure. The SLA should state the parameters for such security arrangements and the performance expectations for any filtering features for virus control and content blocking.

Archiving and Backup

Storage requirements for enterprise messaging are rapidly expanding and are likely to continue to do so in the future as unified messages, video-mail, and larger multimedia message attachments clog mail inboxes. With ever more communication flowing over IP networks in digital form, many companies now need sophisticated message archiving and back-up techniques. The outsourcing provider's hosting infrastructure should have such robust capabilities in case of server outages or corporate audits. The SLA should specify how long it will take to recover the customer's data when needed.

References

Russo, F. (2000). Marketing events and services for spectators, 151-162. In Appenzeller, H., & Lewis, G., *Successful sport management* (2nd ed.). Durham, NC: Carolin Academic Press.

Wong, G.M. (2001). *Essentials of amateur sports law* (2nd ed.). Dover, MA: Auburn House Publishing Company.

Part V

Fundraising

Fundamentals of Fundraising

Introduction

All sport organizations have the need for additional funds beyond the normal revenue streams (i.e., membership fees, ticket sales, sponsorships, luxury boxes, concessions [food, merchandise, and parking], guarantees, postseason opportunities, licensing agreements, franchising fees, naming rights, sale of stock, etc.). There are, of course, many legitimate and logical reasons why additional funding is needed to support organizations, such as program expansion, facility renewal or expansion, inflation, changing priorities, increase in unemployment within the target markets, and a decrease in the purchasing power of the consumers within the target market. Without successful fundraising, the organization could be forced to reduce or eliminate marginal programs, sport teams, layoff personnel, reduce hours of operation, close facilities, as well as other cost reductions. Therefore, it is imperative for sport managers to develop a strong financial development program focusing on a variety of fundraising activities. An effective, efficient, and diversified fundraising program will allow the organization to grow and prosper in competitive financial environments and economic down turns.

Fundraising is the art of soliciting money for charitable organizations, schools, colleges/universities, political parties, as well as other worthy organizations and projects. Many organizations define fundraising as anything that increases revenue streams, including, but not limited to: deferred giving, donations, grants, merchandising, licensing, promotions, naming rights, and sponsorships.

Instructional Objectives

After reading this chapter the student should be able to:
- Describe the function and purposes of fundraising,
- Develop and implement a fundraising program,
- Outline the characteristics of givers, and

•Understand how a direct mail campaign is implemented.

Function and Purpose of a Fundraising Program

A well-crafted, thoughtful and personalized fundraising program can play an important part in an organization's strategic operating plan. It should be regarded as another effective method of targeting and reaching out to important segments of the organization's market. It is a means of explaining the organization's mission and services. It offers the opportunity to strengthen existing relationships and make new ones. It can generate important income through gifts and bequests—income that will become increasingly important in the face of increasing competition.

The Various Roles of Fundraising

The various roles of fundraising can be many and varied depending on the organization. What is important to the donor or grantor is how the dollars are to be used and how many people will benefit from the dollars and the programs. Brayley and McLean (2001) have suggested that there are four common roles related to fundraising. The first role of the fund raisers is to "build a sense of community" among those who are interested in the organization, its values, and uniqueness. The people within this new community will become the foundation for the fundraising plan. This community will grow as the programs and activities continue to grow.

The second role of fundraising is to "invest in the people" who will operate the organization. The organization must also invest in the community that is being built to support the organization. The most important asset that any organization has is its people and supporters, the human capital. The smart sport manager will understand that investing in people will pay the greatest dividends in the long run (Brayley & McLean, 2001).

People, foundations, corporations and the government like to invest in programs and projects that benefit people directly. They like to support organizations that have a strong "humanitarian mission," as well as programming that has a humanitarian focus as it central goal (Brayley & McLean, 2001).

Finally, smart sport organizations and their managers will determine what the aspirations are of donors and establish programming that will "assist the donors in fulfilling their aspirations" (Brayley & McLean, 2001). This effort by the sport manager will allow for a greater vested interest by the donor in providing future funding for similar projects.

The Fundraising Program

Fundraising is a very big business. How can a sport organization tap into this potentially significant source of revenue? As a sport manager of an organization which has never had a fundraising program, how do you begin one? If the organization has a fundraising program, how can it be strengthened?

Initiating a Fundraising Program

The responsibility for initiating a fundraising program must rest with the most senior management of the organization and its governing board. The organization should have a development professional who is part of senior management. The development professional must have policy say. This is a very important personnel decision that should not be taken lightly.

In order to effectively represent the organization to its members and other constituencies, both internal and external, the fundraising professional must be involved in the development of policy. The development officer must have first-hand information about the direction, plans, and management of the organization. Without this status, the development officer's usefulness to the organization will be drastically limited.

Beyond the commitment to employ a development officer, the board and senior management must provide sufficient resources (i.e., time and money) in order to begin the process of establishing a fundraising program. By doing this, the board and senior management will be sending a clear signal to all parties that a fundraising program is or will be an important function of the organization. A fundraising program, if done correctly, will pay for itself many fold. A good development officer will pay for him/herself many times over. Initially the fundraising program will cost the organization a few dollars, but; after a year or two it will be paying for itself easily as well as providing an additional source of revenue for the organization.

Once established, the fundraising office becomes the organization's principal contact with the various constituencies it serves. The fundraising office works closely with the marketing and public relations entities within the organization. The fundraising office is responsible for the development of the "case statement" for the organization. The case statement is the key to success in fundraising. Its development should not be taken lightly.

Developing the Case Statement

A case statement is a clear, concise, and compelling explanation why the organization merits the support of its members and others. It explains the rationale and objectives of the fundraising program. It serves as the primary reference source for the organization's volunteers. It is the basis for proposals, which will be submitted to corporations, foundations and individuals and for related fundraising brochures. The responsibility for writing the case statement falls to the development officer with oversight by senior management and the board.

The process of writing the case statement is as valuable as the document itself. If properly done, it will assist the organization in evaluating and, perhaps, re-assessing its mission, goals, and objectives. It can help renew the organization. The key to an effective process is involvement of all the various stakeholders.

Preparation for writing an effective case statement begins with a critical examination of the organization's mission, beliefs, history, goals, objectives, and its relationship with its members/customers/fans, potential members and other parties who can assist the organization. The critical review is just that. The organization and its people must take off the make-up, look into the mirror, and honestly describe what they see and feel. The following steps should be taken in gathering the information for the critical review:

- Develop a questionnaire to be used to interview a variety of different stakeholders in and outside the organization, including top management, middle management, employees, members/customers/fans, donors and prospects, community leaders (i.e., government, business, education, and industry), and top management from similar organizations,
- Critique the mission and beliefs of the organization and other similar organizations,
- Examine the goals and objectives of the organization and other similar organizations, and
- Survey other case statement from similar organizations and communities.

It is important to define why the organization is important to its constituents and what it can offer to its clients, customers, fans, or members. Further, the case statement should clearly define why this organization is uniquely qualified to meet the needs of its constituents. Finally, the statement needs assure the donors that their dollars will be well spent on humanitarian programs and projects that will improve the community and expand opportunities.

Writing the Case Statement

Armed with the information from interviews and related research, it is time to begin writing the case statement. The statement must reflect the organization's mission and beliefs in compelling terms, which are relevant to its members/customers/fans and to other constituencies. The statement should convey a sense of vision, excitement, and purpose greater than the organization itself.

This can be accomplished by explaining how the organization fits into a larger context. For example, if you represent youth sports, the case statement should clearly indicate how this grant is part of a national effort to encourage fair play, a team effort, and reduce criminal and gang activity in the inner cities. This case statement has a strong humanitarian argument and is something many funding sources can easily support and they may want to become an integral part of the movement. It is a win-win proposition for all involved.

The case statement should be built around sections including challenges faced by the organization, history of the organization, current history and services, unique abilities of the organization to meet the challenges it faces, and plans for financial sustainability in the future.

What the Reviewers Look For in the Case Statement

The reviewers who review for foundations, corporations, and government grants, and individual donors look for a number of key ingredients in the case statement when making funding decisions, including, but not limited to:
- Description of a compelling need,
- Description why the organization is uniquely suited to implement the project,
- The purpose and mission of the organization which enables it to implement successfully this project,
- How and why the organization was started,
- What is the organization doing today in this area that would further support this project, and
- Where will the organization be five years from now.

The Donor Prospect Continuum

The donor prospect continuum stretches from the cold prospect phase to the warm prospect phase to the committed prospect phase. The donors in the cold prospect contact phase are donors drawn from a very large market base who might have a general interest in the organization. This large market is segmented into smaller manageable markets through research, demographics, and cultivation. Eventually target markets are developed for use in specific fundraising campaigns either by direct mail, telemarketing, door-to-door media, or a combination of these methods. The best method for raising money is the old fashioned method of face-to-face contact with a known party.

Once a donor has been cultivated and shows an interest, she/he will be moved into the next group on the continuum—the warm donor prospect. The strategies for this group of donors include personal contact, letter, phone call, or any combination. These prospects are segmented into either upgraded or renewed donor, special or major gift donor, or capital donor. The latter donor is treated by personal contact only—no letters or phone calls.

The final group of donors on the continuum is the committed (hot) donors. These folks, through a personal contact, will make a planned gift donor (i.e., insurance policy, bequest or trust, or gift of real estate). In this group is the "ultimate" donor, the person who has the economic resources to make a major impact on the organization if cultivated the correct way.

The Basic Elements of a Fundraising Program

The fundraising operating plan should concisely explain the organization, methodology, and goals of the organization's fundraising program. The elements of the operating plan should include: (a) management structure to implement a fundraising program, (b) volunteers requirements (see Chapter 18), (c) identification of giving opportunities, (d) overall goal and goals by source, (e) cultivation and solicitation strategies, (f) public relations, (g) prospects at the top end of the funnel, and (h) timetable.

Guidelines for a Fundraising Program

One of the biggest errors made by novices as well as experienced fund raisers, is to seek something new, different, and unique when it would be far better to adopt a program that has been successful. Why invent a new wheel? The challenge should not be to originate activities, but to be creative in the implementation of those that have produced results elsewhere.

It is vital that an overall plan for fundraising be developed using the following guidelines offered by Stier (1994):

"(1) fundraising must be program-specific;

(2) a prospect list must be developed;

(3) an accounting system must be established;

(4) an acknowledgment and follow-up system must be devised;

(5) a time table must be established;

(6) the organization will do better if it is classified as a non-profit or not-for-profit 501(c)(3) tax exempted corporation;

(7) a board of directors must be formed and a legal binding contract drawn requiring the board to review and monitor funds periodically;

(8) the overall plan should have short- [one to two years] and long - [three to five years] range goals and objectives;

(9) the goals and objectives (projects) should be prioritized;

(10) all activities, policies, and procedures should be kept simple;

(11) an attorney and certified accountant should be involved in the early stages of the fundraising program;

(12) in selecting projects, choose those that are cost-effective and appropriate for the organization to sponsor; and

(13) a training program should be established for staff and volunteers to prepare them for the tasks and a formal and informal means of appreciation needs to be established for all volunteers and community members."

Addressing Key Fundraising Issues

A fundraising program is a major commitment for any organization. Therefore, according to Sawyer & Smith (1999) and Stier (1994), it is necessary for the sport manager to be able to answer the following questions in detail:

- Is there a definable financial need?
- Can fundraising activity meet the program's needs?
- Is this the only way, or the best way, of meeting the needs?
- Is the program itself worthy of support?
- Is there adequate and competent leadership?

• Is there a sufficient cross-section of volunteers?

• Is there an organization support infrastructure capable of achieving the successful conclusion of the fundraising effort?

• Is there a support organization in existence?

• Could this organization be recognized as the official representative of the overall business organization in fundraising efforts?

• Is there a positive reputation and image of the support organization in the eyes of the various constituencies?

• How much will it cost to raise the desired amount?

• What are the downside risks and liabilities?

• Will the program be cost-effective in terms of money, time, effort, personnel, and other resources?

• What are the requirements in terms of time to reach the objective?

• Can the objectives be reached in time?

• What legal matters will be of concern (i.e., incorporation, tax exempted status, mailing permit, taxes, special permits, insurance, etc.)?

• Can the end results stand up to close scrutiny of the various constituencies?

• Is the financial and political climate conducive to success?

Key Components of a Fundraising Program

According to Sawyer & Smith (1999), Howard & Crompton (1995), and Stier (1994), there are seven components of a fundraising program. Each component must be integrated in order to develop a successful program. The components include:

• What—is the organization,

• Where—fundraising in what venues,

• Why—the case statement and an outline of justifiable needs,

• When—will the fundraising activities take place,

• By whom—who will be involved,

• Categories or vehicles of giving— what will be the categories of giving and the vehicles for giving, and

• Feasibility—how successful could the fundraising activities be?

All of the above components are essential in developing a successful fundraising program. Each component has a unique importance to the overall program. If one is missing, the program could be doomed to failure.

Common Models Used in Fundraising

Sawyer and Smith (1999) and others (Lewis & Appenzeller, 1985, 2000; Stier, 1993, 1994; Fader & Koehler, 1994; Howard & Crompton, 1995) suggest the most commonly used models for fundraising include:

• Contributor campaigns (i.e., A shotgun approach to gaining a larger number of contributors for the organization by expanding the market to include more possible contributors. Think of it as increasing the size of the top of a funnel. As the top of the funnel is enlarged, the greater the number of potential contributors that can be introduced to the organization, thus increasing the potential number of actual donors.),

• Grant seeking (i.e., government [state and federal] grants, foundation grants, and corporation grants) (see Chapter 16 for more information on grant seeking),

• Major/planned giving programs,

• Product sales (e.g., memberships, Christmas cards, agency services, group insurance, travel packages, audio and video tapes, advertising space, logo-bearing items, etc.),

• Membership campaigns,

• Special events (e.g., parties, workshops, seminars, sport camps,

Table 14.1

Role of Staff/Board Members
Grants

Board Members
- Sets annual goals in consultation with staff
- Identifies grantmakers
- Helps to cultivate grantors
- Uses influence to gain access/appointments
- Asks for gift on solicitation visits

Staff
- Develops and administers plan
- Conducts research on grantmakers
- Organizes cultivation process
- Writes proposal
- Provides information for visits
- Accompanies board member and provides information regarding visit

Table 14.2

Role of Staff/Board Members
Major/Planned Gifts

Board Members
- Sets annual goals in consultation with staff
- Identifies prospects
- Helps cultivate prospects
- Uses influence to gain access
- Asks for gifts on solicitation visit

Staff
- Develops and administers plan
- Conducts research on prospects
- Organizes cultivation process
- Provides information for visits
- Accompanies board member and provides information on solicitation visit

Table 14.3

Role of Staff/Board Members
Special Events

Board Members
- Sets annual goals in consultation with staff
- Serves on event committees
- Recruits additional committee members
- Identifies and solicits sponsorships
- Attends event and recruits attendees/sells tickets

Staff
- Develops and administers plan
- Provides staff support to event committee
- Provides research on sponsorship prospects
- Provides staff support during the event

conferences, exhibitions, auctions, shows, concerts, carnivals, flea markets, car washes, swim-, walk-, run-, or bike-a-thons, novelty athletic events [e.g., Harlem Globetrotters, donkey basketball or softball, King and his Court, etc.], rodeos, celebrity golf tournaments, celebrity tennis tournaments, wine & cheese socials, and many more),

• Person-to-person solicitation (Note: This is the most successful technique for gaining large gifts or increased giving from warm prospects),

• Single-person cultivation (i.e., a very successful technique, the personal touch is always more successful),

• Telemarketing (Note: In today's environment this may not be the best method with cold prospects but acceptable with warm or committed prospects),

• Direct mail solicitation,

• Contests of chance (e.g., 50/50 drawing, raffle, lottery, casino nights, bingo etc.),

• Annual campaigns (i.e., a campaign held annually to raise dollars for the organization of which everyone in the community is aware, such as United Way or Community Chest drives),

• Capital campaigns (i.e., a campaign done specially to raise capital dollars for a building construction or renewal. Many non-profit organizations such as the YMCA/ YWCA or Boys Club or youth sport group have a capital campaign to raise dollars for a new facility), and

• Memorial requests (i.e., a campaign to raise dollars to honor someone in the community who has been instrumental to the organization or community to built a facility, support scholarships, etc.).

Fundraising Committees

Fundraising support groups (i.e., athletic booster clubs or band booster clubs) are very useful tools in the fundraising arsenal. These groups are composed of members, parents, alumni, and community supporters who are all volunteers. They are useful for not only fundraising but also in public relations.

The sport manager needs to understand the role and function of this type of fundraising group. The manager needs to know how to establish a booster group if one is not already established. Further, the sport manager needs to understand the dangers of such groups as well. Lewis and Appenzeller (1985, 2000) outline seven commonly taken steps in the establishment of support groups that include:

Table 14.4

Role of Staff/Board Members
Telemarketing/Direct Mail

Board Members
• Set annual goals in consultation with staff
• Makes thank you calls to large donors

Staff
• Develops and administers the plan
• Contracts with vendors
  • Selects copy and packages
  • Manages program
  • Plans appropriate budget expenditures
  • Tracks and records gifts in donor database
  • Provides regular analysis of results

• "Recognition of the need for a support group;
• Communication with management, board members, and/or appropriate school officials;
• Consultation with representatives of various internal and external constituencies;
• Establishment of general principles and guidelines for the support group;
• Recognition of potential pitfalls that should be avoided (i.e., overzealous boosters, improper accounting methods, failure to establish priorities, poor relations between support group and organization, and failure to organize and plan for continuity);
• Dissemination of information about the organization and its purpose; and
• Determination of the organizational structure of the group through establishment of articles of incorporation, bylaws, and rules of operation."

Athletic booster clubs are very successful fundraising instruments in interscholastic, intercollegiate, and youth sports. They have been around for many years. They can be very useful. Yet, they can also be very destructive unless controlled by the sport manager. A word of advice to sport managers: do not allow these groups to think they can influence how a sports program is operated. The sole function of an athletic booster club is to raise money for the sporting organization.

Benefits Given to Contributors

Contributors to fundraising generally receive some kind of benefit for their donation. These benefits go well beyond a tax deduction. It is important that the sport manager understand that any benefit given to contributor has a tax consequence to the contributor. Normally the contributor's donation is 100 percent deductible if the organization is a not-for-profit charitable organization (501C). However, many of the benefits given today to contributors as a reward for their donation have a monetary value. Therefore, the value of the benefit must be deducted from the contribution. The amount of the contribution after the value of the benefit has been deducted is the amount the contributor can deduct from her/his taxes, not the full amount of her/his contribution. The smart sport manager will have prepared a list of the benefits with the value of each in parenthesis so the contributor is aware of the tax consequences prior to making the contribution. Further, the sport manager might want to provide to the contributor information about how to claim her/his tax deduction and what is legal and illegal. Finally, the manager might want a tax lawyer or tax account to review whatever document is prepared prior to distribution to potential contributors and any follow up letters sent to contributors regarding the value of their tax deduction.

Table 14.5

Role of Booster Club/Support Organization Board

• Help develop plans to involve board in fund raising
• Ensure that the case is strong
• Help develop strategies for cultivation
• Evaluate potential of prospects
• Develop expectation of giving from board
• Solicit gifts at various levels
• Involve other board members and volunteers

The benefits might include such things as:

Items that may have a value and would potentially decrease the contributors tax benefits	Item has no taxable value	Other publications	Away game ticket priority
		Mention and recognition in game programs	Access to press box
Preferred parking	Privilege to purchase tickets in a particular location	Travel with specific teams	A private booth for home contests
		Specific apparel to identify donors and contributors	Auto decal
Complimentary tickets	Special event ticket priority	Free golf at college/university course	Scholarship named after donor
Reduced ticket prices	Dinner & banquet seating priority	Free or reduced membership to college/university	Building named after donor
Special seating	Plaques to recognize donors	Health/wellness center	Room named after donor
VIP Lounge membership card	Invitations to special events	Dinner to honor donors	Perpetual award given in donor's name
Press Guide(s)	Periodic newsletter		

Table 14.6

How Board Members Participate

- Make a personal contribution
- Understand the fund raising plan
- Understand and endorse the case
- Raise money from outside sources
  - Identify prospects
  - Cultivate prospects
  - Ask for gifts

Major/Planning Giving— A Long-Term Fundraising Strategy

The committed (hot prospect) donor is the key target for planned giving. Major/planned giving is an effort by the organization to ensure its future through a long-term fundraising program. The committed donor, once identified, is contacted, nurtured, and made an integral part of a giving program that benefits the organization and the individual. The fund raiser must realize that most planned giving is deferred, with the actual donation occurring years in the future.

The common types of gift approaches for major/planned giving include:

- Bequests—are anything the former owner wishes to leave to the organization as outlined within the last will and testament.
- Trusts—are financial instruments that are established to transfer property, securities, and/or cash with little or no shrinkage due to taxes to a charitable organization. The assets can be transferred all at once (revocable charitable trust) which removes the burden of managing the assets, or over a period of ten years (charitable lead trust). It should be noted that most revocable trusts are not revoked and thus provide future funding.
- Life income gifts—are those that provide a fixed income for the organization throughout the life of the donor. There are four common types of life income gifts: Pooled income funds derived from appreciated securities and cash; Charitable remainder unitrusts derived from real estate, securities, and cash; Charitable remainder annuity trusts derived from cash and securities (upon death of insured remaining dollars payable to organization); and Charitable gift annuity (see death benefit above for organization). The latter instrument can provide a sizeable portion of the funds immediately to the organization as well as ensure future funding. All four instruments provide the donor with good tax benefits.
- Life insurance policies—that are either paid up and are given to the organization, or the organization is an owner and beneficiary of the policy, or the organization is a beneficiary of the policy. In the first two options, the organization may borrow on the policy, cash in the policy, or receive the face value of policy at insured's death. In the latter option, the organization receives the face value of the policy upon the insured's death.
- Outright gift— derived from cash, securities, real estate, insurance, or personal property given directly to the organization.

Summary

Fundraising is the art of soliciting money for charitable organizations, schools, colleges/universities, political parties, youth sports, and many more worthy projects. Many organizations define fundraising as anything that increases revenue.

A fundraising program is a major commitment for any organization. If not properly planned, it can be a resource drag. The successfully organized fundraising program has seven components.

The sport manager should spend a considerable amount of time defining the characteristics of the givers most likely to become involved in a fundraising program or project sponsored by the organization. She/he should understand why people contribute to a fundraising campaign.

References

Brayley, R.E., & McLean, D.D. (2001). *Managing financial resources in sport and leisure service organizations.* Champaign, IL: Sagamore Publishing.

Fader, H.L., & Koehler, J. (1991). *Building a Fundraising Plan.* In Fundraising for Associations and Association Foundations: Background Kit. Washington, D.C., American Society of Association Executives' Association Management Press.

Howard, D.R., & Crompton, J.L. (1995). *Financing sport.* Morgantown, WV: Fitness Information Technology, Inc.

Lewis, G., & Appenzeller, H. (1985). *Successful sport management.* Charlottesville, VA: Michie Company.

Lewis, G., & Appenzeller, H. (2000). *Successful sport management.* Greensboro, NC: Carolina Academic Press.

Sawyer, T.H., & Smith, O. *The management of clubs, recreation, and sport: Concepts and applications.* Champaign, IL: Sagamore Publishing.

Stier, W.F., Jr. (1993). Project Profit. *Athletic Management, 4*(2), 44.

Stier, W.F., Jr. (1994). *Successful sport fund-raising.* Dubuque, IA: WCB Brown and Benchmark Publishers.

Committees: Critical Tools in Fundraising

Introduction

Almost everyone has a pet cliche about committees. There seems to be no other single form of organization that takes as much derision and abuse; and yet, for all the remarks about the inefficiency and inertia of committees, managers go right ahead appointing them. Perhaps the actions reflect the fact that committees are useful. They contribute in ways that would be impossible under any other organizational structure.

A committee can be one of the most productive tools that an organization has to work with. Whether you are chairing a committee or are a committee member, you face the challenge of becoming involved in the work the committee was formed to accomplish.

Your contribution and your participation on the committee will determine its success or failure. If you participate, become involved, and encourage others on the committee to do so, the committee will be successful. Enthusiasm is contagious.

The findings of a committee have a direct impact on the decisions made by the officers and the board of directors of the club. The energy you put into your work on the committee has a direct influence on the direction your club takes.

Committees are clearly one of the most important tools available to executives. More than any other managerial area, management is charged with the responsibility for representing, involving, and serving a vast number of members. A staff that attempts autocratically to establish policy and procedure and to plan is doing a disservice to itself and to the organization.

A committee can provide a vital link with the attitudes of members and the world of actual practice. Committee members can keep personnel attuned to realities of the industry or profession and committees are an excellent training ground and screening device for budding leaders. It would be rare to find an executive who did not experience an upward spiral of committee involvements and chairpersonships on his way to the top office. Any person who demonstrates consistent ability to unify and coordinate the efforts of committees should be tabbed as having high leadership potential.

Instructional Objective

After reading this chapter the student will be able to:
* Appreciate the value of committees,
* Outline the common problems with committees,
* Describe the various types of committees, and
* Describe the role of the chairperson, other officers, and committee members.

Reasons for Using Committees

The most common reason for forming a committee is the desire for group participation to solve a problem. If there is no need to take advantage of the synergism phenomenon, then there is probably no real need for the committee to exist. In smoothly running committees, two plus two can add up to five or six or more, because capabilities tend to multiply. For a committee to feel its existence justified, its product should be something that no member of the committee could have accomplished on his own.

Some committees are necessary because the staff does not have the authority for actions it believes are necessary. In such a case, the board of directors or a committee may be responsible for providing this review and coordination of authority. Both the staff and the board should be alerted to danger when these meetings begin to look like rubber stamp sessions. Even though the board may have absolute trust in the judgment of the executive, it does him and the organization a disfavor by accepting all recommendations without question.

Often committees are brought into being for the purpose of assuring that all of the interests are represented. This is one of the nobler reasons for committee existence. At the other end of the spectrum is the ignoble, but common, reason for forming a committee: to kill an idea. It cannot be denied that many committees come into being for the unspoken, but definite, purpose of sticking some touchy or inconvenient problem in limbo rather than acting on it immediately. Sentencing an idea to sure death in committee may be a diplomatically and politically acceptable tactic, but there is definite tarnish on the ethic of the practice. If the idea is good, grab it. If the idea is bad, kill it.

Committees have their advantages in the realms of unification, representation, motivation, coordination, consolidation, and that all-important communication. Obviously, the disadvantages are of significance, too. Often the frustrations and disparaging attitudes tend to receive more than equal time when committees are mentioned. As a result, many executives minimize the use of meetings that involve the problems of the committee process.

Problems with Committees

Committees almost always cost more than the work of an individual. There is more travel required, special facilities and materials to be prepared, and a large amount of extra time involved. Members of the committee deserve to be heard and the verbal exchanges and refining processes are certainly frustrating and expensive. In some cases, though, the extra cost is necessary because of special needs or long-range benefits. The prime responsibility to involve and represent justifies the additional cost.

A committee decision has a few characteristic disadvantages of its own. If it is unanimous, there arises the concern that both sides of the question were not fairly represented. If the decision is a fair compromise, then it is probably not even a majority opinion and may well be a decision that pleases nobody.

Committees can play havoc with a timetable. Everyone needs to have his say and no one wants to make a decision that might appear to have been forced through. Strange as it may seem, one of the most common avoidance tactics of committees to forestall a decision is the appointing of subcommittees. Such an ad hoc group is charged with checking out the side issues, which may or may not have bearing on the committee's original assignment. Farmers who chase the field mice turned up by their plows may never get the crop planted.

A leadership struggle often has to be completed in the opening rounds of committee action. The bringing together of several individuals who are almost certain to be leaders in their own areas can create a situation pregnant with potential personality clashes and power struggles. Besides the time and effort that can be wasted while the group members establish the pecking order, there is also the problem of the pouting participant who refuses to play at all if he cannot be the captain. Somebody usually gets stepped on in these opening skirmishes, and it is the skilled group leader who greases the friction areas well in advance.

The disadvantages of committee effort can be as synergistic as the advantages. A group can cause more problems than any individual member could possibly have caused alone. This is especially true in the situation of a minority tyranny. Because committees are generally seeking unanimity, there are often a few members who find that they can flex new muscles. They are able to filibuster and sabotage the normal process by simple obstinacy. The hung jury and the ambiguous concluding statement are both results of minority tyranny in groups.

Try these tips for streamlining your next meeting:

- Consider the primary objective—Include only people who have a direct bearing on the issue in question. The subject matter should affect everyone who is invited.
- Distribute an outline beforehand—By creating a meeting agenda attendees can prepare to address the issues. Keeping the meeting focused means less time spent on frivolous subjects.
- Take notes—Summarize discussions, decisions, and action items. Your notes should be clear enough to keep those who could not attend in the loop.
- Start and finish on schedule—Nothing is more powerful than precedence. Concluding the meeting in a timely manner will set the standard for future meetings.

Types of Committees

Committees may be classified according to function or longevity or both. The simplest classifications are involved in telling whether the group is a standing or special committee. A standing committee performs a continuing function and operates indefinitely. This committee usually deals with organizational and operational procedures or with specific permanent features of a program. A special, or ad hoc, committee is organized with a specific objective or problem in mind and usually disbands after its work is completed.

According to function, committees generally fall into four categories: administrative, project, problem, and liaison. Overlapping of functional areas is the rule rather than the exception and some committees are involved in portions of all four functions.

The administrative committee is concerned with organizational and operating procedures of the organization. Some of these committees include executive, nominating, policy, finance, budget, bylaws, membership, and election. A committee on committees, included in this category, deals with the selection and rotation of committee members, drafting of assignments, and coordination of the work of several committees.

The project committee studies and recommends policy and action on a particular program or service. This committee reviews problems and needs in terms of the organization's program of work. Included in this category are committees dealing with public relations, marketing, advertising, research, education, statistics, government relations, and employer-employee relations.

The problem committee is appointed to explore some new problem or to study the feasibility of developing a new activity or service. It can be used to investigate or attempt to resolve some controversial question facing the organization. The value of this special committee lies in its ability to examine and review each new proposal thoroughly, reach a conclusion, and offer suitable recommendations.

The liaison committee is established, when necessary, to promote cooperative relations with other organizations, government agencies, and certain interested groups. The work of this committee is increasing in importance and value to the organization. It may serve to maintain a working relationship between national, state, and local organizations, provide a liaison between trade organizations and professional societies, bring together trade groups with mutual market interests, and provide working relationships between suppliers of materials or services and organizations constituting consumer or user groups.

Functions of a Committee

The primary function of a committee is to contribute to the efficient operation of an organization. In most cases, a committee is concerned with the communication of information and with assisting the leadership in the decision-making process by providing needed information. In order to accomplish these tasks, there are two types of committees that are usually formed by an organization— standing and ad hoc.

The standing committee is a committee that is considered a permanent committee for the organization. This type of committee is delineated in the by-laws and is populated by board members only. There are a number of common standing committees established by organizations including awards, audit, by-laws, finance, fundraising, human resource, maintenance, marketing, and nominations.

An ad hoc committee is a temporary committee established either by the board or chairperson. It is generally a committee that has a single purpose and once that purpose has been accomplished, it is dissolved. The committee is generally composed of board members and non-board members. The non-board members are added as resources or experts. The common types of ad hoc committees are capital campaign, building committee, special event committees for fundraising, special event committees for recognition, and many more.

How a Committee Meeting Is Constructed

Following is the generally accepted sequence, or order of business, that is observed for a meeting:
- Call the meeting to order.
- Roll call (sometimes omitted).
- Minutes of the previous meeting.
- State the purpose of the meeting.
- State briefly the program for the meeting.

•Discuss and resolve agenda items as they appear.
•New business.
•Adjourn the meeting.

Committee Size

The size of the committee is primarily determined by its purpose and the nature of its work. If prompt action is essential, it is best to limit the number of committee members. A smaller group takes less time to organize, communicates more rapidly, and will be able to act faster.

A larger group, on the other hand, will allow more diverse viewpoints to be heard, although it will usually require longer periods of time to do so. A larger group will be able to solve a greater variety of problems because the number of skills available will increase proportionately with the group's size.

Role of the Chairperson

The chairperson usually determines the success of any committee. Much of the chairperson's task is involved with human relations and group dynamics but there is also a significant amount of the pivotal work, which needs to be resolved prior to the first meeting. Anyone who is going to chair a committee meeting or who is responsible for choosing a committee chairperson should realize that the pre-meeting activities can be half the battle—the big half.

The smooth management and creative achievements of any committee often mirror the chairperson's ability and effort. The chairperson needs to be the type of person who readily accepts responsibility, fosters creativity, and can deal in firm but unobtrusive ways to keep the group on the topic and on the move. S/He must not be personally or organizationally in awe of the members of his committee. S/He should pass careful evaluation of his leadership potential, background, ability, and past accomplishments.

Some truly perceptive leaders have wisely disqualified themselves from chairing certain committee meetings. Such action is not a matter of modesty or fear but of honest self-evaluation and recognition of personality traits or other factors that might derail an otherwise productive group.

The Chairperson's Responsibilities

The chairperson's responsibilities and duties can be considered in five general areas:

•Planning the meetings and the methods by which objectives will be accomplished is the first responsibility of the chairperson. Many meetings wander haphazardly because they are poorly planned. The steps of the agenda should lead naturally from one to another.
•Conducting meetings, of course, is the position of the chairperson. S/He stimulates thinking, bridges gaps, and elicits innovation. This responsibility is seldom over looked though there is an unfortunate, but common, misconception that being chairperson means parliamentarian or some sort of honorary, but passive, role. The chairperson must exercise all the great characteristic skills of leadership yet never draw attention to these skills.
•Maintaining records and information is a greatly underrated part of the chairperson's responsibility. Meeting minutes are generally boring. Nobody gets too excited about motions and reports. It is easy to see this task as busywork, but it only takes one incident for the chairperson to see the importance of keeping minutes up to date and accurate and making sure that the written work will communicate accurately the work of the committee.

- Getting action is up to the chairperson. He must ensure that committee members move toward active participation. With overall objectives in mind, he must channel the efforts of multiple individuals into a unified thrust.
- Evaluation of committee efforts is an important, but often overlooked, part of the chairperson's responsibility. It may be as simple as saying, "We were supposed to do such and such and we did it. We succeeded." Whether the evaluation is sophisticated or off the cuff, the chairperson has not completed his job until the committee has some feeling for its degree of accomplishment.

Responsibilities of the Treasurer

- The treasurer is responsible to the committee for monthly budget reports and the annual budget.
- The treasurer attends all committee meetings.

Responsibilities of the Assistant Chair

- The responsibilities of the chairperson will become the responsibilities of the assistant chairperson when he cannot fulfill his duties.

Selection of Members

Once the chairperson is selected, he or she can participate in the next major activity—the selection of the committee members. The first question is how many members to involve. Many experts who have studied committee operations think five is the ideal number with an acceptable variation of three to nine. Aside from tradition and arbitrary numerology, there are several guidelines that might help in determining the most appropriate number for a given committee.

First, if prompt action is required, keep the number as low as possible, making certain that all other requirements are not slighted. Second, if the objective is an enormous amount of information, investigation, or participation, then more people automatically should be brought in. Third, all involved segments should be represented regardless of number. Finally, whenever administrative direction is the object, a smaller committee is definitely advantageous. The ideal committee "should be large enough so the loss of a member can be tolerated and small enough so that such a loss could not be altogether ignored."

Committee members must be selected for more than their ability to fill a chair, represent a faction, or constitute a quorum. Qualifications important for committee members parallel those for the committee chairperson. The following points should also be considered in viewing the total committee makeup:

- Consider the member's executive level of responsibility within his company or level of prestige within his profession. Depending on the scope and objectives of the committee, a blend of top management and lower levels of management responsibility may be preferable.
- Consider representatives of different basic types of members may be essential—the large, medium, and small company or the multi-product line and the single product line. A variety of viewpoints are important in achieving a well-balanced group.
- Ensure continuity. It is valuable to retain certain members who have previously served on the committee; however, avoid establishing a permanent clique.
- Rotate personnel. Include new members and avoid overworking those who have made a contribution over a period of time.

The makeup of certain committees may be stated in the bylaws. On nominating committees, for example, two or three immediate past presidents may be included. Two or three members at large who are not on the governing board are often specified. The executive committee, the chairperson of the board, chief elected officer, vice president, or other official may be designated. Committee personnel can be elected or designated by motions passed at membership business meetings or be elected by the organization membership from a slate of candidates. Most often the chief elected officer or chairperson appoints committee members.

Most organizations do not poll the membership periodically to determine individual preference for committee service. Regardless of how members are selected, the organization staff can play an important advisory role. The staff review can be particularly helpful in larger organizations, when a prospective board candidate's capabilities are not known by the members charged with making the decision. Staff can also supply background information and other factors to be considered in the selection.

Orientation of Chairperson and Members

Orientation of every committee chairperson is a vital responsibility of the organization's executive working in conjunction with the elected officers. The points contained in the following checklist can be the basis of an effective orientation program for the chairperson and committee members:

- Emphasize the importance of the chairpersonship.
- Fully explain the chairperson's duties and responsibilities.
- Review the committee's objectives in relation to the organization's objectives.
- Review and establish the bounds of committee activity and authority.
- Review organization policies, practices, and procedures.
- Have the chairperson review bylaws and constitution.
- Provide a list of other committees and their objectives, including names of respective committee chairpersons.
- Provide a list of members on the organization's governing body.
- Have the chairperson review current committee programs of work.
- Identify the chairperson's role.
- Provide complete background material outlining previous committee activities and accomplishments.
- Chairperson reviews minutes of previous committee meetings.
- Have chairperson review all committee projects and programs—those continuing and those in various stages of development and completion. This includes both short- and long-range plans.
- Review scheduled meetings, locations, and dates.
- Have chairperson review all current assignments of individual committee members.
- Have chairperson review roster of last year's committee and current membership listing.
- Have chairperson review criteria used in selecting new members of the committee.
- Identify staff assistance available.

In general, let the chairperson know what is expected, how the committee's work fits into the total program, and the type of assistance that can be expected from the staff, committee members, governing body, and others within the organization.

Committee Action

Once committee objectives are developed, each should be translated into a specific plan for action. The committee answers its challenges with specific recommendations and steps to be taken. To advance from the charge to the change—from the problem to the solution—certain basic steps of the problem-solving process should be observed.

Objectives must be clear for individuals as well as for the entire committee. Never let a committee member say, "Yes, I understand what the committee is supposed to do, but I don't see why you need me."

- The problem—not just the symptoms—should be carefully analyzed as the group begins its work. Any boundaries or limitations imposed by time, money, rules, or policies of the organization should be made clear.
- A plan of attack should be developed within the committee's own work. Will the members do everything together or will they delegate some tasks to individual members or ad hoc committees? What percentage of time and money are warranted by the various subtasks of the total task?
- Accumulation of facts is important. There is sometimes the temptation to deal in what the committee members think they know.
- Deadlines need to be set both for the completion of the committee's work and for the completion of each subtask. All the meetings and deadlines should be on every member's calendar right from the start.
- Solicit help whenever needed. Outside consultants can be highly valuable as long as they are brought in to help, not just retained to do the committee's work.
- Evaluation is not just for the end of the project. It can be a most valuable tool from beginning to end. Are intermediate goals being reached? Should the process be changed or improved? Is everyone participating? An objective evaluation enhances success.

- Develop a list of alternate solutions. As an intermediate step, the committee will develop and refine a list of possible activities, which would solve the problem. Some of the alternatives may be wildly impractical, but every possible solution should be considered.
- Select the most fitting alternative. The committee should also provide some listing of other alternatives judged worthwhile to avoid the retracing of old steps. Suggestion of a second alternative could keep a project from the costly bounce-back to the committee.
- Translation of the solution into action is the final step in the problem-solving process. The committee has been closer to the problem than anyone else for some period of time. It is logical that the committee should have valuable input in the actual implementation phase of the project.

Communicating Results

One of the real measures of a committee is the report and recommendations that end up trying to communicate the extensive involvements and investigations of the committee. Care should be given to the report lest it become the weak link in a strong chain. No matter how thorough and effective the committee's work has been, it is going to have to be made understandable to the uninitiated.

Meeting minutes are invaluable. Usually, the minutes are kept by the committee secretary or organization staff. Minutes nail down committee decisions, assignments, and become a permanent record for continued reference. Minutes should be prepared for approval immediately following a meeting and distributed promptly to all committee members, and, in some cases, to the governing body for review. Briefly, minutes should include date, time, place of meeting, members present, presiding officer's name, names of guests or outside consultants, decisions reached and follow-up action decided upon, formal motions (indicating members making and seconding motion) and their outcome (passage or defeat), summary of discussions to justify decisions, information on the next meeting, and signature of the committee secretary.

Summary

Committees generally have responsibility for either designing and operating a project or making policy recommendations to the governing body. Tension between committees and governing bodies usually involves issues of emotional commitment and autonomy plus the desire for ratification of committee activities by the more senior governance body.

When denying a request or voting down a committee's recommendation, a governing board must be careful to articulate the rationale for its decision. Otherwise, the committee may take the rejection personally and form an independent organization or become discouraged enough to cease its innovative activities.

Recommended Reading

Ernstthal, H. L., & Jones, B. IV (1996). *Principles of association management* (3rd ed.). Washington, D.C.: American Society of Association Executives.

Techniques for Successful Grant Seeking

Every organization with a fundraising plan in place should be seeking private foundation, corporation, and governmental grants to assist in implementing its overall programming efforts. This chapter will outline for the reader how to obtain a grant.

Instructional Objectives

After reading this chapter, the student should be able to:
- Discuss the process for seeking grants from public and private sources,
- Develop and evaluate proposal ideas,
- Describe the various funding sources,
- Prepare a grant proposal, and
- Appreciate the various grant seeking tips outlined.

"How to" Become Ready to Seek Grant Support

The first item that should be prepared is a proposal development workbook for each project an organization is seeking funding. This workbook is designed to make the grant development process effective and efficient. This approach can save up to 50 percent of the time required to prepare grant proposals. The workbook should include such sections as:
- Developing and evaluating proposal ideas—how to
- Proposal list,
- Redefining proposal ideas to find more funding sources,
- Expanded and redefined proposal list,
- Needs assessment—development of needs assessment tool,
- Documenting need,
- Uniqueness/capitalizing on differences,
- Case statement,

- Advocates—how to use them,
- Advocate list,
- Advisory committees—how to develop community support,
- Advisory committee list,
- Government funding sources—how to contact funding source,
- List of government funding programs with deadlines,
- Private funding source research tools—locating and selecting appropriate funding sources,
- How to contact private funding source, and
- Sample letter proposal.

Developing and Evaluating Proposal Ideas

When you ask someone (funder) for their support (grant), you must look at your organization and your request from their perspective. At the very least, you can try to determine what the grantor values, what the likes and dislikes are, and how to avoid those areas that may be potentially negative while highlighting the areas that make you look competent to the grantor.

The grant proposal must allow for sufficient flexibility to tailor or select alternative approaches (solutions) to the problem. By providing the funding sources with several approaches, you develop credibility and present an image of analysis as a basis for your approach.

The best technique for developing sound proposal ideas and alternatives is brainstorming. The brainstorming group should number no fewer than five or more than nine. If you want more people to participate, organize multiple groups and allow time to report out to the larger group. There are seven steps generally employed to obtain maximum benefit from this technique:

- Appoint a neutral group leader or employ an outside facilitator,
- Appoint a recorder,
- Set a time limit—10 minutes,
- State one question or problem,
- Ask each group to generate answers to the problem,
- Encourage group members to piggyback on each other's answers, and
- Record and post all answers, combining those that are similar.

It is critical in this process not to evaluate or discuss ideas until the process is over. At the conclusion of the process, all the ideas should be displayed on large pieces of paper attached to the walls of the room. Now the larger group is ready for the next step in the process.

After the brainstorming session is completed and all possible approaches are recorded and posted, the group begins the process of elimination and consolidation of the most appropriate approaches to solve the problem. This is accomplished by removing all duplicate ideas and merging all similar ideas into one powerful idea. Once the list is narrowed to ten or less ideas, the group is ready to make the final decisions.

Once the pre-proposal list is established, a detailed review begins. The key to this review is to find the idea(s) that best fit within the organization's mission and uniqueness. The decision makers now discuss such items as:

- Best match to available funding sources,
- Matching funds commitment (i.e., the organization decides what it can commit to the project),
- Space and resource allocations,
- Coordination of contact and use of funding sources, and
- Organizational mission.

Refining the Proposal Ideas to Find More Funding Sources

Do not make the fatal mistake of developing a myopic proposal. Defining the proposal in a narrow perspective will doom the project to failure. Always define the proposal in a very broad sense and this will expand the funding horizons. As the proposal is developed, think about the funding sources and how they can relate to the project. Funding sources may not be obvious when you look at only one way of defining the project. The project should be looked at from at least four perspectives:

- Subject areas (e.g., education, labor, agriculture),
- Constituencies group (i.e., type of constituency or target group),
- Type of grant (e.g., needs assessment, pilot project, seed money), and
- Project location (i.e., geographical location).

Needs Assessment

It is important that the funding source can clearly see there is a pressing problem or need that must be addressed. The needs assessment section provides the back up for the development of a convincing and motivating needs statement in a final proposal. Developing the needs assessment is analogous to a lawyer developing background information for a case. Any good lawyer will select from the database the information that will sway a particular jury toward his or her side of the argument. The purpose of the needs assessment is to provide the planners with a command of the facts to document the need. The planner will select information from this database that is necessary to develop a needs statement depending on the known viewpoints and biases of those who will read and act on the proposal.

The key to needs assessment is choosing the approach. The way the assessment is approached must blend in with the organization's operations and functions. There are five basic needs-assessment approaches commonly used:

- Key informant (i.e., testimony from people),
- Community forum,
- Case studies (i.e., example of clients in a need population),
- Social indicators (i.e., use of data from public records to depict need), and
- Survey.

Capitalizing on your Differences

Many grant seekers forget that the funding source has to choose from among many prospective grantees and that the successful grantee must stand out from the rest of the competition. Therefore, it is to the grant seeker's benefit to be different or unique in the eyes of the grantor.

It is not hard to determine an organization's unique characteristics, but determining differences is a bit more difficult. The uniqueness exercise will result in (1) a list of those factors that make the organization unique, (2) the ability to select those uniquenesses that have particular appeal to a funding source, and (3) a staff that refocuses on the unique qualities, placing the organization above the others.

The Uniqueness Exercise

The following are the instructions for the exercise:

- Give each group the following—use the brainstorming technique.

This organization has many unique qualities. These positive qualities can be utilized to convince a funding source that they are investing in the right individuals when they grant the organization money.

This exercise will result in a combined list of qualities that make you stand out from the competition for grant funds. The group leader will tell the group when to begin recording responses to question 1.

Question 1: What makes the organization good at what it does?

Question 2: Why will a funding (donor) give a grant to the organization instead of some other organization in the same field or what makes this organization a good investment or what are the advantages of funding this organization?

- Combine the responses to 1 and 2.
- Ask each person to look at the list and (1) rank-order their preferences

Chart 16.1

Needs Assessment Approaches
Advantages and Disadvantages

Type of Approach	Advantages	Disadvantages
Key Informant	• easy to design • costs very little • you control input by what you ask and whom • excellent way to position the organization with important people	• most funding sources know you have selected and included comments of those individuals sympathetic to the cause • you may be omitting parts of the population who have not been visible and caused problems that were noticed.
Community Forum	• easy to arrange • costs very little • increases your visibility in the community • promotes active involvement of the populace	• site of forum has profound effect on the number and type of representation • you may lose control of the group and have a small vocal minority slant results or turn the meeting into a forum for complaints
Case Studies	• easy to arrange • cost very little • increases sensitivity to the client's real world • very moving and motivating	• your selection of a typical client may be biased and represent a minority of cases • you must describe one real person —not a composite of several put into one example.
Statistical Analysis	• there is an abundance of studies and data • little cost to access data • allows for flexibility in drawing and developing conclusions • analysis of data is catalytic in producing more projects and proposals as staff sees the need	• can be very time consuming • bias of staff show up in studies quoted • feelings on funder's part, you can prove anything with statistics • if original data has questionable validity, your extrapolation will be inaccurate
Survey	• high credibility with funders • excellent flexibility in design of survey to get at problem areas and document exactly what you want to document	• takes time to do survey properly

1 to ___, and (2) give each individual ten points and request them to allocate their ten points over the entire list (this will produce a weighted list).

- Use the completed list to select uniqueness that will convince the funder that their money will go farther with this organization (e.g., your staff has ____ years experience; your buildings are centrally located; special equipment is available; and your needs population and geographies are broad).
- In addition to use in the grants area, the uniqueness can be valuable in (1) training and recruiting staff, board members, and volunteers, (2) developing case statements, and (3) direct mail, wills and bequests, and other fundraising techniques.

Advocates

Advocates are those people or organizations that support the organization and/or project. A list needs to be developed of advocates inside and outside the organization. This list will be valuable in selecting people to (1) write endorsement letters, (2) talk to the funding sources for you, (3) set up appointments, (4) utilize advocates' expertise (e.g., finance, marketing), and (5) accompany planners to meet with potential funders.

Advisory Committee(s)

Advisory committees are used to develop community support and link the community to the organization and/or the project. Some funding sources require the organization to demonstrate community support for the proposal. The funding source may want to see this support in the form of advisory committees, resolutions, and minutes of meetings or letters of endorsement.

Funding Sources

The key to gaining a grant is knowing the correct marketplace for submitting a funding proposal, understanding the characteristics of government and private grants, and knowing who to contact and how to contact a funding source. Once the proposal is completed, you are ready to determine your marketplace for seeking a funding source. There are three markets for funding sources: (1) federal and state governments, (2) foundations, and (3) corporations. There are four questions the planners should ask when determining where to go for funding:

- What proposals are best for each type of funding?
- How do you find out about the grants?
- Which sources are best for your type of organization?
- How do you apply?

Government grants fall into four categories: (1) formula grants (based on a set of criteria for funding), (2) block grants (federal grants to local governments), (3) contracts for services (Requests for Funding Proposal are advertised for specific programs), and (4) state grants.

There are five basic classifications for foundations: (1) community (e.g., community foundation), (2) national general purpose (e.g., Rockefeller Foundation and Ford Foundation), (3) special purpose (e.g., Robert Wood Johnson Foundation which specializes in health areas), (4) family (e.g., DuPont, Ball, or Rockefeller), and (5) corporate (e.g., Lilly or Ford Foundation).

The Final Source is Corporate Philanthropy.

Characteristics of Government Grants

An unusual characteristic of a federal grant is the requirement for matching funds. Perhaps the most imposing characteristics of federal grants are the highly regulated, detailed rules about the grant management: allowable costs, indirect cost rates, accounting requirements, and the like.

How to
Contact a Government Funding Source

The importance of pre-proposal contact with government funding sources cannot be overemphasized. It is estimated that chances for success go up 300 percent when contact with the funding source before the proposal is written in its final form. Contact is encouraged by letter, phone, and, when possible, in person. The following schedule should be used for pre-proposal contact:

- Week 1—write to two funding sources,
- Week 2—write to two more funding sources,
- Week 3—call the first two funding sources from week 1 and ask for appointments,
- Week 4—call the second funding sources from week 2 and ask for appointments,
- Week 5—follow up on appointments from phone conversations.

If you have trouble locating the names of contacts, contact your congressperson and have her/him contact the agency for you initially.

Questions to Ask Past Reviewers

It is important to be able to speak with past reviewers. The funding agency will provide a list of reviewers that you can contact. Here are a few questions to consider asking:

- How did you become a reviewer?
- Did you review proposals at a funding source location or at home?
- What training or instruction did the funding sources provide?
- Did you follow a point system? What and how?
- What were you told to look for?
- How would you write a proposal differently now that you have been a reviewer?
- What were the most common mistakes that you saw?
- How many proposals were you given to read?

- How much time did you have to read them?
- How did the funding source handle discrepancies in point arrangements?
- What did the funding source wear, say, or do during the review process?
- Did you know about a staff review to follow your review?

Making an Appointment

The objective in making an appointment is to have an interview with a decision maker in the program. The first step is to call and ask for the program officer or information contact. Second, obtain the secretary's name and ask when the officer will be available. Third, call person to person, and if that fails, ask the secretary for help. Fourth, ask the secretary if anyone can answer technical questions on the program. Finally, fifth, when you finally are connected to the program person on the phone, introduce yourself and give a brief (ten words) description of your organization. For example, "Hello, I am _____; I represent _____; the need for _____ in our area is extreme. We are uniquely suited to deal with the problem. We want you to understand that this proposal deals with these needs, and I would like to make an appointment to talk with you about this proposal and our approaches."

An alternative plan might involve any of the following: try to have an advocate set up the appointment; try obtaining congressional assistance with the appointment; or try going in cold in the week to have an appointment for later in the week.

Typical Proposal Sequence

It is important that the proposal be organized in the following sequence:

- Cover letter
- Title page
- Executive summary
- Introduction (i.e., describe the organization, uniqueness of organization, and the project)
- Problem/need

- Goals and objectives
- Methods (i.e., action strategies, person(s) responsible, and timeline(s))
- Assessment or evaluation of the project
- Future funding (i.e., project sustainability after the grant ends)
- Dissemination (i.e., information to be sent to various stakeholders)
- Budget
- Attachments (should include studies/research and tables or graphs, vitae of key personnel, minutes of advisor committee meetings, list of board members, credibility builders, auditor's report/statement, letters of recommendation/endorsement, copy of tax-exempt designation by the IRS, pictures/architect's drawings, and list of other funding sources you will approach for funding).

Writing Tips and Style

Many proposals fail because they are poorly written. The following are a few common writing tips to assist in enhancing the proposal:

- Follow the guidelines exactly.
- Fill in all the blanks.
- Double check all computations.
- Repeat anything they ask for—do not refer them back to what you consider a similar question and answer.
- Your writing style must reflect what the funding source wants and what the reviewers are looking for.
- Begin each section with a strong motivating lead sentence.
- Use an active voice and describe emotions and feelings.
- Use humor (in a non-offensive way).
- Ask the funding source a question and answer it.
- Vocabulary—shorter words are generally better than long, complex words.
- Style—easily skimmable.

- Use short sentences (no more than two commas).
- Use contractions.
- Use short paragraphs (from five to seven lines).
- Visual attractiveness—use underlining, bullets (M), use different **type** *face,* change margins and spacing, use **BOLD HEADINGS**, use pictures, use charts and graphs, and use handwriting.

Dealing with the Decision of Public Funding Source

When you send the proposal into the funding source, send it registered mail and call to be certain the source received the proposal.

You will receive a response to your proposal in several months. The response will be one of the following:

- Accepted (Send a warm, personal thank-you letter, request a critique of the proposal; ask the funding source to visit or arrange a visit to them, request any completion forms and learn what records you need to keep; and ask the funding source what the common problems with grants similar to yours are and how to avoid them);
- Accepted with budget modifications (Send them a warm thank-you letter; call and negotiate budget items; take out some of the methods; drop the accomplishment of the objective; and be prepared to turn down the funds before you enter into an agreement that will cause you to lose credibility later);
- Approved but not funded (Send them a warm thank-you letter; call funding source and ask where the proposal was stopped, ask what you could have done better; request the reviewer's comments; try to obtain additional appropriations; and ask them if they may have discretionary money left over [for unsolicited proposals]; and

•Rejected (Send them a warm thank-you letter; request reviewer's comments; ask for suggestions; ask if the proposal could be funded as a pilot project, needs assessment, or in some other way; are there any ways the funding source would assist you in being ready for the next submission; should you bother to reapply, what are the chances of another try; what would you have to change; could you become a reviewer to learn and become more familiar with the review process?).

No matter what happens, always take the time to follow up with the government funding source.

How To Contact
a Private Funding Source

The strategy is simple: (1) write a letter, (2) make a telephone call, and (3) go and visit them. The information you need to gather about the private funding source is as follows:

•The organization's current granting priorities and changes from past priorities;
•Specific information on how you should change your project and/or proposal to make it more attractive to the funding source;
•Proposal format; and
•The best grant size to request.

There are a number of questions that need to be asked of a private funding source including:

•Would you look at these approaches to the solution of this problem and comment on which are the most interesting to you?
•Last year, the amount of funds from your organization to our type of project was X, and the average size was Y. Will that remain consistent?
•What will be the deadlines this year for submission?
•Do proposals submitted early help you? Do they receive more favorable treatment?

•How do you review the proposal and who does it? Outside experts? Board members? Staff?
•Are these your current granting priorities?
•What do you think of submitting more than one proposal in a funding cycle?
•Is our budget estimate realistic?
•Would you look over the proposal if finished early?
•Can you suggest other funders who would be appropriate for this project?
•May I see a proposal you have funded that you feel is well written?
•Is the amount we are requesting realistic in light of current foundation goals?

Tips for Securing a Grant

The following are tips that will assist you in increasing your chances of securing a grant from a funding source:

Understanding What the Funding Source Wants

•Develop a common interest with the funding source, some link that will make you and your proposal immediately recognized.
•Make certain the proposal addresses exactly what the government, corporation, or foundation wants to fund.

Presentation Format

•Double space as it is easier to read.
•Use tabs to enable the reader to find any part of the proposal quickly.
•Leave a blank page at the back for notes.

Evaluating a Proposal

•When critiquing a proposal, make certain the following questions are answered:
•Has the problem been explained clearly?

- Has the solution been presented?
- Has the document been checked for typographical errors?
- Has someone made certain there are no mathematical errors?
- Have the priorities been outlined?
- Have the priorities been documented?
- Has the application been signed and dated?
- Have the pages been numbered?
- Does the text refer to studies that are documented somewhere else in the body of the proposal?
- Has all the support data been included?
- Is there a time line included?
- Have resumes been included for all personnel?
- Does the proposal state sources of future funding?
- Does the proposal state how many people will be affected by the proposal?
- Is there a description of the people affected?
- Have census tracks of the areas included that will be affected by the proposal?
- Are maps included?
- Are geographic areas explained?
- Does the proposal state how findings will be disseminated?
- Is the travel budget reasonable?
- Is the per diem reasonable?
- Is the overhead included?
- Is the equipment included?
- Is the IRS 501(c)(3) ruling included?
- Has all jargon been removed from the proposal?
- Have the words miscellaneous, et cetera, and hospitality been removed from the proposal?
- Is the proposal neat and bound?
- Is there a table of contents?
- Are there dividers for the various sections?
- Are contact numbers included?
- Is the projector's name visible?
- Is there any place within the document which refers to an appendix instead of a page number?
- Is there a personal letter to the funding sources director included?
- Have enough copies of the proposal been printed?
- Finally, has the proposal been given to someone who knows nothing about this project to learn what he or she finds confusing or out of place?

Submission

- Make certain the proposal arrives at least two weeks prior to the deadline.
- Contact the advocate(s) and Congressperson(s) that the proposal has been submitted and send each one a copy.

Summary

A fundraising strategic plan is not complete without a section devoted to grant seeking. Grants are good for seed money or start-up funds for new projects but are not useful for long-term funding. Grants are meant to be short-term fundraising instruments with a life span of one to three years.

Before an organization can begin seeking grants, it must first determine (a) its needs, (b) a case statement outlining its capabilities, strengths, and uniqueness characteristics, and (c) the problem it can solve because of its unique characteristics. The needs assessment and case statement need to be developed by an advisory committee. The advisory committee, after completing the needs assessment and case statement, will select key advocates to assist deciding the type of grant that should be sought.

The grant proposal should be broad in nature. The preparers should not be afraid to "think outside of the box" and dream. The proposal should be unique and stand out for the reviewers. The proposal must pass the uniqueness test.

There are three funding sources that should be reviewed carefully—government, foundation, and corporation grants. The reviewers need to compare the organization's needs, case statement, and problem(s) with the purpose of the grants or granting agency. There must be a clear, sound match between the organization and the granting agency.

The final grant proposal must be prepared in the appropriate format for the granting agency. It must be concise, clear, creative, and above all, well written. The grant should be pre-reviewed by a strong review team before submission. The grant request must be unique and include a strong plan for future sustainability at the conclusion of the grant.

The Booster Club

Introduction

A booster club is a separate legal entity that serves as a non-profit organization for fundraising. Although it does not exist to make a profit, booster clubs are required to generate sufficient resources to cover their operational costs and create reserves for the future. In order to accomplish this, the booster club looks to volunteers as its lifeblood. Volunteers dedicate their time to raise money to support the sporting organization (see Chapter 18 for more information about volunteers).

Fourteen trends have been identified that will affect profit and non-profit organizations in the 21st century, including (1) leadership's role, (2) value—return on investment, (3) responsiveness, (4) technology use, (5) change loops (actions that result from other actions), (6) revenue sources, (7) generational issues, (8) workforce, (9) outsourcing and co-sourcing, (10) governance, (11) competition and alliances, (12) consolida-tion and mergers, (13) globalization, and (14) image building.

Instructional Objectives

After reading this chapter, the student should be able to accomplish the following:
- Understand the importance of the organization and structure of a booster club;
- Appreciate the process for the development of policies and procedures within an organization;
- Understand the value of consolidating a booster club;
- Appreciate the role of the board members and the board president;
- Understand the role of the organization executive; and
- Develop a booster club for a sport organization.

What Is Booster Club?

A booster club is a not-for-profit entity organized to raise funds for a sport or other organization. It is generally an organization operated by volunteers and, in some cases, a few paid staff. However, at the interscholastic and youth sport levels, these organizations are organized and operated by volunteers, and in rare instances, the organization has a paid staff member.

How Does Booster Club Work?

The booster club is governed by a board of directors. These individuals are supporters of the sport organization who represent the various stakeholders in the sport organization. Each board member serves as a liaison between the stakeholders and the organization. Board members are selected by each group of stakeholders. Elected officers are president, vice president, secretary, and treasurer. The day-to-day operations of the organization are carried out by full-time staff and volunteers following a constitution and bylaws. An annual budget is approved by the board of directors. Each year the board of directors provides the organization with funds for various approved projects.

Booster Club Organization

The booster club executive (paid or volunteer) has the job of orchestrating the time and talents of many individuals to carry out the goals and objectives of the membership. This will require organization. The typical organization executive is responsible to a board of directors which, in turn, is responsible to the membership. Committees report to the board, but the committee is served by a member of the association staff. The chief executive has responsibility for the operation of the staff according to the policies and procedures established by the board. Seldom will a staff member, including all department managers, have any direct responsibility to the elected board. The line of responsibility is through the chief executive officer.

Organization is a word that can be used in a number of ways. Organization is a function of management. Managers are responsible for arranging all relationships between people, work, and resources in such a way that the desired outcome will be achieved efficiently. Organization also refers to people who are united by a common purpose. The term organization is most often used as an adjective—organizational theory, organizational charts, and organizational structure. Organizational theory is somewhat of a catch-all term, ranging from the behavioral scientist's desire to include specific phenomena of interpersonal behavior to the humanist's consideration of organization as anything having to do with the behavior of people.

People Working Together

Organization is simply a matter of people working together toward a common goal. "Efficient organization" goes a step further and involves the grouping of people and processes for the prevention of waste and for maximum productivity.

The creation of a formal booster club is best accomplished by competent legal counsel in concert with those who know the objectives of the group to be served. Qualified attorneys can prepare necessary papers for tax-exempt status as a foundation, for charter applications, constitution and bylaws, and for other necessary legal formalities for proper organization.

In this connection, it should be noted that most organizations meet the federal regulations for tax

exemption as a foundation, such as:
- Promoting a common business interest,
- Becoming nonprofit,
- Having no organizational income that inures the benefit of the members, and
- Complying with existing tax-exempt requirements and claim exemption.

Many booster clubs are incorporated. However, whether the club should incorporate is chiefly a legal question and is governed by the desires of the group. The advantages of incorporation are that (1) it sets a limit on the liability of members, (2) it provides for legal continuity of the association, and (3) it simplifies the negotiating and enforcing of contracts. While these are important legal considerations, many clubs have existed successfully for years without incorporating.

Booster Club Structure

The grouping of members, employees, and their activities into departments and committees makes it possible to manage ever-increasing complexities of club endeavors. Otherwise, it could be physically impossible for the manager to oversee the entire operation. The structure selected for the organization will determine the methods and speed by which the group can move. If all the decisions reside at the top, decision making will move slower and be less interesting for board members. If, on the other hand, the leadership is willing to adopt a structure that redistributes the decision-making responsibility, it changes the entire complexion of the group. There are many types of organizational structure. The choice should be made with care. Structure can set the pace for activity.

The organizational chart is the skeleton of the organization. It is widely used for making organizational principles work. It is a way of spelling out the relationships upon which progress depends (see Chapter 2 for additional information regarding structures and Appendix J for the Articles of Incorporation).

Forming a Tax-Exempt Booster Club (IRS Tax Code)

The booster club should be organized as nonprofit and tax exempt [501 (c)(3)]. The club should be organized for fundraising.

The club will not be recognized as tax exempt if its charter bylaws or other governing instrument or any written policy statement contain a provision that provides for discrimination against any person on the basis of race, color, or religion. No part of the club's net earnings may inure to the benefit of any person having a personal and private interest in the activities of the organization. However, fixed fee payments to members who bring new members into the club are not a part of the club's net earnings if the payments are reasonable compensation for performance of a necessary administrative service.

The club needs to submit with its application evidence that personal contact, commingling, and fellowship exist among members. Members must be bound by a common objective of fundraising. Fellowship need not be present between each member and every other member of a club if it constitutes a material part in the life of the club. A statewide or nationwide club that consists of individual members, but is divided into groups, satisfies this requirement if fellowship constitutes a material part of the life of each local group (see Appendix K for application procedures).

Booster Club
Policies and Procedures

A booster club is established to accomplish certain definite purposes for its members. In order to do so, it must know what it is doing. It must, therefore, be governed in its work by established policies. It must follow sound procedures. It is not uncommon for these two terms—policies and procedures—to be used more or less interchangeably. However, they are not interchangeable; they are not the same thing. Policies are guiding principles. Procedures are working methods.

As a means for accomplishing tasks in an orderly and efficient way, procedures are ordinarily initiated and developed by the club executive—either on her/his own or with the concurrence of the board of directors.

Policies are broader. As guiding principles, policies reflect—or should reflect—the views and thinking of the membership. The club's executive is responsible for providing wise and thorough leadership in the formation of needed new policy. He has a responsibility for initiating needed policy and promoting needed policy; but policy making involves the entire membership, either directly or indirectly, and it directly involves the officers and directors of the association, as well as the chief executive.

Policies are of two kinds: internal and external. Internal policies involve the character, purpose, structure, and operation of the organization. External policies involve the thinking and philosophy of the membership and the position of the association on problems and issues affecting the membership, the community, and the good of the company.

External policies have an influence on internal policies, and for that reason, external policies and internal policies overlap to some extent. Basic internal policies are set forth in the constitution or bylaws of the association and cover such areas as the following:

- Officers, board, committee policies—titles, officers and board tenure, size of board and number of meetings, frequency of board meetings, executive committee, board operating policies, committee structure.
- Membership—who is eligible, categories of membership.
- Financial policies—dues and reserves, financial controls, expenses, membership accounting.
- Personnel policies—retirement, vacation, sick leave, fringe benefits, office hours, salaries, employment.
- Legal policies—counsel, corporate policies.
- General policies—seals and codes, service to nonmembers, conventions.

As this list shows, internal policies look inward. The distinguishing mark of external policy is that it has a bearing not only on the membership of the association, but also on the company and the general public.

In the formulation and implementation of policy—both internal and external—here are some facts that the association executive must never forget:

- The members are the association; the association belongs to them.
- The board of directors, acting in behalf of the membership, administers the affairs of the association.
- As one of its duties, the board of directors, in response to the desires and wishes of the membership, establishes the overall policies of the association—and keeps the policies adjusted to meet changing conditions.
- It is not the responsibility of the chief executive to formulate overall policy for the association by herself/himself. It is her/his responsibility, however, and a big responsibility to know at all times what the members are thinking about and to pass this information on to the members of

the board for their action in establishing new policy or revising existing policy.

- Once policy is established, it is the duty of the association executive to carry out that policy. How well she/he succeeds in implementing established policy determines to a major extent her/his performance and professionalism.

Policies Must Change When Conditions Change

It would be ideal if all policies were consistent and enduring, but the only thing permanent about them is change. As times change, and as the goals of the association change, policies of the club must change, too. It is, therefore, the responsibility of the executive, with the help of her/his staff, to keep abreast of change and to review and recommend to the board adjustments in policy based on his or her knowledge and awareness of changes in the club's objectives and environment.

How Policies Are Determined

A host of factors interplay to affect the association in its determination of both internal and external policies. Policy determination factors might be grouped, artificially, into two broad categories: (1) the immediate club setting and (2) the total environment of the club.

The first group would include such influences as ethical and legal consider-ations, the club's charter, its constitution, its bylaws, and its articles of incorpora-tion. These documents form the founda-tion of the policies as well as many of the procedures that govern and proscribe the association in its day-to-day operations.

While these documents offer general guidance, they may not cover some points that would be desirable for the policy statement to include. Some ethical rules, though carefully observed, may not be found readily in writing. The charter or constitution may be couched in vague or general terms. The articles of incorpora-

tion may be phrased in legal terminology. For these reasons, it is necessary that a policy statement be put in writing so that policy may be understood by everyone in terms that will be easily comprehensible and applicable to the situation at hand.

The second group of factors affecting the determination of policy includes the entire political, economic, and social milieu in which the club operates. A wide variety of environmental factors force the club to formulate policy.

It is important to recognize that in the determination and formulation of policy, the factors influencing the club are not discrete entities. All of the factors that influence policy must be considered. The club membership, board of directors, officers, executive, and staff all share responsibility for the policies of the organization. They formulate policy by responding to environmental factors such as government and consumers and internal factors such as the club's purpose, bylaws, and objectives.

Policy making, then, is a dynamic, ongoing process. Policies are made as the association considers all factors and influences that may or may not endure as conditions change. As circumstances change and policies become obsolete, they should be restudied by the appropriate committee, board, and staff in light of adjustment to new conditions and new precedents. Hence, policy becomes a living body of guidelines, evolving as the needs and circumstances of the club evolve.

Problems of Policy Formulation and Administration

Policies may be mistakenly inter-preted as inflexible rules providing some relief from decision making but also possibly imposing rigidity that may stifle creativity and inhibit adjustment to change. Better policies may be interpreted as general guides that point effort toward a desired goal allowing exceptions where they are in order. Broad policies, or those with too many exceptions, may fail to offer adequate guidance in day-to-day efforts.

A policy, particularly an inner policy, may be stated as consistent and universal, yet be applied selectively. It may be an association's office policy, for example, that employees take one hour for lunch. Yet, the manager may spend more than that time at lunch discussing a problem with a board member. This same manager may require his or her staff to adhere strictly to the one-hour rule. She/he is applying a dual standard; and, where circumstances justify it, she may be right.

If problems arise, the policy may be changed to state that staff at specified administrative levels shall take no more than one hour for lunch; but even so, an occasional situation may arise that justifies an employee taking more than one hour.

In short, policy may not be applied consistently. Policies can be issued with the expectation that there will be variance in compliance. Policies may be changed to bring them into line with practice, but frequent change destroys one of the functions of policy (i.e., to provide enduring guidance).

One effective way of providing flexibility is to regard policies partly as guides that give broad direction and partly as rules to which adherence is required. A policy statement that there be no drinking on the job, for example, might be rigidly enforced. Policies may also be considered as strict rules for the operating people and only as general guides for those at an administrative level where policy can be changed and exceptions authorized. In any case, desired flexibility may be attained if two precautions are taken: (1) making intent clear and (2) establishing rules only where required.

Plainly, the amount of detail in policies should be adjusted to the level and nature of the subject or position and the attitude and ability of the person or organization affected. Where detailed prescription is required, it is well to explain why it is required so that it will be more readily accepted. It appears clear

that policy provides continuity, applying the wisdom and experience of the past to present and future problems, thereby avoiding a trial-and-error approach to each incident.

Policy contributes to consistency of behavior, which makes for a true team effort. It permits the executive to delegate with the knowledge that subordinates can apply the plan of action to specific cases in approximately the way that the executive would act under similar circumstances. When a plan of action is applied repeatedly, the quality of decision making is improved up and down the line, leaving managers free to cope with the truly exceptional situations.

Policy helps to support morale and motivation when each person knows what is expected of him. It also supports individuals when they know that their actions are supported by policy.

Policy and the Greater Responsibility of Executives

In recent years, it has become more and more necessary for the association's board of directors to delegate additional responsibility to the association's executive, especially with government affairs and legislative matters. It is not always possible for the executive to poll the board or executive committee to obtain changes in policy on issues. He must be in a position to compromise and give the association's position on immediate problems and how the association will react to them.

When policy guides operations this obviates the need for extended communication regarding each incident as it occurs. The communications channels are cleared for use in quick consideration on matters that are truly unusual or exceptional. When policy clearly and specifically prescribes or guides action, persons of lesser qualifications may function well in some positions. Further, clear policy helps to avoid lost motion, distraction, inaction, and confusion that may result when policy is inadequate. Policy also facilitates promulgation of controls to ensure that results are not left to chance.

However, any policy carries with it an element of rigidity that can hamper effort or retard action in situations where change is desirable. It also may be used by some as an excuse for inaction where policy considerations, with all their overtones, are involved. Human inertia may cause a person simply to forgo action rather than make the effort involved in changing or making an exception to policy.

The Approval Process

The making of policy should be a team effort to the maximum extent possible. Where possible, everyone affected by the policy should have an opportunity to take part in its formulation. Taking advantage of the contributions of everyone involved also enhances the chances of receiving the best the organization has to offer and should improve the product. It also strengthens the psychological commitment of those involved and facilitates acceptance of changes in policy. Neglecting of these aspects, plus dictation of every policy by fiat, means loss of the advantages of a team effort.

Obviously, there are some relatively minor policy decisions which, in the interest of efficiency, should be made without lengthy consultation and formal referenda. In the trade or employee association, these often are left to the association executive. Other policies are so significant that the board, executive committee, and members participate in their formulation. Hence, everyone makes some policy to some extent.

The board of directors predominates in formulation of major policy for the association. In some groups, an executive committee may make policy, particularly in emergencies, subject to the approval of the board. Typically, a simple change in policy requires a majority vote for approval whereby a change in the bylaws may require a two-thirds vote of the board or may require a vote by the membership.

Some organizations use the policy committee to screen proposed policy to see that it meets established criteria and is lawful. Typically, a policy change might be suggested by a member or group of members to one of the association's committees. From here, it might go to the policy committee, which could send it along to the board of directors.

When the Membership Makes Policy

Members of an association may make or shape the organization's policy in three major ways. First, they may approve or reject policy changes by vote during membership meetings. Second, they may act upon such a proposal by mail referendum. Finally, in less formal fashion, members may shape policy through influence or organization leadership.

When members vote on policy changes at their general meetings, the proposed change, typically recommended by the policy committee, is presented during a business session. The proposal should have been circulated well beforehand so that members have had the opportunity to study and discuss it. This procedure is usually spelled out in the bylaws. The proposal may be accepted as presented, accepted after amendment, or rejected. Other courses are open. The members may order the proposal to a referendum or refer it to the board of directors with a recommendation for further study. The board or the bylaws may specify whether a referendum is conducted by mail or by telegraph and may state the length of the voting period and other technicalities.

The Executive's Role

The association's executive has a major role in the making of policy. Two extremes are possible: the executive who has no voice whatsoever in policy making and the executive who enjoys and employs her/his power to the point that s/he virtually dictates policy. Neither extreme is commonplace. Both extremes have their weaknesses.

The executive who has no part in forming major policy serves an association that is deprived of the useful experience and wisdom that s/he might contribute. The powerful dictator of policy deprives her/his association of the benefits of other people's viewpoints in formulating policy. S/he may achieve apparent efficiency for a while, but her/his reign could end with a schism among members, disruption of the association, or formation of splinter groups.

Ideally, the executive will be of such competence and stature that the board of directors and members will have confidence in him/her and lean heavily upon him/her for policy guidance. Her/his counsel will be sought, and her/his recommendations will be heeded because s/he is regarded as an authority on needs, objectives, and programs. This executive will act prudently and with self-discipline, resisting the temptations of either of the extremes described above.

Most executives are in almost daily touch with at least some members. Thus, they may keep in touch with member needs and interests, but they also may be unduly influenced by a relatively small group.

Administration and Implementation

While the association executive helps make policy, she or he is almost alone in holding responsibility for carrying it out once it is made. The administration of policy requires good communications and control to see that desired results are achieved. The executive may or may not agree with a particular policy, but he must implement it or resign.

The making of policy is a relatively long-term undertaking calling for considerable research, foresight, and creativity. Administration, on the other hand, means carrying out policy by direction or action. This calls for a high degree of practical know-how and experience in accomplishing objectives, and it may be a day-to-day challenge.

Policy, if it is to be effective, must be known to those whom it is to guide. If it is not known, it cannot be effective. Ideally, those affected not only know what the policy is, but how it came to be that way and why. It is important for the association executive to understand that regardless of whether or not he agrees with the policy, the general membership will assume that it is his policy, and she or he must be prepared to take the consequences.

The Place of Procedures

There is a dim and uncertain line between policies and procedures. Each merges into the other and each differs only in degree. Sometimes, the difference between policies and procedures lies only in the eye of the beholder. An upper-level executive or board may set policy and prescribe a method by which it is to be carried out. The implementors may consider the prescribed method as policy and set more detailed procedures to guide the work of their own staffs.

Procedures, being detailed step-by-step instructions, can help in the training of new employees. Guided by an orderly statement of what-to-do-in-case, the newcomer to the position is spared expensive and frustrating trial and error in learning how to perform her/his task. S/he is aided by a statement of procedure that has been worked out by someone of knowledge and experience.

Procedure must guide, rather than misguide. The manager should seek to involve his supervisors and key employees in the search for efficiency, and all employees should be encouraged to suggest improvements and be rewarded when their ideas prove to be of worth. These suggestions, when valid, are adopted into procedures. Such a program will make use of the expertise the experienced worker develops and allow all to take advantage of the improvements s/he discovers.

Improvements mean change, and change often is resisted by those affected, especially if it calls for revision of comfortable habits. However, if staffers are properly motivated, they will accept the change, and they are more likely to accept it if they feel that they had a hand in suggesting it or bringing it about. Motivated to accept change, they can do so more easily if it is spelled out clearly in a well-worded statement of procedure.

The Role of Board Members and the Elected President

The board of directors is the association's most important committee. The director is an individual functioning as part of a unit—the board. The board will serve its association best when its members have qualities of leadership, realize the importance of a good working relationship between the association staff and its members, are aware of the importance of the public's attitude toward the association, and see the value in promoting the business or profession.

It would be nice if the club's executive could count on all directors coming fully equipped with these qualities. She/he can hope that directors will have these qualities, but she/he may have to exercise leadership in developing these skills and attitudes in her/his directors.

The director should be a leader, and often she/he is. It is probable that some qualities of leadership were evident before she/he won election to the board. Once on the board, she/he can refine and develop these strengths and techniques to make herself/himself a more active member, and she or he can take them with her/his to use in her or his own business or profession.

Participation in a variety of board projects and activities will reinforce the director's ability to approach problems objectively. Attitudes may be reexamined, biases may be brushed aside, new viewpoints taken, and new avenues opened to the solution of problems. Ability to delegate authority while retaining responsibility is an essential characteristic of the effective board members.

The success of an association depends in great part upon a live, working partnership between its members and the trained club staff. The board members can help find the consensus of member judgment and can offer the direction needed to help the association meet its obligations to the employees it represents. The board member can also work to develop the membership cooperation and participation required to make the club the accurate and authoritative voice of its company.

The director must remember that, in his role in the club, she/he represents and speaks for not merely his personal interest, but all of the club's members. The director serves as the champion of all members. A balanced viewpoint is essential to make the club useful to its variety of members with their differing emphases and interests. The director can help to provide the guidance that the association's professional staff needs in standing guard for all members and promoting the full spectrum of membership interests. The executive may find it helpful to do what she/he can to keep the director whose department is a large one aware of the needs and interests of smaller members and vice versa.

It is in the interest of the membership that the director works toward continued development of the club as the conscience of the employees it represents. A club may fail because of inadequate or inept professional management or because the directors fail to recognize or assume their obligations and responsibilities to the organization.

In reality, even a failure by the club staff is the responsibility of the board. The most important functions of the board are to motivate the professional staff executive and to be finally responsible for the plans and operations of the organization.

Often the executive helps in the nomination of board members. Her/his research and recommendations may be influential in determining policies regarding the board and its membership. Thus, the executive can help fulfill her/his responsibility to the association by making available her/his knowledge and, to some extent, her/his influence in the nomination of board members who will best serve the club. She/he must do this objectively, with the best interests of the whole association, rather than a faction, in mind.

The Ideal Director

The selection of nominees for the board of directors is extremely important for two major reasons. First, the board of directors serves as the official spokesperson for an entire employee population. As such, every member has the ability to enhance the reputation of the group. Second, directors should be viewed as a potential president. Typically, committees and committee chairpersonships serve to identify potential directors, and meetings often serve as a screening ground to identify those individuals who have the dedication and ability to become effective club presidents.

In selecting among those who may be qualified to serve on a board, a series of questions may be asked. The following guidelines might be utilized by the association executive and the director's nominating committee in evaluating potential members of the board:

- Are the potential board members interested in more than the honor? While every individual is entitled to recognition because of his contributions, selection to the board is not merely a reward for past services. It represents a serious commitment to serve the group, which makes the honor possible.
- Will s/he be able to devote adequate time to the job? Generally, prospective directors will have demonstrated interest through participation in the affairs of her/his club. S/he should have been groomed for this position through experience as a committee chairperson. S/he must also be able to arrange her or his own business or professional and personal affairs to allow time to apply to the demanding role of leadership. The nominating committee should secure a commitment that the individual will give the necessary time. There should also be a written policy to the effect that if a director misses a certain number of meetings, s/he is automatically removed from the board. Many organizations set this at three unexcused absences.
- Does her/his health permit the exertion of energy required to serve as successful directors? Only rarely should a club select an individual to its board of directors as a tribute to him during a period of declining health. There are many other ways to recognize past contributions or to show the affection and appreciation a group may have for an ailing member. Directors should possess a high level of mental and physical energy.
- Will he be able to work effectively with the association executive? In a very special way, the association executive and the elected president form a vital team to lead employees. The two individuals must be able to communicate effectively and relate to each other. The same requirement applies to all members of the board.
- Can s/he stand the limelight and criticism of leadership? Popularity is required for any individual to achieve leadership. Popularity, however, cannot be more important to an individual than his judgment and integrity. S/he must be able to accept the limelight graciously without becoming pompous or self-

centered and s/he must be willing to tolerate the criticism, which is inevitable when change or new courses of action are considered. In almost every group, there is a dissident minority that can immobilize the entire organization if leaders are not willing to move ahead with what they believe is best for the entire group.

• Can s/he communicate effectively? The entire board of directors, and especially its president, must be able to communicate effectively with other directors, with the association as a whole, and with the public as they represent their colleagues. A deep thinker who cannot communicate is not likely to contribute significantly in her/his role as director.

• Can the director subordinate her/his departmental, personal, or business biases for the good of the group? Since the board acts and speaks for all employees, directors cannot be special pleaders for her/his interests. S/he does, however, make use of his experience and may be expected to reflect the special feelings of her or his own constituency. At the same time, she/he is expected to put the interest of the employee first. There should be little concern about hidden motives since each director is assumed to have made her/his individual interests subordinate to the good of her or his group.

• Does her/his personal conduct reflect favorably upon the group? Although the association has no interest in or right to meddle in the personal affairs of its members, a nominating committee should remember that the association leaders represent the group at times other than during board meetings. Members who are notorious for their unorthodox behavior may prove more irritating or embarrassing than amusing.

• Will s/he be able to step down after his term of office? Every director cannot become president, and every president has a limited term. An individual selected for leadership should be capable of playing an important role after her/his term of office has expired. Individuals should be selected in view of their potential continuing contributions as elder statesmen.

The Director Should Be a Proven Performer

High integrity and an understanding of the ethics of his community and his calling are, of course, prime requisites in a director. High on the list of desirable qualifications is business experience, knowledge, and capability. The director should be a proven performer, active in her or his business or profession.

Having the other necessary qualities, a newcomer to the board may also have been selected because he offers balance-bringing abilities that complement the strengths and weaknesses of those already on the board. Even the best director must vacate her or his position after a reason-able time. A portion of the board—frequently about one-third—should be elected each year. There should be a constitutional limit on length of service. This can bring fresh ideas, attitudes, and approaches while preserving stability and continuity.

In a constructive way, the board should be critical of the association, seeking continually to make it more useful to its members and thereby of better service to the public. Representing the highest aims of its industry or profession, the board constantly keeps itself open to new ideas.

To do its best work, the board must operate in a free atmosphere where there is uninhibited, though reasonably polite, exposition of feelings and ideas. Open exchange and honest debate are called for. Once this discussion stage is past and a decision is made, the entire board must work to make that decision effective. The director's efforts are aimed toward influencing the decision and toward carrying out that decision, once made, rather than frustrating the board's effort.

The Role of the Executive

Mutual respect and support are the foundations for a productive working relationship between the board and the executive. The executive has the responsibility of providing information to her/his board that is as complete as s/he can possibly make it. No sycophant, she/he respects herself/himself and her/his calling enough to offer ideas, suggestions, guidance, and proposals when s/he sees a possibility of improving the association and its service. The conscientious executive will develop the best proposals s/he can and will bid for board support of these proposals. Board members must consider this information and these recommendations in the light of their own knowledge, experience, and observations.

The board member and the professional staff must believe profoundly in the validity of the group process to work effectively as a member of a board. Group work, with all of its shortcomings, is the essence of voluntary organization. High regard for the dignity of the individual, including herself/himself, is required of each participant. Each must see the other as a unique person—an individual to be regarded as such, rather than stereotyped or categorized.

Current programs, structure, and staff should be evaluated periodically with changes made as required. The aid of outside consultants may be needed in such an evaluation, but the ultimate decision should reflect analysis and attention from each director. Board members must have full information about the club's work if they are to function effectively. Detailed reports to directors in advance of meetings and minutes of committee meetings help to keep the board informed.

Directors, especially the board chairman, should maintain a close relationship with the club executive, each keeping the other posted on all developments. Board members should also become acquainted with other staff people, even though lines of responsibility pass through conventional channels.

The board of directors deliberates— at least it should. The best deliberation occurs in an environment of comfort rather than tension. At board meetings, the atmosphere should be relaxed, discussion should not jell too quickly, and shoot-from-the-hip motions that quickly polarize the group should be avoided. The aim is to extract the most that each individual can offer. Tension and formalities that inhibit such offerings should be eliminated wherever possible (see Appendix L for tips in grooming new directors).

Grooming the New President

Generally, the elected president will assume her/his position after some experience on the board of directors. Thus s/he will be familiar with the goals, problems, hopes, and fears of the association and its members. In addition, s/he probably has some general idea of the scope of his job and the demands s/he can expect it to make on her/him.

There are, however, sound reasons for providing the president and those around him with some precise indication of what responsibility goes where. The club's constitution and bylaws offer guidance and, to some extent, define responsibilities. So does established custom, which may be more or less well known.

Without some effective guidance, the new president's eagerness and energy may be wasted. S/he should know where, when, and how to apply her/his efforts. The better organized and more readily available this knowledge is, the more useful it will be. Often, it's better to put procedures including custom, objectives, policies, and responsibilities in writing.

A handbook prepared by the club's chief executive, with the help of current and past presidents, can be of inestimable help to the new president. Such a handbook can be a most important tool in the orientation of the new president.

The president's handbook should be designed for the particular work and association, bearing in mind, the organization's objectives, policies, and resources. The handbook should encompass the presidential guidelines set out in the constitution and bylaws, but it should elaborate on these, covering significant points that are omitted in the bylaws. Is a particular responsibility the president's, or does it go to the board of directors or to the executive? The handbook should pin down responsibility. There also may be statements of, and comment upon, such general responsibilities as leadership and the need for delegation of authority. An outline or list of the services and resources available to the president from the club's main office and its staff also might be included. It is entirely possible that the staff could apprise her/him of the limitations on such things as staff resources and facilities.

The handbook can define the president's relationship with other officers and directors, the staff, committees and their chairperson, individual members, other organizations, and the press. Encroachments into the responsibilities of these groups should be eliminated if possible. Yet presidential influence and leadership should come to bear on those with whom she/he comes in contact. The handbook should include a policy manual of the club, a complete listing of all policies drawn from the bylaws, board minutes, and various meetings of the association. Procedures also may be set out, in appropriate detail, for handling complaints from members, speech preparation, expense reimbursements, appointments, and publicity.

The club's chief executive should have an important part in preparation of the handbook, for he probably has experience in dealing with a series of presidents with a variety of interests, needs, temperaments, and abilities.

While such a handbook can be infinitely useful to the president, it is not the complete "how-to-succeed-as-president-in-one-easy-lesson." More is needed.

The new president also may benefit from talks with past presidents, the executive, and other staff members. Whatever the method, he should be equipped to learn from past successes and failures, take advantage of new opportunities, and help the association and its members adjust to new conditions.

Summary

It is the responsibility of the board to maintain an environment for performance by the entire club staff and membership. Every board member shares this responsibility. It is especially important that the board understand its place in the structure of the association. Directors should know the association, of course, but they should also know the management role. The full relationship among the board, the members, and the executive should be understood clearly.

As a plural executive, the board has innate problems, weaknesses, and strengths, which should be recognized. Being a group, a board should be used where a group can apply its best effort—in deliberation, stimulation through interchange, bringing to bear different points of view, and probing deeply into problems.

The board of directors shapes the association's personality, defines its goals, charts its future, nurtures, strengthens, and protects it. The board does this by representing the needs, desires, and attitudes of association members, but members can apply their influence most effectively only if they are well informed on developments and attitudes within and without the association. It is the board's responsibility to do what it can to keep information flowing both ways between directors and members.

In deciding a course and selecting methods of action, the board functions best if it makes full use of all the resources available to it. Especially, it should look to its chief staff executive for there is hardly an area where he cannot provide advice, information, or service.

The directors have a major hand in shaping the public's attitude toward the industry or profession. They do this best by being of genuine, efficient, and conscientious service to the association, to its members, and ultimately to the public.

Volunteers: The Soldiers in Fundraising and Game Management

Introduction

Prior to 1970, relatively little was known about the scope and size of the volunteer sector. Since then, several major national surveys have provided information useful in drawing a profile of the volunteer corps in America (see Table 18.1 outlining characteristics of volunteers).

In youth, interscholastic, and intercollegiate sports, volunteers are very important to the successful operations of these programs. The volunteers are ticket sellers, ticket takers, ushers, swimming and track and field officials, youth sport coaches, and fundraisers. If volunteers failed to be involved in these programs, these programs would not exist. Not-for-profit youth organizations would never be able to employ adequate numbers of paid personnel to operate the various youth sport programs. This chapter will outline everything the sport manager will need to know about volunteers and how to manage the volunteer corps.

Learning Objectives

After reading this chapter, the student should understand how to:
- Deal with volunteers,
- Recognize and recruit volunteers,
- Develop a volunteer personnel management system,
- Design an orientation and training program for volunteers,
- Supervise volunteers, and
- Provide appropriate recognition to volunteers.

Dealing With Volunteers

Before beginning to understand what a manager should put into place regarding the management of volunteers, it is important to understand the characteristics of volunteers as outlined above. Further, the manager needs to consider these characteristics below when dealing

Table 18.1

Characteristics of Volunteers

A recent Gallup Poll outlined the following characteristics relative to volunteers:
- Nearly half of all Americas over 14 years old volunteer (approximately 89 million).
- Volunteers contribute an average of 5.3 hours per week up from 2.6 in 1980, 3.5 in 1985, 4.4 in 1990, and 4.9 in 1995.
- Volunteer activities range from informal volunteering (i.e., helping a neighbor) to more formal volunteering (i.e., working for a non-profit organization, such as Little League, Red Cross, Salvation Army, American Heart Association, Church, YMCA, YWCA, Boy Scouts, Girl Scouts, Boys and Girls Clubs of America). The major areas of volunteering have been religion (23 percent), informal volunteering (19 percent), education (13 percent), youth sports organizations (13 percent), general funding-raising (11 percent), amateur sporting events (11 percent), and recreation (10 percent).
- Most volunteers (80 percent) contribute time to charitable organizations, 17 percent contribute time to governmental organizations, and three percent reported contributing time to for-profit organizations.
- Volunteers do a variety of jobs including, but not limited to, assisting the elderly, performing caretaker duties, coaching youth sports, member and/or officer of the board of directors, financial consultant, and being an officer of an organization. The most popular form of volunteer work was assisting the elderly, the handicapped, or a social welfare recipient, or working for non-profit services agencies and youth sport organizations.
- The primary reasons given for becoming volunteers were wanting to do something useful to help others (52 percent), having an interest in the work or activity (36 percent), or enjoying the work (32 percent).
- People who volunteer their time are much more likely than non-volunteers to donate money to charitable organizations. They are also far more likely to donate money in the area in which they volunteer.

Other characteristics associated with volunteering include:
- The prime years for volunteering are from about age 27-29 through retirement, with the peak being 35-49 years of age.
- Overall, more women than men volunteer.
- Working class ("blue collar") urban people tend to be active in their churches, unions, lodges, and sport clubs. Middle and upper-middle class people tend to be active in general interest areas, career-related business and professional, community-oriented, service-oriented, educational, cultural, and political or pressure groups.
- Married individuals participate more extensively in volunteering than any other marital status group. This group is followed by widows and widowers, single people, divorced, and separated people.
- Having children is associated with higher rates of volunteering and having children of school age produces even greater involvement in volunteering.
- The majority of volunteers are white.

with volunteers. These characteristics have been identified by Meagher (1995), Stier (1993), and Heidrich (1990) including:

- The 25 percent rule—25 percent of the volunteers will do nearly all that is asked of them;
- The 20 percent rule—refers to those individuals who are truly effective, who are the real producers and "result-getters,"
- Volunteers have feelings, so make them feel valuable and wanted. Treat them with respect, and provide them with special privileges to reward them for their contributions;
- Volunteers have needs and wants. Satisfy them;
- Volunteers have suggestions, seek the input;
- Volunteers have specific interests. Provide options, and alternatives for them to do;,
- Volunteers have specific competencies. Recognize these skills and do not attempt to place square pegs in round holes;
- Volunteers are individuals working with other individuals. Encourage them to work as a team, not as competing individuals;
- Volunteers are not (usually) professionals within the organization or profession. Treat them with a special understanding and empathy;
- Volunteers are not paid staff. Try not to involve them in staff politics;
- Volunteers desire to be of assistance. Let them know how they are doing (feedback), answer their questions, and provide good two-way communications;
- Volunteers have the potential to be excellent recruiters, especially through networking, of other potentially helpful volunteers;
- Volunteers can be educated to assume a variety of roles within the fundraising process; and
- Volunteers are able to grow in professional competency with

appropriate and timely training, motivation, and opportunity.

Role of Volunteers

The role of the volunteer should be examined prior to the development of a volunteer management program. Each volunteer position should have a job description with the minimum qualifications listed. Further, there should be a clear description of what the volunteer will be required to accomplish.

Heidrich (1990) suggests that the following initial questions should be asked regarding a volunteer management program before developing such a program:
- "What aspects of the program would volunteers find interesting and rewarding?
- What is the organization doing that would benefit from volunteer participation?
- Are there better ways to organize the way the organization works?
- How many volunteer hours would it take to do each job?
- Is each job a "real" job; would someone want to do it?
- What expertise is needed? Can we offer training?
- Can the existing staff handle the supervision of volunteers?
- Does each job provide for personal satisfaction and a sense of belonging and purpose?" (Heidrich, 1990)

After a preliminary survey, appropriate roles for volunteers should be defined. If volunteer roles already exist, some of the following questions may reveal areas for improvement:
- "Is there an organizational chart that shows how various components of the program relate to another?
- Are there job descriptions for each position?
- Are the job descriptions updated regularly?

- Are they useful in the guidance and supervision of volunteers?
- Do volunteer jobs provide enough challenge, authority, and responsibility to be rewarding?
- Are volunteers an integral part of the planning, implementing, and evaluating process in all programs?
- Is there a systematic approach to recruiting new volunteers that emphasizes matching the volunteer with the job?
- Are there sufficient opportunities for orientation?
- Are there regular, on-going opportunities for training?
- What kind of supervision system is there for volunteers?
- Is there a recognition program that goes beyond annual formal recognition dinners?" (Heidrich, 1999)

Recruiting Volunteers

Once the organizers have determined the structure of the board, you can begin recruiting and retaining a volunteer base among employees. Many volunteers join organization boards because they enjoy serving others and would like to increase employee morale. Look for people who possess qualities such as honesty, trust, teamwork, leadership, enthusiasm, humor, responsibility, and competence. Board members also should have a business interest, whether it be in marketing, coalition building, training, finance, or technology. A balanced board of directors can assist with the growth of the programs.

Recruiting volunteers to help with organizations seems to become harder every year. Most people's time is stretched so thin, leaving no time for an employee to volunteer. A lament of managers is that the same group of people (pre-baby boomers and baby boomers) volunteer over and over. The younger employees (Generation Xers who often ask, "What is in it for me?") rarely are seen volunteering for anything (Sawyer & Smith, 1999).

Ask yourself these questions: Why would I volunteer? How does this appeal to me? How can this be more appealing to me? (Borja, 1999b).

The event where volunteers are needed should be promoted as if it were the event of the year. Emphasize the uniqueness of the challenge, aim to achieve a new goal each time, make it competitive (offer prizes), and throw in a perk or two. It is easy to obtain employee volunteers for high-profile events. It is difficult to obtain volunteers for a simple fundraising project. In the latter case, incentives for people to volunteer are needed, such as discounts on tickets to local events or logo merchandise or a banquet and a small gift. Recruiting must be an ongoing process. The volunteer recruiter needs to inform people that volunteering is a great networking opportunity leading to making new friends and gaining new skills such as communication, organization, planning, time management, budgeting, negotiation, and priority setting (Beagley, 1998). Further, other methods can be used to recruit volunteers, including "(1) making the event or activity fun, (2) finding out what the employees respond to, (3) involving the employee and family, (4) making it easy, attractive, and interesting to volunteer, (5) making the employee responsible for something, (6) treating the employee (volunteer) with respect, (7) asking for referrals, (8) planning social events for the volunteers, (9) paying for a volunteer's training, and (10) placing volunteers' photographs on bulletin boards, Web sites, or in e-mail messages" (Beagley, 1998).

Successful volunteer recruiting is not an isolated activity. Recruiting actually begins with carefully written job descriptions that delineate the volunteers' responsibilities. It is nearly impossible to recruit someone for a job that is not defined.

Before recruiting begins, groundwork must be done to ensure a successful recruiting experience. Meagher (1995), Stier (1994, 1993), and Heidrich (1990) suggest that some of the topics that need to be discussed are:

- Recruiters — Who will do the recruiting? Whoever the recruiters are, they should have or be willing to develop the following characteristics: (1) knowledge of the jobs for which they are recruiting, (2) detailed knowledge of the organization and its programs, (3) knowledge of how the programs are administered, (4) understanding of the culture of the prospective volunteer, (5) ability to communicate effectively with a wide range of people, (6) commitment to the purpose and goals of the organization, (7) enjoyment in meeting and talking with people, and (8) commitment to assisting the organization and its programs to grow.
- Job descriptions
- Prospective volunteers — A system for identifying potential volunteers.
- Match people with jobs.
- Obtain approvals — It is wise to obtain approvals from each volunteer's supervisor.
- Annual plans — Determine the volunteer needs on a year-round basis and use an annual calendar to schedule various steps in the volunteer management system. Take a moment and answer the following planning questions: (1) What times of the year are optimal for recruiting within the organization? (2) When do terms of office in clubs and associations expire? (3) What documents need to be in place before recruiting begins? (4) What methods will be used to recruit? (4) Who will serve as recruiters? (5) What training will be provided for the recruiters? (6) What orientation and training will be provided for the new volunteers? (7) What recognition events will be planned?

- Recruiting Techniques — The following are some useful recruiting techniques: (1) grow your own, (2) appointment by management from within, (3) management for referrals, (4) friendship groups, (5) family involvement, (6) benefits packages, (7) peripheral groups, and (8) use of media to communicate volunteer opportunities.

Job Descriptions for Volunteers

Written job descriptions delineate volunteers' responsibilities and are a key part of a risk management plan for the organization. Although liability rules vary from state to state, it is not likely that the organization is immune from liability merely because an employee is acting as a volunteer. The simple fact is whether a person is paid or unpaid has very little bearing on the case before the bar. If the person works for the organization in the eyes of the court, he is representing the organization. Therefore, the manager has developed specific job descriptions and reduced them to writing for all positions whether or not the people holding the positions are paid.

Many human resource management professionals have indicated the benefits of a job description include: foundation for recruiting, comfort and security, performance, continuity, communication and teamwork, and support a risk management plan. (See Table 18.2 for a description of the common steps in developing a job description.)

Motivating Volunteers

Everyone who has time to volunteer should understand there are many reasons why they should volunteer, including involvement, reward or recognition, networking, companionship, fulfillment, "the next best thing to being there," "nothing else to do," and "it is just plain

Table 18.2

Common Steps in Developing
Volunteer Job Descriptions

There are five common steps in human resource management that should be followed in developing a job description:

- Explain the concept to the chief executive officer and board, and outline the benefits listed above to them;
- Form a committee to develop the job description and have the committee answer the following questions: Does the organization need individual position and committee leadership job descriptions? What job descriptions are needed? What will be the outline for the job description? What will be the procedure for the annual review of job descriptions so they can be updated and improved over time? Who will be responsible for writing the job descriptions? Who will review the job descriptions before they are finalized?
- Establishment of job clusters such as committee chairs, club or league president, trip coordinators, and project leaders;
- Job evaluation system; and
- Job description format: title, function statement, reports to, staff liaison, task to be performed, time commitment, training, evaluation, benefits received, and qualifications.

Table 18.3

Questions for Sport Manager to Ask about Volunteers
before Establishing the Motivation Plan

Before recruiting volunteers the sport manager should ask the following questions:

- Do you have enough time to volunteer?
- How can you help the organization?
- Will you be able to learn from the experience?
- Will you like what you will be doing for the organization?
- What are the rewards and benefits you are seeking?
- Will your time be well spent?
- Most important—Will you have fun?

fun" (Borja, 1998). (See Table 18.3 for questions a sport manager needs to ask before developing the motivation plan.)

Retaining Volunteers

After recruiting volunteers, the next trick is to keep them as volunteers in the future. This can be done by making (1) the event or activity attractive to belong, (2) certain the event is well organized, (3) people feel needed and appreciated, (4) sure there is a friendly atmosphere, (5) certain the volunteer understands what her responsibilities will entail, including time commitments and workload, (6) a special effort to call volunteers by their first names and know something about them or the work they do, (7) sure to obtain volunteer's input, (8) a special effort to recognize or reward their volunteer efforts for the organization, (9) the event or activity fun, and (10) certain that everyone receives an appropriate thank you (e.g., free lunch or dinner and a framed certificate).

Educating Volunteers

A volunteer is no different (except that he receives no monetary remuneration) than any other employee on the staff. It is important to provide training to the volunteers. The training can be simple or elaborate. The key point to consider is that the volunteer should be clearly informed about goals, procedures, schedules, expectations, responsibilities, emergency procedures, and staff rosters.

Information should be provided orally with a back-up hard copy for each volunteer. This material should be placed in a neat folder with the volunteer's name imprinted on it. Personalizing the material gives the volunteer a feeling of self-worth and importance and, in turn, will motivate the volunteer to be a more valuable resource.

Orientation and
Training for Volunteers

Once the volunteers are on board, it is important to provide them with a sound orientation and a continuous education program. Without good orientation and training, volunteers may not be able to do their assigned jobs well or receive the intrinsic rewards they expected. The purpose of orienting and training volunteers is to ensure the highest possible degree of satisfaction with and contribution to the portion of the program that they are to implement.

- Orientation helps volunteers become acquainted with one another and the staff, learn the organization's culture, and learn about their own volunteer role in relation to the entire organization. Orientation differs from in-service training with orientation usually occurring at the beginning of a volunteer's commitment, and in-service training at various times during a volunteer's commitment and in-service training at various times during a volunteer's involvement with the organization.
- Training, on the other hand, introduces new skills, knowledge, and abilities or reinforces existing ones, can be used to plan and manage program changes, and provides opportunities for self-renewal and growth.

The Orientation Program

The orientation program should be conducted by the head of the volunteer management system and a key volunteer(s). The orientation program should be conducted more frequently then once a year if the organization is bringing in new volunteers on a monthly or weekly basis. Many organizations establish cohorts of volunteers who go through the orientation together. It is not uncommon to see an organization scheduling quarterly orientations.

The orientation can be scheduled as:
- Large group sessions,
- Small group sessions,
- Personal, one-on-one orientation sessions, or

- Personal, one-on-one mentoring systems.

The agenda for an orientation session may include:

- Philosophical and conceptual framework of the organization,
- Content of the various organization's programs,
- Organization of the various organization's programs,
- Governance of the organization,
- History of the organization,
- Policies and procedures of the organization,
- Bylaws and the proper conduct of business,
- Ethics issues,
- Benefits of volunteering and special privileges,
- Identification of key people in the organization,
- Telephone numbers of key people,
- Realistic job previews.

Orientation and Training Checklist

The following set of questions should be used in guiding the final plans for an orientation or training session:

- Does every new volunteer have an opportunity to be oriented to their role, either in a one-on-one conference, a small group, or a large group meeting?
- Are there orientation materials prepared for volunteers: job descriptions, handbooks, policies, etc.?
- Are orientation and training meetings planned with plenty of volunteer input and participation?
- Are volunteers offered leadership roles in orientation and training of other volunteers?
- Does the organization provide books, films, tapes, trips, or other educational materials for volunteers?
- Does the organization pay for volunteers to attend appropriate training events or take courses at other institutions?
- Are all orientation and training programs evaluated?

The Volunteer Personnel Management System

The sport manager should ask a series of questions after he/she understands the environment that the volunteers will be asked to work. I think Rudyard Kipling put it best when he said he kept six honest serving men (They taught me all I knew); their names are Who, What, Where, Why, When, and How. If you keep this in mind at all times, whether it be managing volunteer personnel or the budget, Kipling's six honest serving men will make you successful in most of your efforts.

One of the most notable trends in volunteerism has been professionalization. In most organizations using the services of volunteers, there has been a gradual realization that volunteers should be recognized as the valuable staff members they are. As a result, the management of volunteers has taken on many of the characteristics of the management of paid staff. Managers in voluntary organizations perform many of the same personnel functions for volunteers as for paid staff: they design and define volunteer jobs and write job descriptions, recruit and interview volunteers aggressively, orient, train, supervise, evaluate, and reward. (See Table 18.4 for reasons why to professionalize volunteer management.)

Success in working with volunteers depends on the following managerial elements: assessment, job descriptions, recruiting, orientation and training, supervision and evaluation, recognition, and opportunities to influence the system.

Table 18.4

Reasons for Professionalizing Volunteer Management

Heidrich (1990) indicates there are several reasons for this professionalization of volunteer management, including:

- Many voluntary organizations and volunteer program are quite large (e.g., Girl Scouts, Boy Scouts, American Red Cross, Salvation Army, United Way, and others);
- Increasing concern about liability has forced organizations to improve control of programs conducted by volunteers;
- Volunteers have become more sophisticated and discerning about the organizations to which they donate their time and energy;
- Management positions in voluntary organizations have become more professionalized; and
- Managing volunteers is, in many ways, more difficult than managing paid employees; since volunteers are, by definition, not paid, the incentive structure is intrinsic rather than extrinsic.

Table 18.5

Dealing with Difficult Volunteers

When conflict arises, Heidrich (1990) suggests it can usually be traced to one or a combination of the following factors:

- Lack of agreement about the program goals and components.
- Ill-defined and unmeasurable objectives.
- Absence of a preconceived plan.
- Excluding from the planning process those who will be responsible for carrying out the plan.
- Inaccessibility of leaders.
- Distortion of information accidentally or deliberately.
- Lack of trust, which induces people to withhold opinions that are negative or critical; people will play it safe rather than risk the wrath of someone else.
- Hidden agendas and other manipulations that reduce trust in the long run.
- Ineffective listening, which often represents a desire to dominate and an unwillingness to tolerate others' views.
- A belief in absolutes, which leads to a tendency to cast blame.
- A belief that only two sides of an issue exist and that one must be "right" and the other "wrong." This belief precludes compromise.
- Individual differences in race, age, culture, or status. Sometimes it is difficult to appreciate others' points of view.
- Misunderstandings about territory, policy, authority, and role expectations.

Supervision of Volunteers

Supervision is a managerial function that helps to ensure the satisfactory completion of program objectives. The effective volunteer manager maximizes volunteers' expectations by providing support and resources. Further, the manager ensures that the volunteers possess the skills and abilities to get the job done. Finally, the supervisor must discuss problems as well as successes with volunteers and suggest constructive ways to improve.

As a process, supervision involves three elements:

- Establishing criteria of success, standards of performance, and program objectives such as the job description and annual plan of work.
- Measuring actual volunteer performance with respect to these stated criteria of success through observation, conferences, and evaluation.
- Making corrections, as needed, through managerial action.

Working with Difficult Volunteers

Working with volunteers generally is enjoyable. They want to be involved and are not motivated by compensation. However, there are volunteers who create problems and cause difficult supervisory problems. (See Table 18.5 for suggestions for working with difficult volunteers.)

There are four common solutions to conflict used in managerial setting. These include:

- Retraining,
- Reassignment,
- Redesign, and
- Dismissal.

Recognition of Volunteers

Recognizing volunteers for their work is widely accepted as an important aspect of successful management. There is no single recognition event that will make everyone happy. Understanding that different volunteers are satisfied by different rewards is essential to the success of a recognition program. Recognition is not just a way of saying thank you, but it is also a response to individual interests and reasons for being involved in the program.

The common types of awards include:

- Group recognition,
- Individual recognition,
- Informal recognition (i.e., get well cards, birthday cards, send flowers, thank you notes, have a happy vacation note, photographs, take a volunteer to lunch or coffee),
- Public and media recognition, and
- Formal recognition.

The planning for a recognition, in many cases, is as important as the recognition itself. The first step is to appoint a recognition planning committee. The functions of the planning committee would include:

- Planning and conducting recognition event(s),
- Evaluating recognition event(s),
- Determining whether or not to establish formal awards program(s),
- Researching the reasons why people have volunteered to work with the organization so that future recognition can be planned to meet their needs, and
- Maintaining a record-keeping system that will provide data on volunteers' contributions to the organization.

The recognition planning committee needs to address a number of questions as it develops the format for volunteer recognition. These questions include:

- Does the organization see recognition as an event rather than a process?
- Has the organization fallen into a rut with traditional recognition events?
- Are there parts of the awards program that no one understands

because the meaning is lost in the past?
- Is the awards program really fair to everyone?
- How many people are recognized as individuals?

If the recognition planning committee decides it is important to have a formal awards program, a number of items need to be considered. These items include, but are not limited to:

- Each award has a name that distinguishes it from other awards.
- Awards are incremental with some reserved for people with long tenure and distinguished service, including retirees, and others for short-term or one-time service.
- Each award has written criteria that must be met.
- Awards criteria and nominating forms are distributed to all volunteers.
- Favoritism in nomination and selection is scrupulously avoided.
- Volunteers are involved in the decision-making process.
- Award nominations are handled confidentially.
- There is an official time when formal awards are presented to recipients.
- A permanent record of award recipients is maintained, preferably on a large plaque visible to all in a prominent location.
- The formal recognition system is regularly reviewed.

- Name something after an outstanding volunteer (be cautious—this idea has long-term implications).
- Design a formal award program.
- Make a monetary gift in a volunteer's name to his or her favorite volunteer agency.
- Hold a banquet, brunch, luncheon, or party at a unique location.

Summary

No organization has enough staff to adequately raise funds through solicitation; therefore, volunteers become critical to any fundraising effort. The volunteer plays the role of a loyal community supporter of the organization involved in raising funds for vital projects. They can easily influence colleagues, newer members, former classmates, and other community leaders of the importance of a project and the need for the funds. Volunteers are great ambassadors of goodwill.

Stier (1993, 1994) suggests that managers of any organization involved with volunteers must understand how to best involve them in the organization. The organization must develop a strong volunteer management system, which treats volunteers as full-time paid staff. The organization must provide appropriate orientation programs, in-service training, and recognition programs. Finally, volunteers need supervision and attention just as do regular employees.

References

Heidrich, K.W. (1990). *Working with volunteers.* Champaign, IL: Sagamore Publishing.

Meagher, J.W. (1995). Right on the money. *Athletic Business, 19*(8), 67.

Sawyer, T.H., & Smith. O. (1999). *The management of clubs, recreation, and sport.* Champaign, IL: Sagamore Publishing.

Stier, W.F., Jr. (1993). Project profit. *Athletic Business, 4*(2), 44.

Stier, W.F., Jr. (1994). *Successful sport fundraising.* Dubuque, IA: EECB Brown & Benchmark Publishers.

Part VI

Financial Risk Management

Insurance

Introduction

Are you worried that bad weather will cancel the event you have spent days planning for, or that the star athlete will suffer a career-ending injury, or a patron will slip on a spilled soft drink or ice on the sidewalk and break a leg? Today's litigious environment and tight budgets mean managers and owners must take a closer look at insurance and risk-management strategies.

In the past 10 years, there has been a dramatic increase in the number of companies specializing in insurance for the fitness, physical activity, recreation, and sport industries.

The sport management professional should be prepared to cover injuries arising from other areas of possible liability including: (1) building (e.g., fire, lightning, explosion, windstorm or hail, smoke, aircraft or vehicles striking the property, riot or civil commotion, vandalism, sprinkler leakage, sinkhole collapse [i.e., Florida, Montana], volcanic action, flood, mud slides [i.e., California], and tornado or hurricane) and premises, (2) motor vehicles (e.g., medical expenses for driver and passengers, lost income and services for driver and passengers, damage to automobile(s), additional property damaged [nearby structures, telephone poles, guard rails, road signage, etc.], ambulance expense, funeral expense, investigation expense, legal expense, and overhead of automobile insurers), (3) activities (i.e., from incidents due to the nature of the activity engaged in), (4) employee conduct (e.g., negligent acts of employees, employee dishonesty, forgery, theft, computer fraud, and extortion), (5) business general liability caused by employees, users, or spectators (e.g., direct liability [premises and operations, and products liability], vicarious liability [i.e., indirect liability], and contractual liability), (6) bonds for performance and financial security (i.e., surety bonds guarantee performance and fidelity bonds protect employers from loss caused by dishonest acts of employees), and (7) fringes for employees covered by federal law (e.g., Social Security Act, Employee Retirement Income Security Act of 1974 [ERISA], Internal Revenue Code [IRe], The Civil Rights Act of 1964 [as amended in 1970, 1972, 1978], Age Discrimination in Employment ACT of 1967 [as amended in 1986], Retirement Equity Act of 1984 [REA], Consolidated Omnibus Budget Reconciliation Act of 1986 [COBRA], Tax Reform Act of 1986, Health Maintenance Organization ACT [HMO], and the Civil Rights Restoration Act of 1987 [1988]). (See chapter 20 for a discussion of these laws and others.)

Instructional Objectives

After reading this chapter, the student should understand how to:
- Develop an insurance program for recreation and sport operations and programs,
- Select an insurance consultant,
- Describe insurance coverages,
- Select an insurance company or companies,
- Determine insurance companies insurability,
- Determine the cost of premiums, and
- Select a deductible.

Insurance for Sports Programming

The manager should become familiar with some basic insurance jargon before trying to engage an insurance consultant. Further, the manager should know what insurance the organization currently has and its limits. A survey of companies specializing in this type of insurance shows a wide variety of coverages available, including:
- Professional teams, athletes, and events—liability and accident medical cover age, high-limit accidental death and disability insurance, contractual bonus and performance incentive programs;
- Amateur athletes and events (e.g., Olympic Festivals, USOC, National Governing Bodies, Pan American Games, World Games);
- College and high school teams, athletes, athletic associations, club/ recreational sport activities, sorts camps, facilities—sports liability and accident medical coverage, disability insurance, play practice coverage, transportation insurance, catastrophic injury coverage;
- Youth/adult recreational teams and leagues—liability and accident coverage;
- Health clubs, fitness centers, and sports clubs—property, accident and liability insurance for participants/ members and staff, day-care facilities, tanning beds, diving boards, whirlpools, weight rooms, trampolines, food and liquor services;
- Venues (stadiums, arenas, recreational facilities, water parks)—spectator and participant liability, property insurance, casualty insurance;
- Promotions and special events— event cancellation, sponsorship/ prize guarantee, special events liability, weather, and nonappearance insurance;
- General public liability—products liability, watercraft liability, saddle animal liability, liquor liability, personal injury liability, independent contractor's liability, advertiser's liability, and adventure and tripping program liability;
- Liability coverage protecting employees, directors, and officers;
- Vehicle insurance—bodily injury liability, property damage liability, business auto policy, user of other autos, employers non-owned and hired autos, camp bus coverage, medical payments, comprehensive, and collision insurance; and

• Protection of finances and operations—loss of income, discrimination or civil liberties violations, advertising liability, or contractual liability by endorsement (hold harmless agreement or indemnification).

Insurance Consultant

Insurance consultants can be very helpful to the manager. The consultant can keep the sports facility manager out of trouble and assist in selecting insurance coverage as well as companies. The manager should seek a person with the following characteristics to become the insurance consultant: has been an insurance agent, understands commercial property insurance, has knowledge about general liability insurance, understands bonding and crime insurance, has a basic knowledge of automobile insurance, understands employee benefits and health and disability insurance, has a knowledge of insurance contracts, understands the insurance regulations in the specific state, and has a good reputation as an insurance consultant. You can expect to pay between $100 and $150 per hour or a flat fee based on negotiations and scope of work requested.

Insurance Coverage

All too often, owners renew their same coverage without considering new improvements in facilities and equipment, additional programming and services, new staff, and revenue increases. The manager should review with the insurance consultant annually the coverage of each policy in force to guarantee adequate coverage. Insurance is the most valuable way to protect business assets. A comprehensive insurance program should include, but not be limited to: property coverage, business income, commercial liability, machinery and equipment coverage, employment practice liability, special liability, bonding, crime insurance, and employee benefits.

Property Insurance

This covers facilities, equipment, and personal property. The coverage should include improvements (i.e., facilities and equipment), equipment owned or leased, and all inventory (e.g., employee store inventory, office supplies, custodial supplies, and expendable recreational and sport supplies [e.g., balls, bats, climbing equipment, racquets]).

The following should also be covered under property insurance: office equipment and furniture losses from a flood and/or earthquake if appropriate, glass and exterior mirrors, losses from fire and smoke, computers, and losses from hurricane or tornado if appropriate. If you lease equipment and you insure that equipment, make sure to have the broker provide a certificate of insurance that names the insurance company as the loss payee/additional insured, since the leasing company most likely will have also insured that equipment through another insurance carrier.

Business Income/Extra Expense

This insurance provides income during reconstruction after a loss by an insured peril (e.g., fire, flood, hurricane, tornado, or earthquake). The coverage should be written on an Agreed Value Basis with a 90-day extended period of indemnity. The insurance limit should cover a minimum of six months of gross receipts, less non-continuing expenses and ordinary payroll (include payroll for owners and managers). If renting or leasing a facility, be certain to include rent since most lease agreements require payment in full whether or not the leasee is in operation or not.

Commercial Liability

This includes professional liability, fire legal liability, and medical payments liability. Professional liability should include all part- and full-time employees (not independent contractors; they should be required to have their own prior to contracting with them), and tanning bed liability (make sure there are no cancer exclusions). Fire legal liability is insurance to cover losses while renting or leasing a facility. Finally, medical payments liability allows the insurer to file a claim for medical bills although there was no negligence on the operator's part.

Machinery and Equipment Insurance

This insurance covers replacement of HVAC (heating, ventilation, and air conditioning) equipment, pumps, and other mechanical aspects of the facility. It also acts as an extended warranty policy for other equipment such as computers (i.e., desktops and laptops), monitors, LCD projectors, printers, copiers, and scanners. This covers damage caused by water or electrical surges as well as theft.

Employment Practices Liability Insurance (EPLI)

This insurance covers the organization for wrongful termination, employment-related acts of discrimination (e.g., disability, race, handicap, religion, creed, age, gender, sexual orientation, sexual preference, pregnancy, and national origin), wrongful discipline, defamation, invasion of privacy, misrepresentation, negligent evaluation, equal pay violation, wrongful infliction of emotional distress or retaliation, break of employment contract, negligent evaluation, wrongful deprivation of career opportunity, failure to employ or promote, sexual abuse and molestation, and sexual harassment (see Appendix I for additional information).

Special Liability Insurance

This insurance covers environmental impairment including pollution caused by chemicals, waste in waterways, or dispersed into the air. Sporting manufacturers would be more inclined to carry this type of coverage.

Bonding

There are two types of bonds. Surety bonds which guarantee performance and fidelity bonds which protect the employers from loss caused by dishonest acts of employees such as embezzlement of funds.

Crime Insurance

This insurance covers perils such as forgery, theft, destruction, computer fraud, and extortion by employees. This could be as simple as employees stealing products to an employee shooting fellow employees or destroying property intentionally.

Employee Benefit Insurance

Insurances in this category most frequently provided as employee benefits include unemployment (pays laid off or terminated employees up to eight weeks of minimum income), workers' compensation (compensates employees injured during the performance of their jobs covering income and medical expenses), group life (commonly a term life insurance policy purchased for the employee), health (insurance providing coverage of medical, hospitalization, dental, and eye), disability (covers loss of income caused by a disability combined with social security disability provides up to 60 percent of employees previous salary), and pension plans.

The decision as to what insurance is purchased by the organization comes down to overall cost versus potential risk. The manager and insurance consultant will need to develop a careful analysis of potential risk and those that have the greatest potential of becoming a reality will need to be covered in the blanket policy (insurance contract) developed. It is always wise to secure at least three quotes from three reputable insurance companies. Make sure that the bids received address the same types of insurance you requested with the same deductibles.

The Insurance Company or Companies

It is important to select a carrier that has a stable, long-term knowledge of this industry.

Investigate the insurance company because there are companies out there that are not experienced in the fitness/recreation/sport field. The cheapest company is not always the best company. The ideal company will have a reasonable cost, provide risk management assistance and advice, continually review the policies under force, and provide quick user-friendly service when a claim arises.

How Do Insurance Companies Determine Insurability?

What do insurance companies consider before determining if a facility or event is insurable? The insurer reviews information regarding, variety of basic areas: (1) security, (2) maintenance, (3) housekeeping, (4) emergency services, (5) parking and traffic control, (6) conces-

sions, (7) staff training and preparedness, (8) fiscal operations, (9) staff supervision, (10) activity planning, (11) equipment used in building and ground maintenance (e.g., buffers, vacuum cleaners, mowers, power weed eaters, tillers, etc.), and sport equipment (e.g., golf carts, playground equipment), and (12) chemical usage and storage. The company is concerned as to how these areas are managed. Premiums are based on how these areas are controlled. The only reason insurance is inexpensive is good loss experience. If the experience is consistently good, the insurance company does not have to build in premiums to pay losses and take care of routine claims.

Cost of Premiums

The cost of premiums can be reduced by opting for higher deductibles or taking the initiative of hiring a risk management expert to survey the facilities and programs for unsafe conditions. Some insurance companies offer on-site safety inspections as a value-added service.

Insurance remains a confusing entity and may be the reason why so many managers take little time to understand what might be needed beyond the corporation coverage and what might be needed for the not-for-profit employee association/club. It is not uncommon for insurance buyers to go for the cheapest price and not pay attention to coverages, policy limits, and conditions. The insurance consultant will indicate that not being adequately covered could cost the employee services provider its business.

A Checklist for Selecting Insurance

The following checklist contains recommendations for managers when securing insurance:
•Never assume you are covered;

- Always check your insurance coverage;
- Check insurance policy at least twice a year for changes and to be sure you still have adequate coverage;
- File a report on an incident as soon as it happens and submit a proper claim to the insurance company;
- Anyone involved in an activity outside their job jurisdiction or areas of control may seek to secure more personal liability coverage;
- Be aware of potential hazards and report them to the necessary people or group;
- Secure a short-term group accident policy to cover special activities when risk is forseeable;
- Analyze the liability aspects of your program or area and ensure adequate coverage in these areas;
- Have release forms; they may solve small liability problems because the participants acknowledge the risk they are assuming and their voluntary participation in the program, but do not rely on them to solve any negligent actions and have participants in events obtain medicals.

Questions to Ask a Prospective Insurer

Before you purchase any insurance policy, ask the prospective agent the following questions. The answers can help you decide what type of coverage is necessary and which amount is best for the operation in question.

- How many policies has the agent written with similar organizations?
- What is included in the basic policy?
- What is excluded in the basic policy?
- What types of coverage should be considered beyond the basic policy?
- How much insurance can the organization afford?
- Can the agent provide a list of recent claims and losses (say the last five years)?
- What is the carrier's rating?
- How long does it take for a claim to be processed?
- Can the agent recommend a person or firm to assist in loss control analysis, safety issues, and general risk management?
- How often does the agent recommend policy review and updating?

Self-insurance

This option is not appropriate for small organizations, but is quite practical for large and governmental organizations. Self-insurance usually means retaining financial risks to a substantial level through establishing a reserve fund to insure availability of cash when needed.

The amount of such a fund and its management may be controlled by state regulations or statutes. Taxable profit-making organizations rarely establish such a reserve because of the tax structure and usually the working capital is adequate, at least for larger corporations. Some corporations have established trust funds to maintain such funds.

Other Coverages Available

The following are other coverages available: sports liability and accident medical insurance, play-practice coverage, transportation insurance, catastrophic injury coverage (to costs beyond $25,000 up to $1,000,000 or more), dependent care insurance, food and beverage insurance, spectator liability and medical insurance, automobile insurance, event cancellation insurance, special events liability, and weather and non-appearance insurance. (See Appendix M for a listing of a few insurance companies that cater to health/fitness, recreation, and sport programs.)

How Should the Sport Manager Choose the Appropriate Deductible?

Selecting the right deductible requires a thorough analysis by the sport manager. A higher deductible can reduce the premium but, at the same time, increase out-of-pocket expenditures for care that doesn't meet the deductible amount. On the other hand, decreasing the cost of coverage can allow for more liquid funds and provide the option of building a reserve if funds can carry over from year to year. The following are a few recommendations that should be considered when choosing a deductible:

- Access student-athlete's or patron's primary insurance first and once it has been exhausted, the organization pays until its deductible is reached, then the secondary insurer, the organization's carrier, pays the remaining amount. This is called a straight-deductible policy.
- Select a higher deductible since it will mandate a more aggressive management of insurance claims. However, if the organization has a large number of student-athletes or patrons who lack primary insurance coverage, a lower deductible should be chosen.
- The manager should base the deductible on the physical activity involved and gender of the participants. For example, lower deductible for contact activities and higher for non-contact.
- The sport manager should coordinate all medical care through an HMO or a special arrangement with a local hospital. This will assist the sport manager in controlling losses and take advantage of a higher deductible.
- The sport manager should consider placing a physician on a stipend that will reduce overall costs and allow for a higher deductible.
- The sport manager should establish a referral policy to maximize in-house medical services.

This will also allow for the selection of a higher deductible.

Summary

If you follow these steps, you should be able to select an appropriate insurance program for the sport facility that you manage:

- Select a competent independent insurance consultant,
- Be aware of the suppliers of insurance and the relative advantages and disadvantages of dealing with each,
- Secure a number of quotes and review each closely,
- Make certain your sport facility has adequate insurance coverage,
- Identify the risks that your sport facility will face and adequately insure them,
- Ask yourself, "Can our golf facility survive any major losses?"
- Insure the correct risks,
- Always try to keep your insurance costs down by preventing or reducing losses,
- Review your insurance needs and your business risks annually,
- Understand the basic policy (i.e., exclusions, etc.), and
- Understand the many types of insurance policies and their coverages.

Risk Management

Introduction

Risk management is the logical development and implementation of a plan to deal with chance losses. The risk management process encourages managers to place loss exposure in a broad perspective in which insurance is just one of several alternative solutions. The broadness of the risk management responsibility is seen in the fact that many companies view their employee benefit plans, including their group life and health insurance and pension plans, as part of their risk management program.

The risk management process begins when somebody asks, "What kinds of events can damage my business, and how much damage can be done?" After identifying and measuring the exposures to loss, the next logical question is, "What actions should I take to deal with these problems?" After the decisions are made and implemented, the risk manager will probably ask, "Did I make the right decisions? Did my choices prove to be too expensive? Have circumstances in my business changed sufficiently so that past decisions no longer apply?"

Learning Objectives

After reading this chapter the student should be able to:

- explain risk management and its relationship to other management functions,
- describe the steps in the risk management process, and
- explain the main risk management tools for dealing with potential loss.

The Function of Risk Management

A comprehensive risk management program is a disciplined process that involves many areas of the organization and encompasses a range of risks. In fact, a leading trend is to take an integrated approach to risk management, bringing all risks, including financial and insurance risks, under a single corporate umbrella. To accomplish this objective, it is essential to establish a framework that blends financial market and insurance expertise, systems technology, operational planning, and senior management vision through an interactive relationship. Effective communication and information flow is a critical factor in the success of this relationship.

The Role of Senior Management in the Risk Management Process

The key elements of effective financial governance and oversight include the following:

- Defining the roles and responsibilities of the board of directors and senior management in the risk management process;
- Developing appropriate checks and balances for effective oversight and control of risk management;
- Establishing policy and control guidelines; and
- Designing risk measurement and reporting procedures.

The need to more clearly define the Board's roles in the financial governance and oversight area has been heightened due to highly publicized derivative losses that have taken place in recent years. However, in many of these situations, Board members might not have been sufficiently aware of the intricacies of the transactions to voice an informed opinion on their appropriateness. To enhance board level understanding and to add real value to a company's profitability, while managing risk, it is time for all organizations to become more serious about developing formal oversight procedures and responsibilities at the most senior levels.

By following two general guidelines, organizations will be much further along than many are today:

- Recognize the distinction in the use of the term "oversight" rather than "controls." In some recent well-publicized instances, organizations had policies and procedures in place, which prohibited the actions that caused the publicized losses, yet transactions were executed despite these policies. Organizations must recognize that it is not enough to have documentation declaring certain activities unacceptable; they must also have an oversight process in place to ensure the enforcement of theses policies and procedures. In short, a system of checks and balances, which can ensure that unauthorized activities do not, and cannot, occur, must exist.
- Develop a consistent measurement of firm-wide risk. It is not possible or practical for each board member to have detailed knowledge of all aspects of complex financial transactions, nor is it wise to eliminate their use simply because this knowledge level is absent. Rather, measures of the risk inherent in the transactions executed, as well as the risk from underlying business exposure, must be provided to senior management to allow an assessment of whether this level of risk is appropriate for the company and its objectives.

Responsibility of the Board

The responsibility of the Board is to oversee an infrastructure that can define, analyze, and measure risk inherent in the firm's underlying financial risks and the instruments used to manage them. The output of this infrastructure must be synthesized into clearly defined and understood measures which the Board can evaluate and on which it will impose its oversight responsibility. The methodology to develop this infrastructure is where the responsibility of the Board takes on greater dimensions. If the Board feels it lacks the expertise to analyze the underlying risk elements itself, it should consider going outside the company to find qualified, objective sources for this expertise.

Board level risk definition efforts should include the development of a customized measurement and evaluation process that fits the company's risk tolerances, level of complexity, view of materiality, degree of centralization or decentralization, and desired level of detail. The Board must design an iterative process and evolve to a "best practices" approach, meeting the needs of the company while also taking into account its own limitations.

To provide an understanding for the level of detail behind the two general guidelines mentioned above, a Board level checklist is provided below. While not all-inclusive, the checklist is a good start and will set the company's thought process moving forward on these issues.

A Board Level Checklist For Risk Measurement

Boards need to answer the ensuing questions as they develop a sound risk management process:

- Do you have a written Risk Management Policy, which includes a clearly defined and detailed implementation strategy approved by the proper levels of management?
- Does the policy clearly define the underlying business rationale for the company's derivative use or does it leave open the possibility of speculative transactions?
- Is your hedge orientation towards a "market view" or a defined strategy? If a "market view" orientation is chosen, have the entry and exit criteria for trading positions been formalized by proper levels of management?
- Does the policy include approval levels for various dollar levels of transactions? If any of those transactions are complex or leveraged instruments, does the

approval level cover their risk profile or just their simple face value?
- Is there an oversight function to ensure that policies and procedures are being implemented properly and is this function headed by someone other than those involved in the derivative instrument selection and execution (i.e., Internal Audit)?
- Does a study of the derivative execution group's performance measures find that they could encourage speculative or undesired behavior to improve performance?
- Is there clear reporting to senior management of the potential market and credit risk due to derivatives activities and do these risk measures also separately indicate the underlying business risks being managed?
- Is the risk measurement methodology (e.g., sensitivity analysis or Value-at-Risk) appropriate for the company's risk tolerance and exposure complexity levels?
- Do proper expertise and systems reside in-house to identify and quantify risk, as well as to price and evaluate derivative positions?
- If the expertise does not exist within the organization, has it been secured outside the company from knowledgeable and objective sources?
- Is there an effective reporting system in place to inform proper levels of management of position gains or losses?
- Are management reports on program status and performance measures reviewed by senior management at least one level (if not two levels) higher than the level required to approve transactions?
- Does the Board periodically review the program's performance to ensure that it is consistent with the risk profile of the company?

Policy and Control Guidelines

The policy should be viewed as the long-term blueprint for the management of financial risks within the organization. It should provide broad guidelines regarding exposure management, rather than rigid restrictions. Before its implementation, the guideline should be approved by the company's Board of Directors. While each policy must be customized, a sound risk management policy should incorporate and consider the following issues.

Defining Risk Management Objectives

The most important issue to be addressed in an exposure management policy is to define management's objectives with regard to risk. Since they impact the direction of the entire risk management approach, these objectives must be determined and approved at a very senior level within the company. A risk management program begins with a statement of objectives, which is followed by a statement of principles and procedures designed to achieve the stated objectives.

The essential pre-loss objective is to operate efficiently in a risky environment. This means the organization must select the appropriate balance among loss prevention, risk assumption, insurance, and other risk management tools. A second objective is to keep the organization in compliance with government regulations (i.e., environmental, safety, and tax) and insurance company contractual warranties and provisions, and to fulfill other risk and insurance-related obligations. The final pre-loss objective is to see that the risk management principles and procedures are implemented and operate smoothly (i.e., safety classes are held, employees are motivated to perform their assignments safely, a proper attitude towards safety pervades the enterprise, and procedures are in place to protect against interest-rate risk, credit risk, currency risk, and liquidity risk).

The first post-loss objective for the risk manager is to make sure the organization can survive losses. Second, the risk manager should try to lay a foundation allowing the firm to grow and prosper in the same manner after a loss as it would if the loss has not occurred. Finally, the risk manager should try to establish the firm's ability to behave responsibly towards the environment, employees, suppliers, customers, and the community in which it operates.

The risk manager is responsible for the development of statement of risk management principles. The organization's board of directors and senior management should approve the statement. After approval of the statement, the risk manager must develop a manual of procedures to achieve these objectives. The manual of procedures must be detailed and specific. The procedure manual will become the guidepost for management when making decisions and evaluating results.

The Risk Management Process

Risk management must be a continuous process. Managers need to complete much of the process before losses occur. Some of the process is completed while losses are happening. The process continues after the loss, including complying with insurance policy conditions and conducting statistical analysis of loss patterns.

The risk management process begins with identifying and evaluating loss exposures. This step is followed by selecting the most efficient method of dealing with the loss exposures identified in step one. The final task is to monitor outcomes. Figure 20.1 graphically presents a layout of typical risk management problems faced by most sport organizations.

Figure 20.1

Typical Sport Organization
Risk Management Problems

Property Loss
- Stationary property
- Mobile property
- Leased property

Employee Safety and Health
- Accident prevention
- Industrial hygiene

Personnel
- Workers compensation
- Life insurance
- Disability insurance
- Health insurance
- Pension plans
- Key personnel loss (i.e., turn-over)
- Contractual employees

Liability Control
- General negligence
- Vehicle liability
- Product liability

Environmental Protection
- Storage
- Pollution control
- Waste disposal

Emergency Planning
- Crowd control
- Fire
- Bombing
- Spectator health emergencies

Financial Risk
- Interest-rate risk
- Credit risk
- Currency risk
- Liquidity risk
- Theft of product
- Theft of money
- Market risk

Categorizing Loss Potential

There are two types of risks to be considered when discussing an organization's loss exposure. The first is speculative risk. Speculative risks are exposures than can result in gains or losses and usually are not the subject of risk management. Losses or gains that result from good or bad investment decisions, from competitor's actions, or from government intervention in the economy are examples of speculative risks. These are usually risks outside the scope of the risk manager's responsibility.

Pure risks result only in losses and are the usual subject of the risk management program. Pure risks arise from the following sources:

- Direct losses of property,
- Indirect losses of income (e.g., reduction in ticket sales or a shift in the demographics of ticket sales) or increases in operating expenses because normal business activity has been interrupted by a direct loss (e.g., loss of a major sales contract to a competitor, loss of a media contract),
- Liability losses (e.g., loss of an injury civil suit),
- Losses resulting from death or disability of key personnel,
- Market losses, and
- Loss of favorable credit rating.

The pure risks usually can be managed once they have been identified and measured.

Direct Property Loss

Risk managers can identify potential direct property losses in different ways. The risk management procedures manual should establish a system for notifying the risk management department when property is acquired or sold. An analysis of financial statements, as well as the supporting accounts, can highlight assets exposed to loss, as can an analysis of part losses. Table 20.2 describes a checklist that may be used to identify potential property losses.

Loss of Income

The manager usually considers the fact that every direct loss of property usually has the potential for causing an indirect loss of income. For some sport entities, quick resumption of operations after a loss is especially important (i.e., professional sport franchise, retail operations, food operations, etc.). Included as a part of loss reduction programs is knowing of:

- Alternative sites for operations,
- Subcontractors and salvage operations, and
- Alternative sources of funds that may be needed if operations are to be resumed in the shortest period of time.

Figure 20.2

Property Insurance Checklist

- Identify and value owned buildings, equipment, and land.
- Identify and value property leased from others.
- Identify and value property leased to others.
- Identify location and value of stationary inventory (average cost).
- Identify and value inventory being transported (average cost).
- Identify and value property under construction.
- Identify and value owned or leased vehicles.
- Identify special perils to which property is exposed (e.g., radiation, explosion, flood, earthquake, hurricane, tornado, theft, etc.).

Liability Losses

Identifying possible liability losses requires a knowledge of the law as it is being interpreted currently in a specific jurisdiction. In an age when a liability claim may represent nothing more than the imagination of the plaintiff's attorney, this task is not easy. Thus, the risk manager and the legal staff must work closely to protect the organization from this source of loss. Figure 20.3 presents a categorization of the basis of most lawsuits sport organizations face.

There are three types of liability losses that increased rapidly throughout the 1990s and into the new century:
- Worker's compensation claims arising from injury to an organization's employees,
- Product liability arising from allegedly injuring users of its products or sitting in its bleachers, and
- Environmental impairment liability arising from polluting ground, water, and air, or generating obnoxious levels of heat, noise, or vibration.

Loss of Key Personnel

If a key person (i.e., star quarterback, center, pitcher, or goalie) is lost to an organization by unplanned retirement, resignation, death, or disability, the effect may be quickly felt in lost income. If several key employees are killed (i.e., University of Oklahoma plane crash), disabled, or leave simultaneously, the results could be devastating to an organization. When the success of an organization, or in some instances its existence, depends on one or more individuals, the manager must identify these individuals and be ready to take steps to solve the problem if a loss occurs.

Part of identifying the key-employee exposure is developing an estimate of where, at what cost, and how quickly a replacement may be hired and trained. The cost of the replacement would give the firm an estimate of the value of its exposure to loss. Key employees should have well-trained subordinates when this is possible. Key personnel may be identified using an organizational chart or a flow chart.

Estimation of Maximum Loss

When developing a risk management plan, the manager should have a good notion of the maximum possible loss and the maximum probable loss. The maximum possible loss refers to the total amount of financial harm a given loss could cause under the worst circumstances. The maximum probable loss is the most likely maximum amount of damage a peril might cause under the circumstances.

In evaluating and identifying the source and scope of maximum potential losses, it is important that the manager take a broad view of the problem. All

Figure 20.3

Typical Sources of Liability Losses

- Bodily or personal injury to employees, customers, clients, or guests.
- Property damage to the real or personal property of others.
- Intentional injury to people or their reputations, including illegal accusation or restraint of alleged shoplifters.
- Wrongful hiring, firing, sexual harassment, or invasion of privacy of employees or job applicants.
- Vicarious liability arising when a firm hires or authorizes another party to act on its behalf and this party injures a third party.

consequences, indirect and direct, of the possible loss should be considered together to evaluate the total potential for loss and to make plans to overcome the problem. Plans should be in place in advance to deal with such things as employee theft, theft in general, bomb scares, fires, explosions, bleacher failure, or any other disaster where the amount of damage can be reduced by the action of an emergency response team.

Developing and Implementing a Risk Management Program

After identifying and analyzing all potential sources of loss, the manager must develop and implement plans to deal with them before they occur. Accomplishing this task demands some knowledge of the alternative methods of dealing with risk. Figure 20.4 identifies a number of methods for dealing with potential losses.

Risk Avoidance

Risk avoidance means the chance of loss has been eliminated. In practice, it may mean not introducing a new product, ending the production of an existing product, discontinuing some operations, selecting a business location where a particular peril is not present, inspecting bleachers regularly, bonding all persons who deal with large sums of money, or preparing personnel for identifying and preventing risks.

Some risks are unavoidable (e.g. bankruptcy, liability suit, premature death of key personnel). The exposure to loss can often be reduced, but not eliminated. The basic rule that managers need to follow is: When the chance of loss is high and loss severity is also high, avoidance is often the best, and sometimes the only, practical alternative.

Risk Assumption

Risk assumption means that the consequences of a loss will be borne by the party exposed to the chance of loss. Often risk assumption is a deliberate risk management decision. That is, the assumption of the risk is undertaken with the full understanding that these are consequences of a potential loss, and with the understanding that these consequences will be borne by the one assuming the risk. Sometimes risk is assumed because the potential loss was not identified before it occurred.

Sport organizations assume risks when

- Loss costs are small and will be funded by current cash flow.
- Loss exposures are retained and funded with a cash reserve.
- Loss exposures are retained and recognized in an unfunded reserve account.
- A self-insured plan is operated.

Self-insurance

Self-insurance requires risk retention. It implies an attempt by the sport entity to combine a number of its own similar

Figure 20.4

Potential Methods for Dealing with Potential Losses

- Risk avoidance
- Risk assumption
- Risk transfer through insurance
- Risk transfer other than insurance
- Self-insurance
- Loss prevention
- Loss reduction

exposures to loss sufficient to predict the losses accurately. Further, a self-insurance plan suggests that adequate financial arrangements have been made in advance to provide funds to pay losses should they occur. Finally, unless payments to the self-insurance fund are calculated scientifically and paid regularly, a true self-insurance system does not exist.

Self-insurance plans appeal to some organizations because they see one or more of the following potential advantages:
- Improved loss prevention incentive,
- Improved claims settlement procedures, and
- Improved profitability, including the investment potential from investing cash flow.

Although a self-insurance plan may offer an organization the advantages outlined above, other factors must be taken into consideration when an organization is considering whether to self-insure, including:
- Hiring competent personnel to administer the self-insurance program,
- Cost of capital to operate the program, and
- The wisdom of assuming a risk before the financial arrangements are fully implemented.

Insurance
Insurance is an especially appropriate risk management tool when the chance of loss is low and the severity of the potential loss is high. Insurance is more than mere risk transfer; it is risk reduction because the pooling of numerous risks allows loss predictability. Further, insurance allows the purchaser to substitute a small certain premium for a large uncertain loss.

Finally, insurance companies often provide customers with valuable services in both loss prevention engineering and claims settlement.

Loss Prevention
Successful loss prevention activities lower the frequency of losses. An obvious and close connection exists between loss prevention activities and insurance premiums. The more effective the loss prevention, the lower the risk premiums, therefore, the manager frequently has responsibility for overseeing loss prevention activities.

Examples of loss prevention activities include the use of safety guards on saw blades, security guards near financial operations, ushers assisting customers at events, emergency medical personnel at events, safety education programs, warning signs posted, crowd control procedures, and much more. As a general rule, when frequency of loss is high, loss prevention activities should be considered as one alternative for dealing with the problem. Loss prevention measures are feasible, however, only as long as the benefits realized from fewer occurrences of loss are greater than the cost of the loss prevention measures.

Loss Reduction
Loss reduction activities that are successful reduce loss severity. Loss reduction activities aim at minimizing the impact of losses. Loss reduction activities include:
- Automatic fire-sprinkler system,
- Fire walls and doors,
- Training replacement personnel,
- Regular training of all personnel,
- Evacuation plans,
- Crowd control plans,
- Disaster plans, and
- Security plans.

In general, when the severity of loss is great, and when the loss cannot be avoided, loss prevention activities are appropriate. As was the case with loss prevention, loss reduction efforts can be justified only as long as the savings they produce exceed the cost of the effort.

Risk Transfer

Risk transfer means the original party exposed to a loss is able to obtain a substitute party to bear the risk. Risk transfer is a feature of all insurance transactions because of the uncertainty of who will pay for the loss is transferred from the organization to the insurance pool. The distinction between insurance and risk transfer is that insurance involves not only the mere transfer of risk, but also the reduction of risk through the predictability provided by the law of large numbers.

Hold-harmless Agreements

A hold-harmless agreement is a contract entered into prior to a loss, in which one party agrees to assume a second party's responsibility should a loss occur. For example, vendors request hold-harmless agreements before undertaking the sale of a manufacturer's goods, and contractors require subcontractors to provide the contractor with liability protection if they are sued because of the subcontractor's activities.

Regular Evaluation of the Risk Management Plan

After all potential sources of loss have been identified and plans to deal with them implemented, the manager must evaluate the program regularly to be sure it meets current needs and demands. Over time, conditions change in every sport entity (i.e., new assets acquired, old assets lose their value, new personnel, inventories increase and decrease, new products are marketed, and laws change). A review of existing risk management plans is always useful.

The actual results of the plans must be measured against the original goals and objectives. The variety of questions should be asked, including
- Has the insurance company provided all the service expected of it?
- Has the loss prevention program actually resulted in fewer losses?
- Have the risks that were assumed produced losses as expected?

The development and maintenance of accurate details on losses are important to most organizations. These details would usually include
- Date of loss,
- The amount of damage,
- The cause of the loss, and
- What steps were taken to prevent future occurrences.

Financial Risk Management

In addition to the pure risks an organization encounters, there are financial risks. The cost of capital issues and cash flow management issues are common threads connecting financial and pure risk management. There are five common financial risks, including:
- Interest-rate risk: loss potential caused by increasing interest rates reducing value of fixed-income securities.
- Credit risk: loss potential caused by a borrower defaulting on a loan.
- Currency risk: loss potential caused by unfavorable fluctuations in the value of domestic currency relative to foreign currencies.
- Liquidity risk: loss potential caused by having to take a substantial discount to liquidate an investment quickly.
- Market risk: loss potential caused by having to liquidate an investment at an unfavorable price, perhaps during a down part of the business cycle.

Each of these potential loss sources can be managed using some of the generic tools previously described including avoidance, assumption, and transfer. Insurance usually is not an option as these exposures are not predictable, and some exposures could prove catastrophic.

Summary

All firms and individuals face uncertainties caused by the possibility of loss. A risk management program is an organized method for dealing with risks. The program begins with identification and measurement of exposure to loss. The second step is to choose an approach from among the risk management alternatives and then to implement the decision. The third step is reevaluating and updating previous decisions.

The identification process begins with the recognition of four categories of losses: (1) direct losses of property, (2) indirect losses of income, (3) liability losses, and (4) loss of key personnel.

The development of a risk management program includes the choice of the most appropriate combination of risk management tools for a given exposure to loss. Every risk management decision should be reviewed regularly. Losses that were assumed years ago may now have to be insured.

There are seven ways to deal with risk, including risk avoidance, risk assumption, loss prevention, loss reduction, insurance, self-insurance, and risk transfer.

Glossary of Box/Ticket Office Terms

Advanced Sales - Tickets on sale during the days and weeks before the day of the event.

Agency Seats - Tickets, seats that are allocated to ticket agencies for sale, to be paid for by the agency, and released to the producer at an arranged time before each event.

At the Door - Also called "Pre-show" and "Ins," the hour and a half before the start of the event during which tickets are sold, the audience arrives and is seated.

Black Tie - Formal attire is expected to be worn by the audience, often on opening night and should be announced in advance.

Book Office - "The wallet of a theater," the place where tickets are sold. It can be a resident Box Office which is permanently located at the venue, a ticket agency which is an outlet handling ticket sales for several events, or a temporary set up "at the door" before the event.

Box Office Statement - The final accounting of tickets and income for each performance. This report should be created at the end of each performance. Copies should be submitted to the Producer or anyone who is responsible for financial accounting.

Capacity - The total number of audience members a space can hold without exceeding the maximum number set by the managers of the space and/or the fire department.

Comp - Abbreviation for complimentary. Complimentary tickets are free and are usually given to performers, event organizers, members of the press, contributors, and VIPs.

Consignment - Blocks of tickets printed and allocated to the event producers who sell these tickets, usually through members of the group organizing the event. The ticket manager should give out these tickets to group members in small quantities and keep a list of how many tickets have been given out and to whom.

Curtain Time - The time the event is scheduled to begin.

Dead Seats - Seats, locations, tickets deducted from the capacity and intentionally not sold to an event because they offer an obstructed view of the stage (caused by a pole, a conductor, or equipment) or have been removed to accommodate performers, musicians or some special production requirement.

Deadwood - All unsold tickets that remain after the event for which they were valid.

Dressing the House - The practice of selling tickets or placing audience members evenly throughout the seating area in order to avoid large gaps in the house, to give the illusion of a full house if a performance is not going to sell out.

Front of House - The lobby and box office area or any area inside the building to which the public has access except the theater itself.

Front of House Staff - The production staff who deal with the audience coming into the house prior to the start of the event; usually consists of the box office staff, the house manager and the ushers.

General Admission - Audience members do not have a specific seat assignment. Seats are taken on a first-come, first-serve basis. A General Admission House may be divided into sections. For example, the orchestra may have one ticket price and the balcony another ticket price; but there are no assigned seats within the section. A producer may request that particular seats be reserved for VIPs in an otherwise General Admission House.

Go Clean - To sell or give away every ticket for an event.

Group Sales - Sales of tickets usually 10 or more for which a discount is given.

Handicapped Accessible - Ability for the space to be accessed by patrons in wheelchairs or with any disability.

Handling Fee - An additional fee charged to the patron when purchasing tickets, usually for phone orders or credit card purchases.

Hold - (1) To make a ticket unavailable for sale, to put seats aside for use later (also referred to as "pulling" seats); (2) Ticket reservations that have been paid for and will be picked up by the patron at the door (also called "at the door holds").

House - The auditorium section of the theater, or simply put, where the audience sits. You will say the "House is open" to indicate that the audience has been permitted inside the theater or the "House is closed" to indicate that performers and crew may still be in the theater.

House Count - Also called a Ticket Stub Report. At the end of an event, the house manager and/or ushers count the number of ticket stubs collected at the door to determine how many people are in the house. A report recording the information may be required by the producer and ticket manager.

House Manager - The person who oversees the ushers and coordinates with the event producer and box office regarding all audience and seating issues before and during the event.

House Seats - Also called trouble seats, a pre-determined number of seats held aside by the producer in case of emergencies; used at the last moment by the producer, ticket manager, or house manager to solve any unexpected problems.

Intermission - A break taken during the event.

Late Seating - After the event has already commenced, audience members continue to arrive and are seated by an usher or the house manager at an appropriate moment during the event.

Off-Line/Kill - Seats that have been held and are unavailable for sale to the public because capacity needs to be diminished or there are obstructions.

On-Site - The space where the event is taking place.

Online - Seats for an event are available for sale to the public.

Papering the House - If ticket sales are going poorly, giving away a number of complimentary tickets to a wide range of people fills empty seats. It is commonly believed that it is better to fill the House with non-paying customers than for the House to appear empty.

Patron - A customer buying a ticket.

Pre-pull - To print all remaining unsold tickets for an event.

Press Seats - Seats held aside for members of the press who have been invited to the event and offered complimentary tickets for opening nights and other specially designated performances.

Price Structure - The series of ticket prices offered for a particular event including discounts. Reserved seating houses ordinarily have different prices for different seating sections.

Producer - The person responsible for overseeing the logistics of an event.

Producing Organization - The organization responsible for overseeing the logistics of an event.

Production - The event.

Program - A description of the event. The printed material given to audience members as they enter the performance space which describes the event, lists the performers and production staff, and sometimes contains advertisements.

Reconciliation - To settle an event financially by completing and comparing reports of ticket sales and income at the end of the day to make sure that ticket sales correctly match income.

Reservation - Tickets purchased or held.

Reserved Seating - Each seat location has a corresponding numbered or lettered ticket. A patron has "rights" to the specific seat for which s/he holds a ticket.

Run Time - The length of an event from beginning to end.

Seating Chart - Also called seating plan and manifest, the printed version of the seating configuration.

Seating Configuration - The way the seats are set up and numbered in the house; the two basic types of configurations are reserved seating and general admission.

Starter - The cash needed to give change to customers when selling tickets at the door, usually $100 in small bills and change.

Ticket - A legal contract promising that whatever is printed on it will actually occur as printed for the printed price. Should the producing organization be unable to furnish what is promised on the ticket, it must offer a refund.

A ticket is worth the exact cash value printed on it. Tickets should be handled with the same care as cash. If a ticket is lost or stolen, it is the same as if money were lost or stolen. A box office may contain tickets that represent thousands of dollars.

Ticket Agency (aka Point of Sale, Independent Ticket Operation) - An outlet, which is selling tickets for an event, may be operated by the venue itself or may be an independent outlet.

Ticket Stub - Also called audit stubs, usually a small portion of the ticket which is torn off by an usher as patrons enter the House, used for determining the House count.

TTY - Text-telephone used by deaf and hard of hearing people.

Unpaid Hold - A reservation made for tickets which the patron does not pay for ahead of time. They will purchase the tickets when they arrive at the door by a pre-determined deadline or prior to the release deadline.

Usher - A member of the production staff who works in the front of House tearing tickets, showing patrons to their seats, handling late seating and helping the House Manager to resolve seating issues as they arise.

Venue - The space where the event is taking place.

VIP Seats - Seats held for special people who have been invited and offered complimentary tickets. VIPs can be performers, guest artists, soloists, pre-concert lecturers, donors, people who need to be specially thanked for goods or services they rendered, faculty, administrative staff, and certain production staff such as directors or conductors.

Voucher - Sometimes called hardwood tickets. Documents presented at the Box Office in exchange for actual tickets. Can be used for complimentary tickets or special discounts. May also be printed as a blank form on which the appropriate information is written in lieu of actual tickets.

Appendix B

Sport Sponsorship Preparation and Proposal Outline

Preparation

Before embarking on a sponsorship drive the sport organization should identify the following:

- What type of support is the organization seeking (i.e., cash or in kind)?
- What types of businesses could provide the appropriate support?
- What benefits could be offered to sponsors?
- What links do members of the organization have with any potential sponsors?

Suggested Proposal Outline

Below is a typical outline of headings for a sponsorship proposal:

- Cover letter
- Overview (executive summary)
- Objectives
- The investment (i.e., amount of funding or in-kind support being sought)
- Time period
- Sponsorship benefits (i.e., naming rights, promotional strategies, signage, advertising, brand awareness opportunities, articles in newsletters, placement of the website, etc.)
- Target market (i.e., provide a target market profile and identify how it matches the target market of the proposed sponsor)
- Exclusivity
- Servicing the sponsors needs
- Evaluation strategy
- Renewal options
- Conclusions

Other Issues to Consider

The following tips will also help improve the overall proposal:

- Provide a clear and attractive cover page outlining the proposed sponsor and the organization requesting the sponsorship.
- Provide adequate space in the content so that it can be easily read.

- Provide a table of contents, proposal dividers, and a three-ring notebook.
- Examine additional information and determine whether it is best placed within the body of the document or as an attachment.
- Number pages
- Provide examples of programs, newsletters, web sites, etc., which show how previous sponsors have been acknowledged.

Appendix C

A Concession Lease Agreement

A Concession Lease Agreement covers many areas. It contains: Definitions, Terms of Agreement, Operational Condition, Special Conditions, and Legal Requirements.

Each part of the Concession Lease Agreement is important to your operation and the success of your concession. Be sure you know what will be required before you bid on any concession, and be sure you will be able to meet the obligations if you commit to it.

In order to give you some idea of what you will find in a Concession Lease Agreement, we are providing the following general information that we hope will help you decide on whether or not the operation of a Bureau of State Park concession should be in your future.

Length of the Concession Lease Agreement

A Concession Lease Agreement is generally awarded for a maximum period of 10 annual terms. In a few instances, agreements have been awarded for a lesser number of terms. This is based on circumstances as determined by the Bureau of State Parks that warrants a shorter period of award. These agreements can be awarded directly by the Bureau of State Parks.

Depending on the type of concession operation and if substantial capital development (permanent improvements or development that become the property of the Bureau at the termination of the agreement) is required by the concessionaire that will exceed at least $100,000, it is possible to award up to a 35 year agreement, if approval is granted by the Governor's Office.

Rental Payments

There are generally three different types of rental payments received from concessions: 1) Annual Lump Sum Payment only; 2) Annual Lump Sum Payment + 5% of the annual adjusted gross receipts; and 3) Annual Lump Sum Payment + 7% of the annual adjusted gross receipts.

Selecting which of the above listed methods is used is determined by the Bureau of State Parks prior to the solicitation of competitive bids and is based on the financial history of the involved concession.

Rental payments are required on a time schedule that is contained in the concession lease agreement. It may differ based on the type of concession operation and/or the operating season.

Consumer Price Index (CPI) and Increases to Rental Payments

Concession Lease Agreements that contain an Annual Lump Sum Payment of $500 or more are usually subject to a CPI increase at the beginning of each two year term the agreement is in effect.

The CPI increase is not applicable to Annual Lump Sum Payments of less than $500.

The CPI increase is not applicable to the payment of any required percentage of the annual adjusted gross receipts.

Pouring Rights

In 1999, the Bureau of State Parks designated "soft drink" products of The COCA-COLA Company of America as the official "soft drinks" of the Pennsylvania State Park System.

The Bureau now requires a Concessionaire who is awarded a new concession agreement to provide the public only those "soft drink" products available from The COCA- COLA Company of America.

Concessions that operate under agreements that existed prior to the official designation agreement may not contain the pouring rights clause. Many of these concessionaires have voluntarily switched to providing COCA-COLA products. If an addendum to an older concession agreement is processed, the pouring rights clause is added and becomes a part of the concession agreement.

The Bureau may periodically designate a different soft drink company and, as a result, a concessionaire would be required to change product lines.

Leased Premises

Each Concession Lease Agreement specifies the area of the park that is designated as the leased premises. A concessionaire is only permitted to operate and conduct business under the terms and conditions of the Concession Lease Agreement in the facilities or areas specified.

Maintenance of Leased Premises

The Concession Lease Agreement will specify the type of maintenance work to be done and whether it is required to be completed by the concessionaire or the park maintenance staff.

This can range from daily litter pickup to grass mowing, to building repairs, etc.

Some Concession Lease Agreements require the concessionaire to undertake all maintenance on their leased premises while others may allow for maintenance of certain items by both concessionaire and park staff.

Required Submittals

Each concessionaire, based on the terms and conditions of the Concession Lease Agreement, is required to submit certain payments, forms, financial statements, and other items on a timely basis. Failure to submit any of the required items in a timely fashion can result in the concessionaire being assessed liquidated damages for failure to comply with the agreement.

1. Rental Payment - The rental payment is required by specified dates, as listed in the Concession Lease Agreement. Failure to do so can not only result in the assessing of liquidated damages, but an interest charge of 18% will also be imposed on late payments.

2. Annual Financial Statement - Each concession operation is required to submit an Annual Concession Financial Statement (#6000-FM-SP0024), or any revisions thereof, by the due date listed in their agreement. This provides the Bureau of State Parks with a financial statement of the concessionaire's operating season.

3. Liability Insurance Policy - Concession Lease Agreements usually require the concessionaire to carry specified amounts of liability insurance with the Bureau of State Parks listed as a certificate holder and additional insured.

4. Fire Insurance Policy - If a building or buildings are leased to the concessionaire as a part of the concession operation, the concessionaire may be required to provide fire insurance in an amount equivalent to the replacement cost of the building, as determined by the Bureau of State Parks.

5. Performance Guarantee - A performance guarantee equal to the annual lump sum rental payment or an amount established by the Bureau of State Parks is required for most Concession Lease Agreements. Should the concessionaire fail to provide the concession services agreed to or meet the conditions of the agreement, and it results in the termination of the agreement, the performance guarantee will be liquidated and used to finance the process necessary to secure another concessionaire or to repair or replace facilities that may have been neglected by the terminated concessionaire.

6. Other Documents or Payments as Required by the Specific Concession Lease Agreement - It is the concessionaire's responsibility to meet all due dates and deadlines for submitting the required information, reports, and payments. The involved park staff is not required to send notices or reminders that items are due.

Concession Lease Termination

If a concessionaire wishes to terminate an existing agreement, they may do so by notifying the Bureau of State Parks, in writing, according to the time frame listed in their Concession Lease Agreement.

The Bureau of State Parks will not terminate a Concession Lease Agreement unless: 1) it becomes necessary due to the continued lack of concessionaire's compliance with the agreement terms and conditions; 2) it becomes necessary to close park facilities for safety or economic reasons; or 3) there are unforeseen circumstances that dictate a closure.

If the Bureau requires closure and the concessionaire is not able to operate for most or all of a season, it has been the Bureau of State Parks' policy to extend the existing agreement for an additional year, if acceptable to the concessionaire.

Pricing

A concessionaire may charge prices and rates that are reasonable and fair. A copy of all prices and rates must be submitted annually to the involved park office. The Bureau of State Parks must approve all charges, prior to opening each season.

Non-exclusive Rights

A concessionaire **does not have** exclusive rights to all concession operations within a particular state park, but rather, only to the specific operation at the specific location as described in the Concession Lease Agreement.

Concession Operation

A concessionaire is required to operate at specific times and on specific days as listed in the Concession Lease Agreement.

Any early closure or reduction in operating days or hours must be approved by the Park Manager.

If a concessionaire wishes to operate on additional days or additional hours, approval must also be requested from the local Park Manager.

Americans With Disabilities Act

Each Concession Lease Agreement contains a clause that requires the concessionaire to comply with the Americans with Disabilities Act Accessibility Guidelines (ADAAG). Any service-oriented concession, such as watercraft rental, would be required to provide access to watercraft and watercraft capable of serving disabled visitors that wish to rent a watercraft.

Appendix D — Request for Proposal for Food and Beverage Services

THE GOLF CLUB AT GLEN MAURY

I. PURPOSE

The City of Buena Vista is requesting proposals to provide Food and Beverage (including alcohol) Concession Services at The Golf Club at Glen Maury.

Proposer will not be allowed to submit proposals after the closing date of this Request for Proposals. The City shall evaluate all proposals as to what is in the "City's Best Interest."

II. DESCRIPTION OF FACILITIES AND EQUIPMENT

The Golf Club at Glen Maury is located within the City of Buena Vista and owned by the City of Buena Vista. This is an 18 hole, championship golf course with practice facility. The course was designed by Rick Jacobson and is currently being built by Wadsworth Golf Construction

Company with a scheduled opening date of summer 2004. The course is operated as a public, daily fee golf course and is open year-round. It is estimated that there will be 20,000 golfers the first year, increasing up to 30,000 golfers in the first three years.

Plans for a clubhouse are currently being designed. The clubhouse with the current design contemplates three different food and beverage outlets. The City is requesting bidder for Food and Beverage Services to bid on any of the following outlets:

A) Snack Bar - Counter Service - Snack Bar with at least 20 seats,
Including appropriately sized kitchen and all necessary equipment. Open from 7:00 a.m. to 6:00 p.m.

B) Club Dining - (including A above) - Sit down restaurant experience; with waiter service, serving lunch and casual dinner at minimum dining during the eight month golf season.

C) Banquet Pavilion (including A & B above) - Outdoor enclosed Banquet Tent (no HVAC) which would seat at least 180 people and would be serviced by Club Dining/Snack Bar Kitchen.

III. SUBMITTALS

Proposer shall submit proposal to include the following:

1. That the Proposer is qualified and eligible to secure an Alcohol Beverage Commission (ABC) License under applicable laws and regulations and applicable permits for such services.

2. Proposer will pay to the City and proposed annual incremental increases for the operation of The Golf Club at Glen Maury Food and Beverage Concessions for Snack Bar; Snack Bar/Club Dining; Banquet Pavilion/Snack Bar/Dining Club Dining.

3. The Proposer must provide a Cash-Flow analysis. An analysis of the Proposer's ability to provide sufficient revenue to recapture the Proposer's investment, cover operating expenses, service any other debt, yield adequate return and profit to manage the golf course concessions operations.

4. Business Resume. A resume including business activities of the Proposer's major business should be submitted. A statement should be provided given the Proposer's experience in food concession services. In the event that the Proposer has provided such golf course food and beverage and concession services on a contractual basis to a public agency or to a private entity, the Proposer shall submit the name, address and phone number of such clientale, and a brief description of the services provided and other pertinent data. Further, the Proposer must identify any such contracts within the last five (5) years, that have been cancelled or not renewed. Failure to provide this information shall be cause for disqualification of the proposal.

5. Proposed Menu Price List. Proposer shall provide sample menu for established prices for the three (3) options outlined.

6. Sample of menu of existing food service operations.

IV. TERM OF AGREEMENT

The term of Agreement may be for one two-year term with three optional one (1) year extensions, at the discretion of the City.

The proposed starting date to begin operations is June 1, 2004. Although lease payment will not begin until course is open.

V. SCOPE OF WORK

Proposer is to insure continuous sanitary conditions and safe and proper food handling measures are taken so as to protect workers and patrons.

Proposer is to insure that buildings, including restrooms and common space, but excluding golf pvd-shop, are cleaned no less than daily and more frequently if use is heavy.

Proposer is to insure interior and exterior walls of the food preparation areas shall be kept clean and sanitary.

Proposer is to insure the walls and equipment shall be cleaned when soiled and sanitized at the close of each business day.

Proposer is to operate concessions at the course in accordance with local, state, and federal laws; and to obtain necessary permits to allow lawful operations.

Proposer shall make every reasonable effort to provide the safest operation possible.

Proposer to maintain a dress code for concession employees (approved by the City Manager) insures that the staff is courteous and have an excellent professional attitude toward the public to insure the best possible public relations for the City of Buena Vista.

All signs in clubhouse should be neatly prepared and of a professional caliber.

Clubhouse public utilities including but not limited to gas, oil, telephone, fuel, electricity, and any other services furnished to the leased premises, unless otherwise specified, will be paid by the City.

The Proposer shall provide and arrange for the collection and removal of all garbage, litter, and trash collected within leased premises at his/her expense.

The proposer shall provide complimentary lunch for the Director of Golf Operations and Superintendent of Greens.

VI. ACTIVITIES AND HOURS OF OPERATION AT THE COURSE

The Proposer will have exclusive concessionaire rights on the golf course and the clubhouse facilities.

The hours of operation shall be:

A. Clubhouse from 7:00 a.m. - 6:00 p.m. (April to October).
B. Club Dining Services 11:00 a.m. - 9:00 p.m. (April - October).
C. Pavilion/Banquet - based upon demand.

VII. INSURANCE

A. The successful Proposer shall carry the required amounts of insurance specified below throughout the contract period and submit a Certificate of Insurance certifying this and naming the City of Buena Vista as an additional insured:

A. General liability $1,000,000 combined single limit bodily injured and property damage including liquor liability $3,000,000 aggregate.
B. Workers compensation statutory.
C. Automobile liability $1,000,000 combined single limit.
D. Hold Harmless-Indemnification:

Proposer shall assume the entire responsibility and liability for any and all damages to persons or property caused by or resulting from or arising out of any act or omission on the part of Proposer, its agents, or employees under or in connection with this contract or the performance or failure to perform any work required by this contract. Proposer shall save harmless and indemnify City and its agents, volunteers, servants, employees, and officers from and against any and all claims, losses, or expenses, including but not limited to attorney's fees, which either or both of them may suffer, pay, or incur as the result of claims or suits due to, arising out of or in connection with any and all such damage, real or alleged. Proposer shall, upon written demand by city, assure and defend at Proposer's sole expense any and all such suits or defense of claims.

Fire Insurance - The Proposer must provide fire coverage insurance on the Proposer owned contents and equipment at its own cost.

Appendix E

Job Description

SUPERVISOR, FOOD CONCESSIONS

The following statements are intended to describe the general nature and level of work being performed. They are not intended to be construed as an exhaustive list of all responsibilities, duties and skills required of personnel so classified.

SUMMARY:

Under general direction, oversees the concessions programs at university sports facilities, including supervision of concessions workers and maintenance of inventory, supplies, and equipment.

DUTIES AND RESPONSIBILITIES:

1. Expedites concession operations during sports events and intervenes in crisis situations; recommends methods and procedures to improve sales and services.

2. Supervises the preparation and sale of food and beverages for university athletic activities.

3. Supervises personnel, which typically includes recommendations for hiring, firing, performance evaluation, training, work allocation, and problem resolution.

4. Oversees handling and balancing of cash sales and maintains expense and income records.

5. Develops record keeping procedures and manages appropriate department records in accordance with applicable regulations, policies, and standards.

6. Orders, stocks, and maintains concession food and supplies inventories.

7. Cleans equipment and performs routine maintenance.

8. Assists in the annual budget planning process and regularly monitors expenditures.

9. Performs miscellaneous job-related duties as assigned.

MINIMUM JOB REQUIREMENTS:
High school diploma or GED with 3 to 5 years experience directly related to the duties and responsibilities specified.

KNOWLEDGE, SKILLS, AND ABILITIES REQUIRED:

- Ability to communicate effectively, both orally and in writing.
- Expediting skills.
- Knowledge of food preparation procedures.
- Skill in the use of computers, preferably in a PC, Windows-based operating environment.
- Knowledge of supplies, equipment, and/or services ordering and inventory control.
- Knowledge of customer service standards and procedures.
- Ability to supervise and train staff, including organizing, prioritizing, and scheduling work assignments.
- Ability to foster a cooperative work environment.
- Records maintenance skills.
- Employee development and performance management skills.
- Skill in budget preparation and fiscal management.
- Knowledge of maintenance and care of culinary facilities, equipment, supplies, and materials.
- Knowledge of cash management principles and/or procedures.

CONDITIONS OF EMPLOYMENT:
- Successful candidate must submit to post-offer, pre-employment physical examination/medical history check.

WORKING CONDITIONS AND PHYSICAL EFFORT:

- Work involves moderate exposure to unusual elements, such as extreme temperatures, dirt, dust, fumes, smoke, unpleasant odors, and/or loud noises.
- Moderate physical activity. Requires handling of average-weight objects up to 25 pounds or standing and/or walking for more than four (4) hours per day.

Work environment involves minimal exposure to physical risks, such as operating dangerous equipment or working with chemicals.

Appendix F

Organizational Assessment

A first step in initiating a volunteer management system is organization assessment. An organization assessment is simply a systematic examination of one or more aspects of operation using Kipling's "six honest serving men." According to Heidrich (1990), a total organization assessment may include:

- review or development of the mission statement;
- development of a statement delineating the relationship of fundraising and/or financial management to the organization;
- collection of community data (e.g., trends in the community at large, social problems, housing, education, population growth);
- evaluation of factors in the macro-environment (e.g., political arena, regulatory parameters, economic environment, cultural foundations, technical issues);
- evaluating facilities (i.e., age, condition, maintenance, future needs);

- evaluating personnel (e.g., paid, full-time, part-time, volunteers, independent contractor);
- evaluating the volunteer personnel management system (i.e., job responsibilities, recruiting methods, orientation and training opportunities, supervision, retention programs, recognition);
- evaluating sources of revenue (e.g., growth, decline, potential for development, threats); and
- collection of workforce data (i.e., age, number of workers in various categories, gender, martial status, salary review).

Organization Assessment Checklist

The following organization assess-ment checklist should be implemented prior to deciding whether or not a volunteer personnel management system should be established:

- Mission statement: Is there a mission statement? Does it provide guidance for all programs including the volunteer program?
- Leadership style: What is the leadership style of those in charge of the organization?
- Red tape: What about the program rules, regulations, procedures, red tape, layers of authority, complexity? Too many? Too much? Not enough?
- Atmosphere: Is the atmosphere formal or informal? Friendly? Relaxed? Hurried? Competitive? Is there an "inner circle"?
- Decision making authority: Where is the authority? Who has the "final say" on any issue? How are decisions made?
- Reward and recognition: How much, what kind, and from whom?

- Risk: What is the atmosphere for new ideas? Are new ideas encouraged or discouraged? Are programs and individuals evaluated?
- Support: Who receives what help from whom? Is there an atmosphere of caring? What about burnout? Is there training that not only helps volunteers do a better job but also encourages their personal growth?
- Standards: How high are the standards of conduct and expectations for volunteers and staff? What about safety standards? What about the quality of programs?
- Conflict: How are conflicts handled? Resolved or ignored? Openly? Behind the scenes?
- Identity: Is there a sense of belonging to a group? How strong is group loyalty? How carefully are newcomers oriented to the group?

Source

Heidrich, K.W. (1990). *Working with volunteers.* Champaign, IL: Sagamore Publishing.

Appendix G

Retirees: A Good Source of Volunteers-Retirees Clubs

Some of the greatest sources of expertise and volunteer assistance are a company's retirees. They have many years of experience, loads of knowledge, and for the most part, are loyal to the company. The sport manager needs to tap this well by establishing, organizing, and implementing a "retirees club."

The purpose of the retirees club would be to have fun while assisting the organization and to gather for social activities regularly. The depth of structure would be left up to the club membership.

Club responsibilities might include (1) updating the membership list, (2) collecting dues and handling funds, (3) producing a newsletter on paper or through electronic media, (4) coordinating trips, (5) event planning, (6) securing restaurant reservations, (7) reserving meeting rooms, (8) sending out meeting notices, (9) producing mailings, (10) writing letters, and (11) making phone calls.

Finally, the retiree volunteers could do the following tasks for the organization: (1) answer phones, (2) barbecue foods for picnics, (3) collect raffle tickets, (4) coordinate pickup and drop-off of photo finishing, (5) fill temporary positions, (6) greet attendees at events, (7) help run the golf range, (8) lead art projects at children's events, (9) park cars at events, (10) plan events, (11) serve as costume characters at children's events, (12) stuff envelopes for mailers, (13) take pictures at events, and (14) track sign-up sheets for events.

Appendix H

Developing Volunteer Training Programs

Volunteer training sessions may be conducted by a variety of people from both inside and outside the organization. Usually the subject matter of the training dictates who does the teaching. Often volunteers respond well to an "outside expert" who can bring a fresh perspective to the subject of the training.

The best way to design a training session is to work with a planning committee. Here are a few topics to consider:

- How to conduct a meeting,
- Leadership,
- Group dynamics,
- Event planning,
- One-on-one fundraising, and
- Dealing with difficult people.
  Meagher (1995), Stier (1994, 1993), and Heidrich (1990) suggest the following are the basic steps to be taken when planning a training program:
- Identify the target audience and assess needs,
- Form a planning committee,

- Have a goal,
- Have objectives,
- Identify the program content,
- Plan the instructional approaches to be used (i.e., lecture, lecture and discussion, small group discussion, etc.),
- Plan the agenda,
- Decide how you will know when the goal is reached,
- Arrange for instructors, speakers, presenters,
- Make a list of the equipment needed,
- Make a list of materials to be given to trainees,
- Decide on location for the training,
- Know the estimated cost of the training,
- Publicize the event,
- Invite special guests,
- Check back with resource people,
- Double check the equipment,
- Conduct the training,
- Evaluate, and
- Write thank you letters.

Appendix 1

Questions to Ask Prior to Purchasing EPLI

- How does the state treat EPL punitive damages?
- Does the policy allow the insured choice of defense counsel?
- Does the coverage extend fully to the entity and its owners, partners, officers, directors, shareholders, and employees?
- Does the policy exclude coverage for "intentional acts"; and if so, would coverage still be denied if an intentional act committed by an employee results in the entity being named in the lawsuit?
- Are defense costs outside the policy limits? If not, a sizable chunk of the policy limit could be used to pay for defense costs which could be problematic if a sizable award is determined.
- Does the policy include a participation clause (i.e., requiring the insured to pay a percentage of the settlement)? This could prove to be costly to the entity owner.

- Will the policy respond to EFI lawsuits out of the actions of leased employees?
- Is coverage "retroactive" (i.e. will it respond to lawsuits arising out of "prior acts" allegedly committed but not discovered prior to the policy inception date, assuming another EPLI policy was in place at the time)?
- Does the policy offer an extended reporting provision allowing the owner to report a claim during a redetermined period of time after the policy period for incidents that occurred while the policy was in force?
- Does the policy compel the insured to accept settlement terms as agreed to by the insurance company as a condition of coverage?
- Does the policy promise to pay on behalf of the insured, in which case, the insurance company would pay for EPL expenses as they occur, or

does the policy promise to "indemnify" the insured, which would require the entity to payout all EPL expenses up front, and be reimbursed by the insurer?

Appendix

The Articles of Incorporation of a Non-Profit Organization

Of great importance in the determination of organizational activity is the paper-work upon which the club stands. Whether the organization is incorporated or not, the articles of incorporation or association usually define the objectives, functions, and responsibilities and may include a constitution and bylaws.

The name and purposes should be contained in the charter and constitution and should be stated in general terms. The constitution is important because it provides for inevitable changes in activities and programs of the association and helps to avoid subsequent changes in legal documents. The organization's papers should define membership eligibility, voting control and rights, the methods of electing governing boards, and similar essentials.

Since all of these procedures are basically legal in character, it is clear that competent counsel should be retained to ensure proper compliance with the legal requirements.

Club membership should be representative. All who qualify should be eligible for membership. There should be no membership restrictions. Membership should be voluntary, with no pressures, economic or otherwise. Most organizations maintain the principle of one vote per member, regardless of size, income, volume of business, or contribution to the financing of the organization.

Defining the Constitution and Bylaws

The constitution and bylaws contain provisions for the election of a governing board which is generally named a "Board of Directors" or "Board of Trustees" or "Executive Committee." Regardless of the name of the governing group, the number, method of selection, terms, duties, and responsibilities are provided for in the constitution or bylaws.

Before becoming incorporated, the booster club must draft a constitution and bylaws. Although each booster club's constitution and bylaws vary, here are some common subjects to include:

- Statement of purpose: Includes the reason for existence and mission statement.
- Forms, types, and qualifications of membership: Describes the membership opportunities and requirements.
- Dues structures: Explains the membership cost and the renewal process.
- Elected officers: Lists the board of directors' titles, including descriptions of their terms, powers, duties, and rules for filling vacancies.
- Chief executive officer: Details this position's responsibilities and powers, including reporting procedures.
- Voting qualifications: Provides descriptions of procedures, proxies, and quorum provisions.
- General assembly: Explains when a general assembly is in order and how it should be structured.
- Standing committee: Defines the purpose and responsibilities of a standing committee, as well as who can participate.
- Accounting, fiscal, and reporting procedures: Outlines how funds will be tracked and recorded.
- Corporate seal: Explains how the organization can obtain the corporate emblem and in which context it can be reproduced.
- Amending the constitution and/or bylaws and dissolution: Describes the necessary procedure for revising the bylaws.

Defining the Board

There are a variety of methods for selecting board members, ranging from direct election by the membership to selection through the sport organization's administration. Board sizes vary, with the optimum being in the range of 7-11 members. Aim for an odd number of board members to avoid tie votes during an election. Some of the leadership titles that will need to be filled include president or chairperson, secretary, treasurer, and various vice-presidents; titles that can be determined by specific needs.

When structuring the board of directors, consider recruiting members with various expertise and talent. This will allow the booster club to offer a variety of programs and services. With the sports organization's activities in mind, ask yourself if it would be beneficial to have a lawyer, banker, sport physician, retail executives, etc.

Another issue to consider when assembling a board is members' geographical locations. Members located away from the sport organization should have geographical representation on your board. To offer opportunities for more participation, consider organizing standing committees, special interest groups, or ad hoc groups. These groups are formed for special purposes or functions. They are self-limiting in time and scope, focusing only on the short-term needs of the association. The tasks and decision making involved in these groups will relieve the board of certain responsibilities and provide a new perspective in board discussions.

The size of governing boards varies widely. In general, the larger the club, the larger the board. The principle followed is for the board to reflect adequate representation of members with the number fairly proportional to the size of the association and its interests. Most organizations provide fixed terms for board members, although some do not. With fixed terms, the length of service of a board member is known. Rotation of part of the board at regular intervals allows for changing the membership on a systematic basis, thus allowing for the retention of some experienced members and the continuity of policies and stability of the program.

Provisions are generally made in the club's documents for an executive committee consisting of a small number of members of the board and including the principal elective officers. In some clubs, the committee structure affecting the government of the association is clearly spelled out in the organization's documents, but there is no general common practice. Usually, the top authority is vested in the governing board; and, except for meetings of the full membership of the club, the board decides the policies of the association. Of the board, the elected chief officer, usually the president, is the association spokesman, although there are exceptions to this practice.

It is appropriate to say that the most important criterion for the evaluation of any organizational system is: "Does it get the job done?" Obviously, the really worthwhile manager does her/his own thinking and decides her/his own needs and cures. The manager listens carefully, reads numerous articles, makes mental notes of the methods that have proven effective or troublesome for others. But, when the chips are down, and the manager is face to face with an organizational need, the last thing he can do is to find the book on the shelf that provides a cookbook solution.

Organizational structure and procedure must never be considered final, unchangeable, or irrevocable. The innovative association executive knows that there is always one more wrinkle to be ironed out and two more corners to be turned. In fact, it is her/his appreciation for the very process of wrinkle-ironing and corner-turning that makes the manager worth her/his salt to her/his club.

Incorporating a Booster Club

After gaining the support of the club being supported, the booster club board requests a letter of understanding be-tween the booster club and the organization being drafted. This letter should outline the guidelines for operation of the booster club, including who pays for space, which products and services the organization will provide, whether the organization will pay for the printing of the club's newsletters and distribution, and so on. Decisions between the management and the club also will center on reimbursement for staff time and organizational events, as well as reporting mechanisms. Once management support has been formalized, the organizers can begin developing a strategic fundraising plan and seeking incorporation.

In order to incorporate the booster club, the organizers must contact their state commerce department or department of state. Each state has different requirements regarding incorporation. The state will want to know the governance details and structure of the booster club and will ask questions about the organization's mission and objectives, the leadership of the organization, and the first year's budget. The organization, after successfully incorporating, will need to request a federal employer identification number. This task is completed after submitting to the IRS form 504. The booster club can be organized in any state. There are several advantages to incorporating the booster club (Schools, 2000):

- Eliminates volunteer leaders' personal liability,
- Establishes continuity of the organization,
- Creates a business environment,
- Provides protection under libel laws,
- Makes it easier to obtain liability insurance, and
- Enforces guidelines for administration and organization.

Appendix K

Application Procedures (IRS Tax Code)

Most organizations seeking recognition of exemption from federal income tax must use application forms specifically prescribed by the IRS. One of the requirements is the employer identification number (EIN), whether or not the association has any employees. If the association does not have an EIN, the application for recognition for exemption should include a completed Form SS-4, "Application for Employer Identification Number."

Each application for exemption must be accompanied by a copy of the association's articles of incorporation, constitution, bylaws, or other enabling document. Bylaws alone are not organizing documents. However, if the club is a corporation or unincorporated club/club that has adopted bylaws, those bylaws should be included in the application.

Each attachment should show the name and address of the club, the date, an identifiable heading, and that it is an attachment to the application. Do not submit original documents because they become part of the IRS file and cannot be returned.

A full description of the purposes and the activities of the club should be included in the application. When describing the activities in which the club expects to engage, include the standards, criteria, procedures, and other means that the club adopted or planned for carrying out those activities.

Financial statements showing receipts and expenditures for the current years and the three (3) preceding years (or for the number of years the association has been in existence, if less than four years) must be provided. For each accounting period, a description of the sources of the receipts and the nature of the expenditures is also required. A balance sheet must be included for the most recent period. If the club has not yet begun operations, or has operated for less than one year, a proposed budget for two full accounting periods and a current statement of assets and liabilities will be acceptable.

The description of the sources of receipts should show whether support will be from public or private sources. The club should also indicate whether the support will come from contributions, grants, or other means. If the club anticipates income from fund-raising events, ticket sales, rentals, or other business or investment sources, it should fully explain the nature of such activities.

When describing expenses, the club should distinguish between expenditures made directly for furtherance of exempt purposes and those made for administration and general operations. Finally, the criteria to be used for selecting recipients of funds or other benefits from the club also should be fully explained.

The financial data included in the application must be in sufficient detail to show how activities will be financed. The club should furnish a statement of actual and proposed fund-raising activities.

The IRS may require the association to provide additional information necessary to clarify the nature of the organization. Some examples of such additional material are (1) representative copies of advertising placed; (2) copies of publications, such as magazines; (3) distributed written material used for expressing views on proposed legislation; and (4) copies of leases, contracts, or agreements into which the association has entered.

Appendix

Grooming the New Booster Club Directors

Every director once was new to the job. The newcomer may be all the more valuable to the board because she/he is new, contributing new ideas, new approaches, and possibly fresh expertise. Certainly, she/he should not merely sit tight. She/he has a contribution to make, and the top staff executive is responsible for stimulating her/his maximum contribution.

Many organizations/clubs have a formal orientation program for new directors. This program discusses the purposes and history of the association, reviews past activities and programs, and explains anticipated problems and trends of the association. This orientation process enables the new director to be a contributing, responsible board member at an early date.

The newcomer should be encouraged to read again the constitution and bylaws of the club and review its stated objectives and rules as well as the responsibilities of directors. It will usually be helpful for her/him to review minutes of board meetings for the past two or three years. This will help her/him learn something of what has been accomplished and, in many cases, how success was achieved or how failure occurred.

Part of the learning process can come from simply getting around. The new director should be encouraged to visit with the club's chief executive and, if possible, spend some time with the president. At least one of these visits may be combined with a look around the club's headquarters with the new director meeting the staff and noting the available facilities. Probably the new board member is already generally acquainted with the president and the staff executive through service on committees or other association business. An opportunity to question the executive and her/his fellow directors can help the newcomer to the board as s/he seeks to determine how his talents would best serve the club.

The new director should be encouraged to make contact with other members. Visits with members can help the director learn how they feel the club might serve them better, and thus she or he can improve his touch and contact with his constituency.

When the board meets, the new director, like the veteran, should be as well informed as possible on the issues to be discussed. The preparation of a board book will help her/him be more comfortable, confident, and effective in promoting programs he deems essential. Yet, the views of those who differ should be respected.

It is important that the newcomer to the board approach her/his work with an objective viewpoint and the realization that the director represents not her/his own company or office, but members of an association who embrace a wide range of thinking and interest. The club executive can help encourage this objectivity.

Appendix M

Insurance Companies Offering

Insurance Programs for Health/Fitness, Recreation, and Sport Programs

The following are a few groups that offer insurance programs for health/fitness, recreation, and sport programs:

Allied Specialty Insurance, Inc.
10541 Gulf Blvd.
Treasure Island, FL 33706
800/237-3355

Bollinger
499 Bloomfield Avenue
Montclair, NJ 07042
800/526-1379

Continental Insurance Co.
One Continental Drive
Suite 600
Cranbury, NJ 08570
609/395-2429

Dexter & Company
5910 N. Central Expwy,

Dallas, TX 75206
214/891-6400

Health Special Risks, Inc.
880 Sibley Memorial Hwy., #101
Mendota Heights, MN 55118
800/328-1114

Hughes & Associates, Inc.
Rt. 202 & Meadow Brook Lane
Chalfont, PA 18914
215/822-8700

International Accident Facilities
One State Street
Boston, MA 02109
800/272-7488

ISU Hoffman Insurance
200 Linden Street
Wellesley, MA 02181
800/277-6052

K&K Insurance Group, Inc.
1712 Magnavox Way
Fort Wayne, IN 46804
219/455-3000

Rollins Hudig Hall of Utah, Inc
2180 S 1300 E., Suite 500
Salt Lake, UT 84117
801/488-2550

Appendix N

Forming a Limited Liability Company

What is a limited liability company?

A limited liability company, like a corporation, is a legal entity existing separately from its owners. A limited liability company is created when proper articles of organization (or the equivalent under the laws of a particular state) are filed with the proper state authority and all fees are paid. State laws typically impose additional pre or post-creation requirements as well.

A limited liability company is not a partnership or a corporation, but it combines the corporate advantages of limited liability with (normally) the partnership advantage of pass-through taxation.

The organizational structure of an LLC

A limited liability company is owned by its members who may (member-managed) directly manage the limited liability company, or who may (manager-managed) appoint managers to directly manage the limited liability company for them.

The members may also apportion duties amongst themselves as they see fit and may even appoint one of their members president, or vice president, or secretary, or treasurer with the appointed member to have the duties normally associated with such title or titles. One of the virtues of a limited liability company is the ability (in most states) to structure the limited liability company; however, its members want it to be structured.

The advantages of forming a limited liability company

The primary advantage of a limited liability company is limiting the liability of its members. Unless they personally guarantee them, the members are not liable for the debts and obligations of the limited liability company. In a partnership or sole proprietorship, creditors may seize personal assets of the participants to pay debts of the business.

Additionally, (1) pass-through taxation is available, meaning that (generally speaking) the earnings of an LLC are not subject to double taxation but are treated like the earnings from partnerships, sole proprietorships, and S corporations and (2) the members have greater flexibility in structuring the limited liability company than is ordinarily the case with a corporation including the ability to divide ownership and voting rights in unconventional ways while still enjoying the benefits of pass-through taxation.

The disadvantages of forming a limited liability company

The primary disadvantages are (1) the work involved in, and the expense of, forming a limited liability company, and (2) after-formation record keeping requirements. While limited liability companies have not been in existence in this country for nearly so long as corporations and there is thus less law interpreting the limited liability company statutes and the rights of limited liability company members, it is very likely that the development of the law will be similar to the law as it has developed over the years in the case of corporations.

Paper work involved

First, articles of organization according to state law must be prepared and filed with the proper state authorities and filing fees, initial franchise taxes, and other initial fees must be paid. Second, if the limited liability company is to be structured properly, an Operating Agreement and organization minutes of the limited liability company must be prepared.

If you form your limited liability through us, you have two choices: (1) "bare-bones" formation (like most non-lawyer services) where we take care of the first item above and you deal with the second or (2) complete service, where we take care of both the first and second items, do membership interest documents and investment letters, provide a Right Of First Refusal Agreement and provide you with tax information and check lists for immediate and future use. For the difference in price, see fees.

Is an attorney necessary?

No, but if you are going to pay as much for non-lawyer assistance, why not have the benefit of competent professional help? There is a reason all the big guys use lawyers.

LLC compared to S corporation

S corporations and limited liability companies both permit pass-through taxation when properly structured and the proper tax forms are filed, but a limited liability company is more flexible in allocating income amongst the members: (1) a limited liability company may offer several classes of interest while an S corporation may only have one class of stock, and (2) the interest in a limited liability company may be owned by any number of individuals or entities whereas ownership interest in an S corporation is limited both in number and in the entities which may participate.

Where to form your limited liability company

You should probably form your LLC in your home state, just as you should probably incorporate in your home state, for the same reasons we cited when advising that you should probably incorporate in your home state.

Naming your limited liability company

The name you select must not be the same as or deceptively similar to an existing limited liability company in your state. For example, if a limited liability company named Hyperlinks Limited Liability Company exists in your state, you very likely would not be allowed to name your business Hyperlinks LLC, and you probably couldn't call it Hyperlinx LLC either. Since it is possible that the name you select will not be distinguishable, we ask for a second choice on the

LLC formation order form. Additionally, the name you choose must show your business has limited liability. Most states require that the limited liability company name be followed by Limited Liability Company or by the abbreviation LLC.

Number of people needed to form an LLC

The IRS does allow one member LLCs to qualify for pass-through tax treatment; however, taxation of one person LLCs at the state level may be different, and many states require that an LLC have at least two members. In view of the recent change in IRS rules permitting one member LLCs, however, it is likely that more states will recognize them, and you should always check with us at the time of formation.

Taxation of limited liability companies

You should consult with your tax preparer concerning taxation issues. Generally speaking, LLCs are permitted (under federal law) to elect whether to be taxed as corporations or to have pass-through taxation.

Getting Started

After you have dealt with the questions above, articles of organization must be filed with the state government and initial fees must be paid. Your attorney will take care of that for you, professionally and promptly.

After your Articles are filed, your limited liability company should hold an organizational meeting and must have an Operating Agreement in order to complete the formation process. Membership interest documents should be distributed to the members and records kept of such distributions.

Non-lawyer formation services typically sell you a book with a sample operating agreement, sample organization minutes, and sample membership interest documents. With them, it's your job to do the actual Operating Agreement, the actual organizational minutes, and the actual membership interest documents. Moreover, you are left on your own as to subsequent record keeping.

In most states, neither an expensive book nor a seal is required. For $185 instead of the $60-$100 you pay for these normally unnecessary items, we will do the actual Operating Agreement, do the actual organization minutes, do the actual membership interest documents, do a Right Of First Refusal Agreement, provide you with checklists to assist you in subsequent record keeping, and provide you with the forms and instructions you need to obtain your federal tax identification number.

Appendix O

Sample Trademark Licensing Policy

Nottingham University Trademark Licensing Policy

Summary

Nottingham University owns and controls its name(s) and other marks, logos, insignias, seal, designs and symbols (hereafter, "marks" or "trademarks") that have become associated with the University. Examples of NU's trademarks are NU, the stylized N and NU, the N-Cat head design, the Nottingham official seal, the name Nottingham and Nottingham Wildcats, Purple Pride.

The primary purpose of the Nottingham University licensing program is to protect the integrity of the University's identifying marks. The Licensing Program also serves Nottingham University by:

- Ensuring that products bearing NU's marks are of good quality;
- Ensuring that each licensed use reflects positively on the University, and
- Generating revenues for the University.

The purpose of this policy statement is to provide guidance on permissible use, as well as restrictions on the use, of the University's names and marks, and to clarify responsibility for granting permission and licenses required. Any individual, organization or company wishing to use Nottingham's marks must be licensed and shall be regulated by the Nottingham University Trademark Licensing Office.

Licensing Requirements

A license is required for any individual, organization, or company wishing to reproduce Nottingham University's name or trademarks for a commercial or non-commercial venture. The trademarks of Nottingham University may not be incorporated into the name or mark of any commercial company. Permission is required for the name or marks of the University to be incorporated into the name or mark of any organization. A license is not required for advertisements promoting the sale of licensed products. Such advertisements, however, shall not imply any relationship other than that of licensor/licensee and should include the licensing label which identifies officially licensed goods.

Merchants may be allowed to use the University's name in newspaper advertisements that welcome or congratulate students provided the copy does not contain either an implied or explicit endorsement connecting the University with the advertiser, its products, or its services. Additionally, there must be no violation of National Collegiate Athletic Association regulations. Licensees and merchants must obtain approval for each use of the University's name and marks on a per-product, per-design basis.

University Schools, Departments, and Affiliated Organizations

University schools, departments, and affiliated organizations may not assign, sublicense, or modify the name Nottingham or Nottingham University or any marks of the University. All products which University schools, departments, or affiliates wish to have produced bearing the name and marks of the University are regulated by the Trademark Licensing program.

Athletic Department Official Sponsors

Nottingham University Athletic Department official sponsors may use the University's name and marks in conjunction with the sponsor's name and marks when accompanied by the term "Official Athletic Sponsor" according to the contract terms reached between the Athletic Department and the sponsor.

All items produced with the term "Official Athletic Sponsor" on promotional items to be given away by a for profit or not-for-profit third party entity must be produced by a licensed company.

In the case of a promotional item that is sold or redeemed with proof of purchase certificate, a royalty fee payable to the Trademark Licensing Office will apply.

Unacceptable Products/Services

Nottingham University will not approve the use of its name or marks to promote the following products: tobacco, controlled substances, sexually oriented products, religious products, bathroom articles, or games of chance. In addition, the University will not approve the use of its name or marks with text or graphics that are judged to be sexually suggestive, denigrate any group, including another college or university, or infringe on the rights of other trademark owners. The University will not license products that do not meet minimum standards of quality and/or good taste or are judged to be dangerous or carry high product liability risks.

Advertising in Publications

Nottingham University and University-affiliated organizations that accept commercial advertising for their publications and programs will screen all advertisers for compliance with the University's Trademark Licensing Program. Advertising from non-licensed manufacturers of trademarked products or advertisements using NU's marks without a license will not be accepted for publication.

Compliance Program

The Trademark Licensing Office will maintain a compliance program in the local area. National compliance will be handled by the University's licensing agent.

Royalties and Fees

The University assesses royalties on net, wholesale sales. Royalties will be charged for promotional and/or advertising licenses. Royalties generated by the licensing program are transferred to the University's General Fund.

Royalty Exemptions

University schools, departments, students, and affiliated groups that order items imprinted with NU's name and marks may be exempt from paying royalties if:

- The items will be used for internal University purposes,
- Will be given away at no charge, or
- Will be sold for University-related fundraising.
- To become eligible for the royalty exemption, contact the Trademark Licensing Office stating how the item will be used and the name of the company the item will be purchased from.

Please note that only licensed manufacturers may reproduce the University's name and marks. If the company you have chosen is not licensed, the Trademark Licensing Office will recommend a licensed company or license the company of your choice on a special, limited-term basis.

Trademark Licensing Office

University Services has been designated as the division responsible for the administration of the Nottingham University Trademark Licensing Program. The Trademark Licensing Office maintains the official inventory of the University, approves and registers new marks, and maintains a list of licensees authorized to manufacture and distribute goods bearing the marks of the University.

The Trademark Licensing Program serves to:

- Protect and control the use of the University name and marks,
- Promote the image of the University to the public, as well as to the University community, and
- Establish a cooperative relationship with licensees.

The Program provides the University with a formal means to protect the use of its marks and to ensure that the University shares in the benefits derived from commercial use of its marks.

Definitions

- Trademark means a word or device associated with a person, company, association, or business.
- Registered mark means a trademark that has been registered with the Federal government at the U. S. Patent and Trademark Office. Federal registration provides additional protection against the remedies for trademark infringement.
- Infringement means unauthorized use of a trademark that belongs to another, or use of a trademark so similar to that of another as to cause the likelihood of confusion in the minds of the public as to the source affiliation or sponsorship of the product or service.
- Licensor means one who contracts to allow another (licensee) to use licensor's property (trademark) in exchange for payment, usually royalty as a percent of sales.
- License Agreement means royalty bearing contract between licensor (NU) and a manufacturer or manufacturer's representative who is licensed to produce specific products bearing one or more of the Licensor's trademarks.

Label Awareness

Faculty, staff, students, and friends of Nottingham University are asked to cooperate with the licensing program by purchasing only from manufacturers who have been licensed by the University.

Nottingham University requires that anyone manufacturing products bearing its marks or logos become a licensee. Licensees manufacturing a Nottingham product must attach a label or tag to the product to let the consumer know that the product is an officially-licensed item.

Buyers should look for the label when purchasing Nottingham products.

Be sure that the item you purchase is as authentic as your support for Nottingham University.

Correct Use of Marks and Colors

The Trademark Licensing Office is responsible for considering the use of Nottingham University marks on products, including the appropriateness of the use of University marks as well as the quality of products, legal liabilities, production, and distribution. Before the University's name or mark is reproduced, whether the imprinted item is for internal use or for resale, the product and the associated artwork must be approved by the Trademark Licensing Office.

The following rules shall be used in determining the correct use of University marks and colors:

•Nottingham University Seal and Signature

Nottingham University's official seal and signature is a single unit; the two elements of the seal and the words "Nottingham University" are always to be present together.

Neither the name Nottingham, Nottingham University, nor any design may be imposed on the seal. No other marks may be used with the University seal. The NU seal must be used on a solid background. The seal must be white, purple, grey or black. Exceptions must be approved on a case-by-case basis by the Trademark Office. The wording must be very readable with maximum color contrast.

The typeface used in the seal and the signature is a version of Goudy that has been altered slightly for improved reproduction and legibility at all sizes.

Nottingham University "N"

When used alone, and not as part of the word Nottingham, the University's stylized, registered "N" must be used. No other "N" will be approved by Nottingham University.

The University's stylized, registered "N" should be white, purple, or black. Exceptions must be approved on a case-by-case basis by the Trademark Office. The "N" must be very readable with maximum color contrast. Grey accent is acceptable.

•Wildcat Logos

The N-Cathead must be used as a unit. The name Nottingham or Nottingham University, Nottingham Wildcats, or Wildcats may be used with the N-Cathead.

•Clothing and Manufacturer's Logos

Manufacturer's logos will be limited to one inch (1") square. Exceptions must be approved on a case-by-case basis by the Trademark Office. No more than two manufacturer's logos may be placed on any item of clothing. No more than one manufacturer's logo may appear on the front side of the clothing. No more than one manufacturer's logo may appear on the back side of the clothing.

•Color Use

Purple: PMS 267

Grey: PMS 408

White

Black.

Exceptions must be approved on a case-by-case basis by the Trademark Office.

•PMS: Pantone Matching System

Use of University marks by the news media for informational purposes is not subject to Trademark Licensing. Schedule cards and photographs of campus scenes are not subject to licensing unless they feature the University's name or marks and are exploited commercially. These items will be reviewed on a case-by-case basis.

Trademark Licensing Services

The Trademark Licensing Office has camera-ready artwork, a list of retailers that carry NU imprinted products, and a list of licensed manufacturers. If a school or department would like to use a non-licensed manufacturer to produce an item as a giveaway or for internal use, the Licensing office will grant the company a short-term license.

Licensing Agents

Nottingham University has joined a consortium with other universities throughout the country to bring about consistency in the American marketplace for officially licensed collegiate products. The Collegiate Licensing Company helps administer this group. The objectives of the group are:

- To ensure that the names and logos of the participating universities are protected;
- To ensure that alumni, students, and supporters can easily recognize authorized merchandise; and
- To guarantee that the quality standards of products offered remain high.

Outside the United States, Crossland Enterprises, Inc. assists with the coordination of Nottingham University's Trademark Licensing program. In coordination with both the The Collegiate Licensing Company and Crossland Enterprises, the University also offers a direct licensing agreement.

The services of The Collegiate Licensing Company and Crossland Enterprises include:

- Knowing potential licensees (suppliers and manufacturers).
- Providing licensing information to potential licensees.
- Executing the licensing agreement with licensees.
- Notifying retail outlets about the licensing program and recruiting their vendors.
- Finding potential licensees from other schools and markets.

- Attending manufacturers' trade shows.
- Contacting local retailers to get their support.
- Mailing lists of current licensees to retail buyers.
- Assisting in promotions with internal audiences (faculty, staff, students and alumni) and the general public, and helping with press releases and public presentations.
- Searching for infringers.
- Establishing a series of "Cease" letters which end with the intent to file suit.
- Having "Officially Licensed Collegiate Product" labels or tags placed on licensed goods which are for sale.
- Ensuring timely payments by licensees.
- Conducting on-site audits of licensees.

Licensed Manufacturers

Nottingham University requires that all persons, companies and manufacturers who wish to reproduce the University's marks sign a non-exclusive license agreement. The Trademark Licensing Office maintains a list of manufacturers by type of product they are licensed to imprint with the University's name and registered marks.

Index

About the Authors

Thomas H. Sawyer, Ed.D.
Professor of Physical Education
Professor of Recreation and Sport Management
Indiana State University

Dr. Sawyer is a professor of Physical Education, Recreation and Sport Management at Indiana State University. He has been a high school and university coach in the following sports: baseball, soccer, and track and field. He was an associate athletic director for a NAIA, Division II institution, intramural and recreational sports director at three different institutions of higher education for over 15 years, a student recreation center director, and a department head for an HPE department as well as a department chairperson for physical education for over ten years with two institutions.

He has had over 160 professional articles accepted that were published in state, national, and international professional journals. He has authored 10 chapters in a variety of textbooks and authored or co-authored seven textbooks including this book. His textbooks have included an edited work, *Facilities Planning for Health, Fitness, Physical Activity, Recreation, and Dance: Concepts and Applications* (9th and 10th eds.), co-authored works, *The Management of Clubs, Recreation, and Sport: Concepts and Applications*, and *A Guide to Sport Nutrition for Student-Athletes, Coaches, Athletic Trainers, and Parents*, and authored works, *Employee Services Management*, *Indiana LANSE* (2nd ed.), and *Golf and The Law*.

Dr. Sawyer has given over 80 presentations at state, national, and international professional conferences, and nearly 125 workshops including How to Become a Writer, The Role of the Reviewer, The Lower Back and Employee Absences, Health and Wellness Programs for Corporations, NCA School Improvement Process, Aquatics Management, Coaching Education, Risk Management and Safety in Sport Programming, and Sport Nutrition.

He has been actively involved in professional organizations serving as President, Indiana AHPERD; President, American Association for Active Lifestyles and Fitness (AAALF); Chair, Council on Facilities and Equipment; Executive Director and Treasurer, The Society for the Study of the Legal Aspects of Sport and Physical Activity (SSLASPA) (now known as the Sport and Recreation Law Association); Editor, *Indiana AHPERD Journal and Newsletter*; Former Editor, *Journal of the Legal Aspects of Sport*; Former Editor, *Journal of Physical Education, Recreation, and Dance's Law Review*.

Dr. Sawyer has been recognized by his colleagues including 1995 Caleb Mills Distinguished Teaching Award (Indiana State University), 1995 Howard Richardson Outstanding Performance Award (Indiana State University), 1997 Faculty Distinguished Service Award (Indiana State University), 1994 Indiana AHPERD Leadership Award, 1998 Indiana AHPERD Honor Award, 1998 SSLASPA Leadership Award, 2003 SSLASPA Honor Award, 1996 Council on Facilities and Equipment Leadership Award, 2002 Council on Facilities and Equipment Honor Award, 2003 AAALF Honor Award, and 2004 AAHPERD Honor Award.

Finally, Dr. Sawyer is President of the Indiana Center for Sport Education, Inc. (ICSE). The ICSE provides the following services: coaching education seminars, risk management and liability seminars, sport and recreation safety consultation, and risk management audits.

Michael G. Hypes
Assistant Professor of Sport Management
Department of Health, Physical Education and Sport Sciences
Morehead State University, Morehead, Kentucky

He earned his D.A. in Physical Education at Middle Tennessee State University. Dr. Hypes received his B.S. and M.A. degrees in Physical Education from Appalachian State University.

Prior to his teaching responsibilities at Morehead State University, Dr. Hypes held teaching positions at Indiana State University, Peru State College and Austin Peay State University. He has coached basketball and baseball and worked in sports information, ticketing and event management at the college and high school levels.

Dr. Hypes has written chapters for five textbooks, published articles in peer-reviewed journals and has presented at the state, regional, national and international levels. Further, Dr. Hypes has served as the chair of the Council on Facilities and Equipment, member of the board of directors for the American Association for Active Lifestyles and Fitness, and as assistant editor of *Indiana AHPERD Journal and Newsletter*, the *Journal of the Legal Aspects of Sport*, and the *Tennessee AHPERD Journal*.

Julia Ann Hypes, Ph.D. candidate
Curriculum, Instruction, and Media Technology
Indiana State University

She earned a M.S.S. in Sport Management from the United States Sports Academy and a B.S. in Mass Communications (concentration in public relations and advertising) from Middle Tennessee State University.

Mrs. Hypes has worked as Sports Information Director at Saint Mary-of-the-Woods College while also teaching at Indiana State University. She has held positions in facility/event management, team travel, budgeting, and fund raising at the college level. She has also been active by authoring chapters in textbooks and giving presentations at the state, regional, national and international levels.

Julia Ann Hypes is an Assistant Professor of Sport Management in the Department of Health, Physical Education and Sport Sciences at Morehead State University in Morehead, Kentucky.

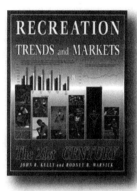